Buddhist Scriptures as Literature

Buddhist Scriptures as Literature

Sacred Rhetoric and the Uses of Theory

Ralph Flores

State University of New York Press

Published by
State University of New York Press, Albany

Printed in the United States of America

For information, contact State University of New York Press, Albany, NY
www.sunypress.edu

Production by Judith Block and Eileen Meehan
Marketing by Michael Campochiaro

Library of Congress Cataloging-in-Publication Data

Flores, Ralph.
Buddhist scriptures as literature : sacred rhetoric and the uses of theory / Ralph Flores.
p. cm.
Includes bibliographical references and index.
ISBN 978-0-7914-7339-9 (hardcover : alk. paper) — ISBN 978-0-7914-7340-5 (pbk. : alk. paper) 1. Buddhist literature—History and criticism. 2. Tripitaka as literature. 3. Tipitaka. Suttapitaka—Criticism, interpretation, etc. 4. Buddhism and literature. I. Title.

BQ1020. B83 2007
294.3'8—dc22

2007016827

10 9 8 7 6 5 4 3 2 1

Contents

Acknowledgments

I am grateful to many persons for inspiring this work, including teachers at the Barre Center for Buddhist Studies, San Francisco Zen Center, the Buddhist Society in London, and Wat Pa Nanachat in Ubon Ratchathani. I was encouraged at the beginning of this project by help from Professor David Kalupahana, and by conversations and correspondence, mostly about Paul de Man's work, with Professor Rodolphe Gasché. I am appreciative of readers who helped by commenting on the text: Stephen Batchelor at Gaia House, Dhammanando Bhikkhu at Wat Benchamabophit, the anonymous readers for SUNY Press, and Senior Acquisitions Editor Nancy Ellegate. I would like to thank her assistant Allison Lee, my colleagues in literary studies at Thammasat University, and my family. For their interest and good cheer, I am grateful to Emily and Kevin Silver, Matthew Sullivan, Anne Smith, Erik and Tetje Falentyn, Apichaya Wuttipongpreecha, and Thanutvorn Jaturongkavanich. I am pleased to thank Martin Perenchio for years of Buddhist discussions, and Michael Beard of the University of North Dakota for an always informative and congenial correspondence. Any errors or misreadings are mine.

1

Fictions of Reading

Westerners and Buddhist Texts

> *The Sun—the Light—rises in the East. Imagination has often pictured to itself the emotions of a blind man suddenly become possessed of sight. . . . By the close of day the man has erected a building constructed from his own inner Sun, and in the evening . . . esteems it more highly than the original external Sun.*
>
> —G. W. F. Hegel, *Encyclopedia*

The Sun, after rising gloriously and providing sight to the blind, is setting in the twilight of the West. Buddhism, with its signs of light, equanimity, ultimacy, and peaceful fulfillment, has found a place in the Western imagination. Certain questions, however, persist. Can the Buddha's teachings be truly viable without native monastic traditions, in an era of ego therapy and showy individualism? Can they truly take root in alien ground? Have we reconstructed and packaged the teachings especially for ourselves—and how much has been lost in the process?

The Fate of Non-Reading

There are no easy answers. Signals are clear, though, that Buddhist ways, recently Westernized, have been sucked into a whirlpool of global economics, New Age therapies, and neo-Buddhisms. This situation is manifested in glossy magazines and newsletters supported by advertisements for meditational supplies, along with services that include matchmaking, financial management, and even dentistry—all somehow "Buddhist." Such foibles may constitute a recent phase in the process, depicted by G. W. F. Hegel, in which the Sun is now setting into the twilight zone. The "Oriental Renaissance" of the first half of the nineteenth century (when India was seen to be the cradle of all civilizations and the source of all nourishment) was followed in the second half, with the entry of Buddhism, by worries that Asian religions could be toxic. Hegel's work was itself a setting sun. With access in 1827 to a multitude of reliable sources, he was neither a careful nor a respectful reader. What he "read" was guided mainly by the demands of his System.[1] Buddhist texts teach *nirodha*, or "cessation," leading Hegel to conclude too quickly that for the Buddha "*nothingness [das Nichts] is the beginning and the end.*"[2]

Negativism was viewed merely as a dialectical moment in the Absolute Spirit's journey. For other interpreters, however, so-called Buddhist "nihilism" was not to be taken lightly; it posed a threat to cherished beliefs and to Western civilization itself. Friedrich Nietzsche spoke of "*the desire of the Buddhist for nothingness, Nirvana—and no more*," warning ominously of a "*plunge into gloom and unmanly tenderness under whose spell Europe seems threatened.*"[3] Other writers—including Victor Cousin, Eugène Bournouf, and Jules Bathélemy Saint-Hilaire—also warned of (or in Schopenhauer's case, welcomed) "nihilism," and were somehow able to ignore or dismiss the Buddha's emphatic rejections, in the early texts, precisely of nihilism (*natthikavāda*) or annihilationism (*ucchedavāda*) (SN 42.13.3.1; 24.5.5).[4] Out of ignorance, fear, or missionary zeal, they were unable to read Buddhist texts. Yet, by the end of the nineteenth century, much had changed: Buddhism was no longer considered a threat. On the contrary, its teachings were seen as an uplifting way of life and a consolation for pain.

What lingers on, though, in the reception of Buddhism in the West, is a tradition—from at least 1820 until recent times—of ignoring or misconstruing Buddhist scriptures, and using them as a launching pad to project common fears, hopes, and fantasies. Desire, in reading, wanders, and is far from direct sight, or insight. For many popular Western teachers today, a detailed study of the texts is frequently deemed unnecessary: close readings may be dispensed with, in favor of vague anecdotes about "what the Buddha says somewhere" or what he or his disciples are said to have done. Today, Buddhist teachings, despite a plethora of fine translations and exegeses, are still often read casually or ritualistically, or discussed in ways soothing to recent mindsets.

The fiction of Westerners reading points to the unlikelihood—the fiction even, given our history—that we are capable readers of Buddhist texts, with energy, time, and motivation. But the fiction of reading may, in another sense, point to the results of imaginative engagement—that is, to useful figures engendered by filling in gaps and constructing passageways of communication.

Focal Points

With such a situation in the background, this study has three focal points. First, it is an effort to move against the long-standing tendencies, just mentioned, of the non-reading or poor reading of Buddhist texts. It does so by providing something like a guidebook to potential readers who may not fully know, or who would like to review, some major Buddhist scriptures. Second, it goes beyond a guidebook level by proposing to read Buddhist texts slightly askew, in a corrective to commonly accepted protocol. It proposes to read the texts not as primarily philosophy, doctrine, therapy, or even as advice for better living, but rather as literature. My assumption is that such an apparently marginal or parallax approach, informed by literary theory, will yield a harvest of fruitful ways of revising conventional formulae. Third, the readings here are part of a critical strategy meant not only to uncover sites of lyricism, drama, or compelling storylines but to illustrate, along the lines of contemporary theory, how Buddhist ideology and rhetoric are at work in shaping reponses in listeners and readers.

Cultural Encounters

Those responses are important, but we seem to have heard mostly what wanted to hear. The mood of the present epoch is in most ways, and despite a huge upsurge of interest, not particularly Buddhist, and what works as medicine in one part of the world in one epoch, might not work for another part, in a different epoch. The retooling of Buddhist ways for the West, especially in counseling and mental health, has been a troubled process.[5]

The picture, even so, is not entirely bleak. Despite a large distance from Buddhist texts in time and place, a "fusion of horizons," to use Hans-Georg Gadamer's phrase, may be in progress, with our own biases mixed into the exchange.[6] The Buddha, not an author in the usual sense, left his spoken words for monks to recite in formulae, and centuries later those formulae were turned into texts and, much later still, translated into other languages. My inquiry will deal with whether or how a contemporary Westerner reads, or would be likely to read, Buddhist texts. Such an inquiry is fraught with difficulties, and we need to be aware of varying ways in which the West attempts to attain hegemony over its other.[7] In particular, as Philip Almond points out, "through the West's progressive possession of the texts of Buddhism, it becomes, so to say, materially owned by the West, . . . [and] ideologically controlled by it."[8]

Pointing this out is not a neutral act, and here part of the ideology is to concur with such claims but also to suggest that an outsider's perspective is of positive value. As Mikhail Bakhtin argues, "the person who understands [needs to be] *located outside* . . . in time, in space, in culture." New meanings emerge when a culture comes into contact "with another, foreign meaning," and a sort of dialogue ensues in which both cultures are enriched, overcoming one-sidedness:

"we raise new questions for a foreign culture, ones that it did not raise itself."[9] For the encounter to be creative, we need to assert, all the more confidently amidst the transformation described by Hegel, that going "back to the texts" is a usefully contrarian movement. It may be a way to offset ideological fabrications in New Age and other recent discourses.

I propose to take account of nuances in key terms. This is especially crucial, given that Westerners come to Buddhist texts mostly in translation. Regional literatures are often studied by philologists or native speakers, who call for analyses of the finer points of diction, syntax, wordplay, and rhyme. Some of these matters are bypassed here, and most Westerners are unlikely to encounter these texts in the original languages. But literary value, some have contended, is precisely what is *not* lost in good translations, while literary response is crucial on the levels of rhetoric, plot, character, image, archetype and genre. At times I have made reference to Sanskrit terms in preference to Pāli, have often preferred more recent translations to older, more stilted ones, and in the interests of clarity, have have italicized major terms. This book, then, making use of widely available translations, and referring for clarification to earlier languages, shows how Buddhist sacred texts might be interpreted today. What kinds of texts, though, are they?

Truth, Myths, and Folktales

All cultures have stories, legends, folktales, and songs, the most important of which, the *myths* (and so some extent the epics), help illustrate what is of deepest concern to that society. They explain the laws, customs, history, and religion, and are not held to be imaginative, nor even of human origin.[10] Other stories, deemed less important, the *folktales*, are recounted for entertainment or amusement, and are said to be imaginative structures, independent of belief, in which any real or implied beliefs are a matter of indifference.

In our own times, with the decline of local communities and the growth of science, myths have declined or gone underground, while literature, overwhelmingly secular, has broken free from belief systems. Where "truth" was once something of great import, conveyed in myth or legend, it has now become the verifiable, usually mundane, statement. Truth, however, Northrop Frye argues, is not a literary category: "the anxiety of society, when it urges the authority of myth and the necessity of believing it, seems to be less to proclaim its truth than to prevent anyone from questioning it."[11] This declaration is resonant not only for Platonic texts, where a "noble lie" is meant to assure social harmony, but also for Buddhist texts, where the four Truths are designated as "aryan," or "noble." Might there be some anxiety lurking behind the confident equanimity of the Buddha's, if not Plato's, claims about nobility? Is there perhaps a repressed violence, a pressure to "come and see"—not just anything, but this particularly precious saving way?

Despite renunciation and a tight guarding of desire, does not the wandering Prince Gautama move desiringly in his quest? In the wisdom of *Ecclesiastes*: "*Better is the sight of the eye than the wandering of desire.*" This overlaps in part with Buddhist wisdom, where attentive seeing brings direct insight. Yet the sight of the eye may also, at times, be precisely what instigates new desire and continued wandering. Monks are taught to guard their senses—that is, to see in what is seen, only the seen, so that desire does not lead one into errancy. But can the wandering monk always see only the seen, or rather does he wonder, and thus, wander? Here a folkloric thrust makes its deepest cut into the Buddhist ideology and its aryan, noble ways. "I have a notion," Frye muses, "that if the wandering of desire did not exist, great literature would not exist either."[12] And Buddhist texts, whatever else they may be, are also great literature.

There might be some uncertainty then, especially today, as to whether Buddhist texts are primarily imaginative (with the freedom of folktales), or primarily mythic (with the constraints of important truths). In either case, though, the issue of nobility is still alive. Wallace Stevens argues that the apparent decline, even the disappearance, of nobility may be little more "than a maladjustment between the imagination and reality. We have been a little insane about the truth .... In its ultimate extension, the truth about which we have been so insane will lead us to look beyond the truth to something in which the imagination will be the dominant complement."[13] Such a movement, through and beyond truth, is suggestive: perhaps we enter into the Buddhist world most fully and accurately by apprehending it as literature, and not simply as doctrine or as practice.

Any such position may be viewed by some as a compromise, as a way of becoming reconciled to our disenchanted world, so manifestly lacking in buddhas. Yet we need not claim, as Matthew Arnold did, that poetry will now be needed as a substititute for religion, to console and sustain us.[14] Religion, despite changing assessments of it, may all along have been an unacknowledged form of poetry—myth to be taken as truth. Arnold brings to the fore, however, sad symptoms of desperation and unbelief. Many of us today cannot help but be warily skeptical, and discussions of religion are no longer welcome in polite secular society. As Slavoj Žižek remarks, "When it comes to religion, . . . we no longer 'really believe' today, we just follow (some) religious rituals and mores as part of respect for the 'lifestyle' of the community to which we belong."[15] At the other extreme, not far from "polite society," there are those "who live their culture immediately," as Žižek puts it, or who believe to the extent of terror and war. There is thus much at stake in our involvement, even as mere readers, in Buddhist matters

The Reader's Role

First we must learn about reading. How do we read and, if we read poorly, how can we read otherwise? Questions of textuality, reading, and interpretation, so crucial to religion, have loomed large in recent literary thinking. The advocates of *reader-response criticism* maintain that a text is not simply written words on the page but an activation of those words. "Reading can be characterized," Wolfgang Iser writes, "as a sort of kaleidoscope of perspectives, pre-intentions, recollections. Every sentence contains a preview of the next, and forms a kind of viewfinder for what is to come; and this in turn changes the preview."[16] As we read, our progress is impeded at times by puzzling gaps in the story. We need to "fill in the gaps" to allow for the continuing flow of sentences, plot elements, or ideas. Whenever gaps occur, readers are called upon to use imagination or speculation to close up, or jump over, the gaps. The process of reading is thus a search for some sort of consistency, pattern, or explanation.

In reading, Iser comments, familiar illusions are promoted, and then punctured: "What at first seemed to be an affirmation of our assumptions leads to our own rejection of them, thus tending to prepare us for a re-orientation."[17] This could well be a sketch of the Buddhist path: illusions are punctuated, one after another, about comfort, self, pleasure, beauty, goodness, and eternity. Only then can there be a more open-eyed beginning. Here we will welcome gaps, rather than being eager to close them. Gaps or blanks in the texts will be taken as occasions for reading between the lines, for venturing speculations about what might be going on. The speculations may, of course, vary immensely. Norman N. Holland, a reader-response critic, shows how readers' reactions to literary phrases and themes correlate with their varying personality structures, adducing the formula, "unity is to text as identity is to self."[18] By this theory, there will be widely differing responses to any text.

Those responses are crucial to the text's identity and survival. Tristram Shandy, the writer-as-hero of Sterne's novel *The Life and Opinions of Tristam Shandy, Gentleman*, tries to mitigate his outrageous authorial antics (blank or black pages, squiggles, unfinished episodes, interruptions, digressions) by "noticing" any readers foolish enough to have persisted for so long in their shared adventure with him. Nor is the reader today, though rarely addressed directly, any less important. An issue of *The New Yorker* magazine shows a cartoon in which someone, presumably in a bookstore, sits at a desk with a large sign: "*Meet the Reader.*" A number of substantial-looking persons, no doubt authors, are lined up, books in hand, for the reader to sign.[19] As the cartoon's humor implies, readers are not usually given much attention, except perhaps indirectly, when best-seller lists are being compiled.

More than for sales receipts, readers are crucial, especially when cross-cultural or religious matters are at stake. In an age of disenchantment, in the wake of stories of war and terror, readers are likely to harbor ambivalence; they are intrigued yet suspicious of shining promises—of future lives, of relief from suffering, and of nirvana. To read the Buddhist texts "as literature" would ideally lighten the burden of suspicion, allowing the promises to gain a hearing.

Suspension of Disbelief

Literature, especially about magical or supernatural events, requires what not all readers are prepared for. Samuel T. Coleridge called it, in 1817, the ability "*to transfer from our inward nature a human interest and a semblance of truth sufficient to procure for these shadows of imagination that willing suspension of disbelief for the moment, which consititutes poetic faith.*"[20] With that term, *suspension of disbelief,* Coleridge has in mind the supernatural spirits and ghostly figures in a poem much like his own *Rime of the Ancient Mariner.*

The statement could apply more broadly, though, to all literary texts, and to texts containing what some readers may consider to be the "shadows of imagination"—stories of past lives and supernormal powers. Perhaps we need not gravitate inevitably, at least not yet, toward a Buddhism without beliefs.[21] We might instead allow some leeway for temporary suspensions of disbelief or, more positively, for the aesthetic belief we sometimes give, enthusiastically, to literary stories and figures. Perhaps habitual beliefs can come under temporary or experimental scrutiny when we read literary or Buddhist texts. Nor is this situation unfamiliar, since art and literature are all around us. We are tacitly presumed, as readers, to play the game, to walk the walk, to use our imagination, to suspend disbelief. A particular type of reading, then, may be helpful to an inquiry into the Western reception of Buddhist scriptures. That type of reading is of Buddhist texts as literature.

We need not go far to find examples of Buddhist literature. One of the first meetings of East and West is dramatized in the *Questions of King Milinda,* in which a figure said to be the Greek king Menander, given an Indian name, is depicted asking questions about Buddhist doctrine to the monk Nâgasena. The King's requests are perpetually for an illustration or an analogy, and Nâgasena, versed in canonical texts, is admirably fecund in his imagery. The analogies are highly regarded by the King, who, when not entirely satisfied, can always ask for another. Since analogies are images or similes, the ability to persuade the King (who eventually converts) is based on a skill with words or, more specifically, with poetry or rhetoric.

The Buddha as Storyteller

More so than Nâgasena, the Buddha is a master of images, and he frequently speaks as a poet or parable-teller, preferring to cast his message as a lyric or story to illustate what could also be stated discursively. He thereby taps into wider, archetypal dimensions. To many, images may matter more than extended arguments; often, when he is making an abstruse or repeated point, we wait impatiently for an example or story.

One typical story is of the young Kisā Gotamī, who comes to the Buddha carrying her recently deceased baby in her arms. Not willing to accept death, or assuming perhaps that the Buddha may be a miracle worker, she hopefully demands medicine. Instead of preaching about impermanence, non-self and suffering, he tells her to make rounds of the entire city, asking for a mustard seed from any house in which no one has died; if she finds a seed, he will do what she wishes. She makes the rounds but, since in every house, someone has died, she garners no seeds.[22] As in many folktales, the protagonist must undergo a trial, and here she learns by direct experience that death is universal. The dramatized action makes the Buddha's point far more memorably than if he had stated the teaching in a sermon, as he usually does to his monks. The literary dimension thus enlivens and clarifies the teachings.

The story is notably allegorical, and has a mythical or "truth" dimension in Frye's sense. It arises out of the discourse and is strictly subordinated to it: we are told that the Buddha knows by supernormal vision, in advance, the outcome. There is no possibility that Kisā could have stumbled upon (or slyly chosen to knock at) the doors of newly constructed houses with young residents, no deaths, and a plentiful supply of mustard seeds. For if she did indeed get the seeds—and folktales usually have variations—would the Buddha then display shamanic powers, bringing the baby back to life? And if so, what would happen to his teachings of impermanence and karma: would they still have the same import?

At first glance, readers or listeners may gain the impression that the Buddha, a worthy raconteur, may have kept a supply of personally experienced anecdotes on hand, and pulled this one out, as the occasion required. Perhaps a more likely possibility is that the story about medicine was itself composed as "good medicine," so as to reinforce the point about death's inevitability. The story is mythic or highly ideologized, and not open to much modification, if any.

Something similar could be said about the arrow parable, in which a man is struck by an arrow and is in mortal danger. If that man were to insist, before allowing himself to be treated, on knowing details about the arrow and who shot it (and here the Buddha elaborates at length), then the man, while making these inquiries, would die (MN 63.5),[23] the point being that suffering needs to be treated urgently, and that peripheral questions can only get in the way. Just as the wounded man is not able to ask questions, as an examining sheriff might do, so we readers, if we know the genre conventions, are expected to get the point, and then stay quiet. We are not to speculate about whether, for example, suddenly removing the arrow might lead to the man's death, or if perhaps he had been wisely shot at, if his further living might bring vengeance or war upon others. Any elaboration of the tale has already been given within the tale, in lists of possible poisons, arrow types, shooters, etc. The story speaks with one voice—it is monoglossic—and only much later in the Buddhist tradition, we will find, are contending voices permitted.

Contemporary Approaches

To heighten an awareness of the issues at stake in what follows, some recent literary theories will be put to work: reader response theory, Russian formalism, deconstruction, rhetorical analysis, archetypal theory, semiotics, psychoanalysis, poetic influence, mimetic rivalry, ideology critique, and dialogism. The theories are meant to shed light on the Buddhist texts, and not vice versa—that is, my intention is not to comment on the theories, but rather to use them in acts of reading. Particular theories are invoked at various points, but always to assist in reading, and thus perhaps with only reader-response and rhetorical analysis in the foreground. In addition to theory, another aspect of literary study will involve allusions to typical Western texts—often canonical ones, just as many of Buddhist texts here are canonical. The comparisons might seem distracting at times, but the larger task here is discern in Buddhist texts the cross-culturally understandable work of literary figures, storytellers, dramatists, rhetoricians, and poets.

How, more generally, does one read Buddhist texts as literature? The Bible, to take a familiar example, is usually received as sermon, liturgy, prayer, or inspiration, and is believed, by many, to be literally true. But a growing discipline has lately emerged about the Bible "as literature," where literary, rather than religious, meaning is the center of attention.[24] More than those who are committed to the doctrine, those who read Buddhist scriptures as literature may read freely and creatively, since they temporarily suspend disbelief, or indeed belief, in the text's solicitations. They read with due respect, but less piously, less pedantically, and more playfully, more critically. Reading the texts as literature allows and encourages readers to imagine and speculate—in ways which dogmatists or scholars may disdain—about the existential pathos behind the texts' formulaic repetitions.

Those who dare to imagine may be held in suspicion by traditionalists. In a discussion of this issue, Jeff Humphries asks, "Is there any place in a genuine Buddhist practice for literature . . . ?" and "is there any valid place for Buddhism in literature?"[25] He gives a negative answer to both questions, invoking the figures of Nāgārjuna and others who warn against treating the Middle Way as literature or philosophy. True enough, the delights of poetry were considered dangerous distractions by the Buddha, and later by Nāgārjuna. We might be wary, though, of mystifying or essentializing terms such as "genuine . . . practice," "valid place," or indeed, "Buddhism." The Buddha, who taught emptiness with an open hand, deploys parables, songs, similes, and anecdotes in his practice, while later traditions had recourse to koans, verses, tales, visualizations, and chanting. Who can possibly say, then, that there is no literary dimension in the teachings and practices, or that literary texts have no Buddhist points to make? Indeed, to cite Humphries, "the closest thing in Western culture to the Middle Way of Buddhism . . . is the practice of literature—of reading and writing."[26]

Heroic Archetypes

Suspension of disbelief is not always a requirement for the creation of literature. For earlier cultures, gigantic, legendary figures were perceived as real, and one esteemed theory of literature is that all great figures and plots are descended from earlier mythic *archetypes*—that is, recurrent images stored in all psychic constitutions.[27] The power of literature derives from such archetypes, taking us beyond our limited cultural or linguistic spheres. The fact that archetypes are communicable, Northrop Frye points out, "largely accounts for the ease with which ballads and folk tales and mimes travel through the world, like many of their heroes, over all barriers of language and culture."[28]

According to Joseph Campbell, the career of a hero—be it Oedipus, Electra, Aeneas, Arjuna, Jesus, Orlando Furioso, or the Buddha—follows a similarly patterned sequence in all myths, which he calls "monomyth": a communal crisis (plague, sin, war, suffering); a call requiring some courageous response; a difficult journey with occasional help into unknown, supernatural territories (leaving home, wandering, initiation); confrontation with an enormous enemy (Māra, Satan, a dragon); a horrendous life-disturbing battle out of which the hero emerges victorious (enlightenment, resurrection, a defeated dragon); returning home (nirvana, heaven, a palace) "to bestow boons" amidst great acclaim, including marriage into a royal family.[29] The pattern, not always completed, may have peculiar variations, but is generally applicable. The sequence may be refined specifically for World Saviors: royal ancestry and a miraculous birth; prophecy; childhood deeds; possible marriage and propagation of an heir; a calling; departure; forest or desert discipline; battle with a supernatural adversary followed by the performance of miracles, teaching and making converts, founding an order; a sacred death; heavenly ascent or nirvana.[30]

As a literary form, Northrop Frye classifies this kind of life story as a *quest-romance*: "The complete form of the romance is clearly the successful quest . . . in three stages": first, a perilous journey with minor adventures; second, a crucial struggle; third, an exultation of the hero. A "ritual death" is followed or accompanied by a "recognition scene." The three stages of quest may be called, "using Greek terms, the *agon*, or conflict; the *pathos*, or death struggle; and *anagnorisis*, or discovery, the recognition of the hero."[31] In the Buddha's case, recognition (*nirvana*) precedes and is completed by death (*parinirvana*): he knows, with overwhelming conviction, that he achieved his goal, and will not be reborn. Such a story may be read in a number of ways, and Frye finds that "the nearer romance is to myth, the more attributes of divinity will cling to the hero."[32]

Indeed, as centuries passed the Buddha did become a legend, and was "less an example to be followed . . . and more and more a symbol to be venerated."[33] Siddartha Gautama is archetypal, and he himself claimed to be following the "ancient path" of earlier Buddhas. As the Buddha becomes mythical and legendary, his titles are emphasized and, like other epic heroes, such as Homer's, he is known by familiar and oft-repeated epithets: "*Well-Farer, Knower of the worlds, incomparable Trainer of men to be tamed, Teacher of gods and humans, enlightened and blessed*" (DN 2.40).[34] One appealing aspect of the literary text, then, is the very familiarity of its traditional, formulaic, heroic figures and plots.

Defamiliarization, or Making Strange

Interestingly, another specifically literary aspect is almost the opposite. A literary text is evocative to the extent that it speaks of a strangeness different from our customary, familiar world. The Russian formalist, Victor Shklovsky, claims that the purpose of art is "to impart the sensation of things as they are perceived, not as they are known; the technique [used for this purpose] is to make objects 'unfamiliar,' to make forms difficult."[35] *Defamiliarization*, or *making strange*, by which literature is thus defined, avoids names. It represents familiar objects in peculiar ways, so that we see them as if for the first time.

These two different features are not incompatible. A royal prince, that familiar figure of epics and fairy-tales, is in this case a future Buddha, who "goes against the stream," and abandons his lavish palace. His teachings, when eventually offered, acknowledge common facts of conditioned existence (birth, sickness, death) but propose a radical deconditioning as the way to overcome those facts. In both cases, a defamiliarization takes place: the prince behaves in an unprincely manner and inverts his position: he becomes a homeless vagrant, and in his teachings, suffering (*dukkha*) is seen from the perspective of an extraordinary being. Precisely because the perspectives were (and are) unfamiliar for ordinary folk, recourse was taken to various kinds of pedagogy, persuasion, and "skillful means" (*upāya*).

In the West, the ways of persuasion come under the rubrique of "rhetoric," which has been linked at various times with sophistry, legalism, and propaganda, as well as with eulogies, ceremony and political counsel.[36] Recent theorists have shown that literary texts are replete with rhetorical strategies, often deployed in overdetermined or inconsistent ways.[37] One may have doubts, as these theorists often do, about strict distinctions between literature and rhetoric. Sacred rhetoric, for example, is part of a highly performative religious and literary discourse that preaches, consecrates, ritualizes, praises, proselytizes, narrates, sings, confesses, prays, advises, consoles, prophesies, heals, accuses, curses, forgives, memorializes, exhorts, warns and, above all, inspires.

Most earlier listeners or readers are likely to have differed from us in their responses to such discourse. "We" do not constitute a unity, however, and in what follows, I consider possible reactions to Buddhist scriptures by various types of contemporary readers. Those types are schematic, not exhaustive: there are countless strategies of reading, and countless readers. Readers generate readings that range from strict exegeses to mild or radical transformations. In all cases, readings have both literary and rhetorical dimensions. Paul de Man has argued that a critique of metaphysics—a critique that could be extended to dogma, or indeed dharma—is founded on "the rhetorical model of the trope, or if one prefers to call it that, literature."[38] Such a critique, whether mild or rough, whether implicit or explicit, provides fruitful strategies for reading, and for a probing of Buddhist ideology.

Rhetoric and Ideology

Society at the Buddha's time was in turmoil, and competing ideologies frequently came into conflict. A great migration was taking place from small-scale communities to the more impersonal life of urban centers. Wealth was being earned by enterprising merchants, who made business trips from one urban center to another. A new sense of freedom and individualism had a price, however, in a growing sense of aloneness and malaise.[39] The newly emerging Buddhist ideology appealed mainly not to the lower classes but to an increasingly well-off merchant class impressed with the possibility of gaining merit by performing right actions oneself rather than having Brahmins make sacrifices. The Buddha's teaching seemed reasonable, empowering, and calculable. As Richard F. Gombrich argues, spiritual matters could be monetized, and what Max Weber called the *Entzauberung* (disenchantment, demystification) of the world substitutes quantity, be it in money or acts of merit, for quality.[40] The goal of merit-making—better future lives and, ultimately, nirvana—provided a vision of escape from the crowded, unhealthy confines of samsāric life.

Does Buddhist rhetoric disguise its mercantile roots, however, with a conjoined (and seemingly inconsistent) ideology of renunciation? As Terry Eagleton shows, in many literary texts "the ideology seems to determine the historically real, rather than vice versa," so that while ideology pre-exists the literary text, the text transforms that ideology, condensing and displacing it, and thereby indirectly commenting upon it.[41] These processes of troping, visible in Buddhist texts, and much like Freudian dreamwork, can be deciphered by rhetorical analysis. In its basic shape, an ideology emerges in the Buddha's story and in his subsequent teachings. A well-to-do young man leaves home, as commonly many of his counterparts did at the time, to become a *śrvāka*, or wanderer, in search of fulfillment. The text's rhetorical thrust will be to extol and amplify his departure and quest, in implicit comparison with those of other wanderers; it will demonstrate and commend his achievement, in particular, of ultimate freedom. Although the Buddha's biographical narrative is fragmented, the focus on a single divinized figure through a series of disparate episodes is typical of the epic genre in India.[42] The text honors not only the hero, moreover, but also his teachings. Those teachings are repeatedly described as being "*lovely at the beginning, lovely in the middle and the lovely at the end*" (DN 14.3.22).

Hyperboles of the Sacred

The term *lovely* (or "good") has an aesthetic dimension, but it is more than aesthetic. It signals a new world of possibilities. The loveliness, sometimes in the form of "inspired utterances," breaks away from the ordinary world of conditioned experience. It is a "making strange": Buddhist discourse, though often restrained, as befits the Middle Way, at times verges on the incredible, excessive, and hyperbolic. The Buddha performs magical feats—walking across rivers, flying through space, reading minds, instantly disappearing and reappearing elsewhere (DN 14.3.29). Such behavior might seem far-fetched, and the language describing it is hyperbolic.

It should come as no surprise that the language of religion is in general hyperbolic, or marked by a blessed excess. It may be a tool for persuasion and ideology, but it also is more than that. Stephen Webb observes that today we live in a world in which discourse has become flat, rational, technical, and uninspired. The figure of hyperbole, intimately connected with religion, inspires us, by contrast, "to imagine more than we know, say more than we dare to believe, act more boldly than is wise and rational, see more than realism displays."[43] Hyperbole is any apparently excessive or overstated language. It complicates the process of filling in gaps as we read; they may, at times, need to be left open. The language of hyperbole is incomparable, beyond our usual conceptions, straining and elevating our imaginations—in what Longinus calls the sublime style.

Hyperbole, so prominent in rhetorical handbooks, is a manner of speech that exaggerates the truth. The "exaggerated truth" may be all the more true, as in the following passage attributed to the Buddha:

> "*Which do you think is more: the flood of tears which, weeping and wailing, you have shed upon this long way—hurrying and hastening through the round of rebirths, united with the undesired, separated from the desired—this, or the waters of the four oceans?*
>
> "*. . . For a long time have you suffered the death of father and mother, of sons, daughters, brothers and sisters. And whilst you were thus suffering you have, indeed, shed more tears upon this long way than there is water in the four oceans.*" (SN 15.3.3)[44]

The addressees are specified as "*the brethren*" ("*forest-dwellers, almsmen, rag-robed*"); they are monks, but perhaps like most of us, not yet liberated. The "*you*" is gradually built up into a cosmic person who is both selfless and samsāric. Suffering and grief, recurring in so many times and places is—and is not—the "you" of the listener or reader. "*You*" are here and everywhere, and a sense of urgency is all the stronger on that account.

Passages like this, and interpretations that notice hyperboles, are especially provocative in a study of Buddhist texts, which are customarily seen as moderate, realistic, sober, and rational. Yet those texts, especially in the Mahāyāna traditions, are often unfathomably hyperbolic. Even in the earliest, arguably more "rational" schools, we are asked—hyperbolically—to abandon household life, and to employ contrarian, defamiliarizing methods of emotional detachment and sensory renunciation. In all cases, we may decide, as readers or as practitioners, to deflate the hyperboles and reduce the demands. But if so, how well are we reading or practicing?

Skillful Means

Our situation as readers of Buddhist texts as literature is paradoxical. On the one hand, literature is fictional, and its plots, characters, and verbal constructions, however realistic, are meant to be viewed as not literally true. This being so, we may misread Buddhist or other sacred texts if we believe that they are only literature. They are not to be read, some may tell us, as mere fiction or poetry like other fiction or poetry. On the other hand, many Buddhist texts are adapted to the audiences addressed—that is, they are contrived as *skillful means*, thus complicating any uniform message they may be assumed to have. John Schroeder convincingly takes exception to commentators who examine the content of the Buddha's discourses without paying attention to pedagogical contexts, who all too readily assume that the message can be understood as a series of statements apart from any rhetorical context.[45] Buddhist sayings are therapeutic and pragmatic: they meant for the urgent task of relieving suffering.

The therapy's true purpose might not always be clear. For many people, the Buddhist goal is perforce an imagined, if not a fantastic, idea. Many of them, even if practitioners, have not reached the higher jhānic states in meditation, and they can only imagine nirvana on the basis of scanty, often negative, adjectives: "*not-born, not-brought-into-being, not-made, not-formed*" (It 43).[46] Such an idea has been viewed as the locus for projected hopes, wishes, and aspirations, while the path-to-goal structure has been called a quasi-fictional invention, an imagined analogy for the career of ideal persons.[47] Both the path and the goal may have a strong kinship, it seems, with literature.

In a famous, archetypally Buddhist parable, the teaching itself is imagined, again by analogy, to be like a raft:

> "*Bhikkus* [monks], *suppose a man in the course of a journey saw a great expanse of water, whose near shore was dangerous and fearful, and whose further shore was safe and free from fear, but there was no ferryboat or bridge going to the far shore. Then he thought: 'There is this great expanse of water, whose near shore is dangerous and fearful, and whose further shore is safe*

> *and free from fear, but there is no ferryboat or bridge going to the far shore. Suppose I collect grass twigs, branches, and leaves and bind them together into a raft, and supported by the raft and making an effort with my hands and feet, I got safely across to the far shore.'"* (MN 22.13)

The man then does what he intends, described in precisely the same words, and thereupon he reaches the far shore. Repetitions perform a reinforcement and, as with other parables, preclude deviation. The words to describe a hypothetical state ("suppose a man . . .") are exactly repeated by what the man thinks, thereby validating his thinking, just as his activities will exactly repeat, word for word, his thoughts. No symbolic dimension is as yet specified. We are simply offered concise, practical thinking, and an activity that directly stems from that thinking.

Once having crossed the river, what is to be done with the raft? The man can lug it around with him, which would cumbersome. Or else, preferably, he can leave it on the shore or set it adrift, and thereby, according to a significant motif, "lay down the burden" (of suffering). The raft has served its purpose, and he no longer needs it, since he'll have no wish to go back across the river. The moral of the parable is clear: "*the Dhamma is similar to a raft, being for the purpose of crossing over, not for the purpose of grasping*" (MN 22.13). If so, however, the story—the raft, the Dhamma—is to be taken as something tentative, hypothetical, even experimental, very much like a literary text, which we are to see as fiction or illustration, and not as history or news reporting.

The Epic Quest

The reader is aware of the man "in the course of a journey," and here we come to the literary genre of many Buddhist texts, including the founder's biography. The journey or quest-romance, as a type of desire fulfillment, has a peculiar position in Buddhist expositions, since a certain type of desire (*tanhā* in the second Noble Truth) is a great enemy to followers of the path. When the young Prince, and Buddha-to-be, embarks on a quest-romance, what are his motives?

One may pause before tackling this question, and ponder what sort of hero he might be. Frye, who follows Aristotle in classifying heroes according to their elevations, claims that if the central figure is superior "in kind" both to other humans and to the natural environment, the hero is divine and his story is a myth. If superior "in degree" to others and to the environment, the hero is typical to romance; if superior in degree to others but not to the environment, he is an epic hero or a leader.[48]

The Buddha varies in his superiority to us. In making use of supernormal powers, he is closest to the heroes of romance and epic, moving "in a world in which the laws of nature are suspended."[49] At other times, he is not above his natural environment: his teaching—the *dhamma*—is sometimes called the natural or normal "law," and he dies, as other humans do, at the end of his life span. Though starting as a human, albeit a royal prince, he becomes elevated upon achieving enlightenment, and thereafter, especially in later traditions, is turned into a divinized, mythical figure. Even in the apparently earliest stories, he is legendary from the outset. Prophecies that accompany his birth and his career are marked by the paraphernalia of the quest-romance: "unlikely conversions, miraculous transformations and providential assistance."[50]

Much of the Buddha's story has an epic dimension. Prominent in the Pāli texts are stock epithets, oral formulae, speeches and counterspeeches, gods, prophecies, and praises of great deeds or sayings. Passages in those texts often seem to be, as T. W. Rhys Davids has observed, fragments of a "Buddha Epic," or potential forerunners of such an epic.[51] The episodes are not connected, however, and they are far calmer and more concise than those in the *Mahabharata* or the *Ramayana*. Even so, we discover a narrative that might be termed "epic" (or *mahākāvya*) in the *Nidanakathā* or, more surely, in the Sanskrit verses of Aśvaghoṣa's *Buddhacarita.*

The high mimetic epic, as in Homer or Milton, has "an encyclopedic range of theme, from heaven to the underworld, and an enormous mass of traditional knowledge."[52] Classical epics, and Dante's *Commedia*, all begin at a low point, and the central figure is gradually, cosmically educated to make efforts in an archetypal quest. Frye's scheme applies, too, to Indian legends: the prince and future Buddha begins at a low point—a depressing recognition of ubiquitous suffering. The subsequent quest, as in all epics, is not simply self-centered: "an objective and disinterested element enters into the poet's vision of human life," which gives his legend its authority.[53]

The epic often includes a quest-romance dimension, which is heightened in later genres. Intriguingly—and here we return to our question about the Prince's motives—the quest-romance is defined by a strong libidinal element, and is akin to rituals and dreams: "translated into dream terms, the quest-romance is the search of the libido or desiring self for a fulfillment that will deliver it from the anxieties of reality but will still contain that reality."[54] What the Buddha promises is deliverance, precisely from anxieties: the raft parable describes how the "unsafe shore" is "dangerous and fearful." The realization or place of refuge and safety is, or so we would imagine, libidinally satisfying—where I can "*go wherever I want*" (MN 22.13). The typical quest-romance fills in the "want" dimension, however, with rather non-Buddhist items: luxurious banquets and sexual romance, all constituting "the victory of fertility."[55]

The Buddha's quest-romance, then, is atypical. In literary-critical terms, we need to offset a reading of archetypal patterns with a sense of making strange, or defamiliarization. The Buddha's quest-romance is precisely a relinquishment, not a victory, of fertility. And so we might need to ponder the degree of relevance, in this case, of the heroic paradigm.

2

A Prince Transformed

The *Nikāyas*, the *Nidānakathā*, Aśvaghoṣa's *Acts of the Buddha*

Meaning is present to the self in the life . . . that has not yet gone forth from itself into the world, space, or nature. [But] . . . "goings forth" effectively exile this life of self-presence in indications. We know now that indication, which . . . includes practically the whole surface of language, is the process of death at work in signs.

—Jacques Derrida, *Speech and Phenomena*

The Buddha, not long after his awakening, goes out in search of those who would listen to his teachings. He meets Ājīvaka Upaka, a wanderer on the road who notices his clear faculties, and inquires about his teacher. In response, the Buddha, who of course has been his own teacher, breaks into triumphant verse:

"I have no teacher, and one like me
Exists nowhere in all the world
With all its gods, because I have
No person for my counterpart" (MN 26.25).

Despite the exalted exclamation, or possibly because of it, Ājīvaka Upaka is unmoved: he shakes his head, saying, "*May it be so friend.*" The Buddha's very first listener or interpreter thus turns away in doubt, as occasionally others would do in later times.

The Buddha walks on, eventually meeting five of his former companions, who also have reservations. They are wary but polite, believing that Gautama had betrayed his ascetic discipline, and thus could not possibly have reached the goal. They address him by name and as "friend," but (perhaps displeased by his encounter with Ājīvaka Upaka) he sternly informs them that their mode of speech is improper! He is not to be addressed as a mere friend, he says. But how are they to know—that is, by what signs is his new status to be recognized? The Buddha asks, "*have you ever known me to speak like this before?*" (MN 26.28). His force of assertion and tone of voice are indications, he suggests, of achievement. These are matters of persuasion or rhetoric, along with his announcement that he now has a title, or several titles: "*the Tathāgata is an Accomplished One, a Fully Enlightened One*" (MN 26.27).

Who Is the Buddha?

Who, then, is the erstwhile Gautama, and what makes him so special? This question will reverberate throughout history, and already had started to do so when the Buddha was alive. Direct questions about his identity are perpetually deflected, in a naming process that is violent and always incomplete. The Tathāgata (not a proper name) is described as "*deep, immeasurable and unfathomable*" (MN 72.20), while in relics or images, he is always in the mode of a symbol or sign.[1] When a wayfaring brahmin sees his footprint, he politely asks Gautama whether he would become a deva, a gandhabba, a yakkha, or a human being, to which the answer was, none of these—he would become a Buddha (AN 4.36). A highly perfected human, the Buddha has popularly been called a *devātideva*, or "god beyond the gods." For Emile Sénart, he was perceived to be (or was made into) a mythic deity, and the historical person was irrelevant.[2] According to solar mythology, the sun-hero issues from the clouds of night, Māyā's dark womb. A flash of light pierces the world as he is born, and Māyā dies like a morning cloud, vanishing with the morning sun. The sun-hero conquers the thunder-demon, Māra the tempter, in terrible battle under the sacred tree, and when the battle is won, the sun-god sets turning the wheel of dharma, careening across the universe. In the end he dies in the fires of a funeral pyre, extinguished by streams of water, as a sun-hero dies in his own sea of fire.[3]

This legendary account chimes with a literary reading of the story—or, more accurately, with one kind of literary reading, since it falls far short of specifying the more mundane contexts of the Buddha's achievement, and is based on a selectively grandiose reading. One may be tempted, of course, to take precisely the opposite tack, minimizing the mythic dimension, or setting it to one side. Étienne Lamotte, for example, tries to give separate treatment to "the life" and "the legend," while still other commentators account for the Buddha and his experiences entirely in psychological or historical terms, taking an agnostic stance, as Ājīvaka Upaka does, toward claims of enlightenment.[4]

Two Strategies of Reading

Corresponding to such varied evaluations, there are—to simplify—at least two different types of readers, embodying two strategies of reading. There are readers who imaginatively accept the mythical or epic dimensions in the story, and readers who would doubt or ignore those elements as they investigate surrounding circumstances or look for some historical kernel of "real truth." The first type of reader, whom we might call the "*traditional reader*," is open to the text as literature, and pays attention to all aspects of the text. The second type, whom we might broadly call the "*recent reader*," while still often a literary reader, is more reductionistic and chooses to filter out the legendary accretions. These two types of reader correlate with Paul Ricoeur's distinction between the two poles of hermeneutics: "At one pole, . . . the manifestation and restoration of a meaning addressed to me in . . . a message, a proclamation or a kerygma; at the other pole, a demystification, a reduction of illusion. . . . Hermeneutics [is] animated by this double motivation: willingness to suspect, willingness to listen: vow of rigor, vow of obedience."[5] In the case of Buddhist texts, the two attitudes may come into conflict, and together they represent an ongoing ideological process.

There is much for a suspicious recent reader, if so inclined, to be doubtful about. Early hagiographers set out to glorify the Buddha, and they engaged freely in hyperbolizing his story. Later researchers, like many recent readers, work assiduously toward the opposite goal of uncovering the "real" story, and are always suspicious of exaggeration and magic. Thus, for example, A. Foucher, when confronted with the hagiographical *Lalita-vistara*, which claims that the young prince had thirty-two nurses, wonders with some amusement whether to divide by the number by 4 or even 8, while 84,000 wives is of course unacceptable, "out of respect for both the prince and verisimilitude."[6] Clearly a flexible, literary imagination is called for at times, and seeing an interaction between the two types of style, legendary and realistic, is crucial to locating the Buddha's achievement.

Knowledge of the historical Buddha is largely speculative. Among the most recent dates given for his life are 566 to 486 BC; we are largely ignorant about a figure who lived so long ago. Birth-to-death biography, moreover, is not entirely apt if previous lives, as recounted in the jātaka tales, need to be taken into account. The Buddha lived through countless samsāric cycles without beginning. Indeed, one recent "life of the Buddha" starts with a canonical statement about how "*inconceivable . . . is a beginning to this wandering on.*"[7] Devotees take refuge in the Buddha, among other refuges. Yet information about him is scanty and scattered, and does not constitute a detailed narrative line: T. W. Rhys Davids comments, with a touch of amazement, that "there is no life of Gotama the Buddha in Pali scriptures," adding provocatively that precisely this situation indicates "the meaning of true Buddhism."[8]

Certainly there are suggestive autobiographical stories, especially of high points in the Buddha's career, but shifts in stylistic levels may prove bewildering (for some) or mutually reinforcing (for others). His mythical status is entwined with his cosmic mission in a beginningless world of suffering for which he comes as a savior and torchbearer. A Buddha, allegedly in his own words, is "*A sage who knows by direct knowledge, / Who knows his mind is purified, / Entirely freed from every lust, / Who has abandoned birth and death, / Who is complete in the holy life*" (MN 91.33).

In the *Digha Nikāya*, the Buddha's cosmic status is magnified with his appearance as one among a multitude of recurrent Buddhas, whose similar lives he is able powerfully to apprehend: he knows their birthplaces, clans, names, life spans, and even the trees under which they sat: "*The Lord Buddha Vipassī gained his full enlightenment at the foot of a trumpet-flower tree; the Lord Buddha Sikhī under a white-mango tree; the Lord Buddha Vessabhū under a sāl tree*," and so on, for a few more Buddhas, until "*I became fully enlightened at the foot of an assattha-tree*" (DN 14.1.8). Aside from each sitting under their respective trees, the careers of all Buddhas have the same archetypal shapes, with the same incidents, slightly renamed, as in a familiar ritual. We like sets of things: books, stamps, cards, and yes, Buddhas. They provide a soothing sense of familiarity and order.

Sākyamuni, "our" Buddha, is thus not a once-only freak accident but is part of a universal pattern, part of the world's provision for repeated opportunities to be saved. His light-filled descent from Tushita heaven is, like most divine births, a very special occasion, surrounded with prophecies and miracles. It is special, yet so similar are the circumstances, with so many predecessors, that it is rule-governed: "*it is a rule that when a Bodhisatta has entered into this mother's womb, his mother becomes by nature virtuous*," "*It is a rule that . . . the Bodhisatta's mother . . . gives birth standing up*," and so on, with the phrase "it is a rule" being reiterated in all stages of his unfolding (DN 14.1.17, 24–30).

Māyā, the Buddha's mother, is pure in conception and in giving birth: "*she has no sensual thoughts connected with a man, and she cannot be overcome by any man with lustful thoughts. That is the rule*" (DN. 14.1.19). Presumably owing to childbirth complications, "*it is a rule that the Boddhisatta's mother dies seven days after his birth . . . and is reborn in the Tushita heaven*" (DN 14.1.22). Pious Buddhist redactors may have quietly removed Māyā from the scene after she gives birth; she could not properly return to married life, nor have other children after Gautama.[9] The newborn baby, pure like the mother, is not defiled by mucus, blood, or any impurities. Two streams of water pour out of the sky; and he takes seven strides, scanning the four quarters, making an announcement (as he will on later occasions) of his grand destiny, declaring "*with a bull-like voice: 'I am chief in the world, supreme in the world, eldest in the world. This is my last birth, there will be no more re-becoming.' That is the rule*" (DN 14.1.29).

The precocious newborn is also identified by his having "*the thirty-two marks of a Great Man*," which include the soles of his feet having "*wheels with a thousand spokes*"; also "*his legs are like an antelope's, . . . his male organs are enclosed in a sheath, and . . . his tongue is very long*" (DN 14.1.32). Amidst the multiplicity of marks, the "Great Man" still seems ambiguous or even monstrous, and a later text, the *Nidānakathā* (the "story of antecedents" introducing the *Jātaka* collection) recounts in detail how eight Brahmins were summoned to foretell the child's future. Seven of them hold up two fingers, indicating a "*double interpretation*": the child could follow two careers, becoming either a Universal Monarch or, if he goes forth, a Buddha.[10] But one of the Brahmins held up only one finger, "*and gave but a single interpretation*" (W 52), namely that the child would become a Buddha.

Here we are, then, in the realm of hermeneutics, or reader-response: the wise men read the marks, and their raised fingers are signs of the signs (one or two possible careers). The child at his birth is already puzzlingly semiotic, giving rise to debatable construals. Semiotics is closely linked with reader response, and unlocking the crucial code, or highlighting the telling sign are dicey tasks, calling for some degree of magic or luck, since the meaning of every sign is yet another sign.[11] In this child's case, are thirty-two marks enough—and why those marks? The very signs meant to clarify the newborn's identity also complicate it, putting it in need of interpretation. The child as he matures is no less mysterious. A reading of the Buddha is unending.

Naming and Signs

Do we even know his name? We all are assigned names, whether we like them or not, and undergo an originary violence.[12] But the future Buddha's case seems extreme. His given name, Gautama (or Gotama), was almost immediately eclipsed, in a second violence, before and at his birth, by prophecies and by thirty-two marks that, like medals worn by a military officer, define him as a type. He was eclipsed, too, by titles, some of them self-endowed—Buddha, Tathāgata, Lord, Blessed One, World Conqueror.

The Buddha, then, is less a personal character than an plenitude of signs. Derrida, in this chapter's epigraph, points to "death in signs," or the capacity of signs to indicate without needing expression or intention. Signs are "fissured in value," but a "privation of presence is the condition of experience."[13] In a departure from his aristocratic life of presence—that is, from auto-affection, or hearing only one's own royal self—Gautama chooses, in his "going forth," to efface his given names, as monks still do, and remains with nothing proper—little personality and almost no property. Such a condition is quite fitting, surely, for an uncomfortable visitor whose chief lesson was depersonalization. Neither did he have a mother, not only on account of a mythically pure birth, but because another woman was substituted to fill her role. As for wife and family, he abandoned them in a radical reductionism, turning them into phantom figures as he sets out to live a free life, without props or property.

In leaving home, however, there was nothing special, for at the time many ordinary young men did the same. The episode needed to be elevated, hyperbolically, into "the Great Departure." An enormous rhetorical task incumbent upon the author(s) of the Buddhist text was to exalt, in any and all ways possible, this cipher of a figure. The splendor of the Buddhist text—deploying huge resources of stock epic phrases, prophecies, regal birth, charismatic speech, quick conversions, and supernormal powers—is to make a hero out of someone who was close to nothing. With his departure, Gautama was a dead man walking. A renunciate is socially deceased: "one who renounces the world performs his death-rites."[14] Perhaps the deepest suffering of Gautama is that he was cracked and empty—the Lacanian split subject writ large. That may also be our suffering as well, and so we read on.

The Four Sights

Despite diligent scholarly and archaeological efforts, little is known of the man who called himself the Buddha. We must make do with only a few well-known scraps of highly scrutinized, yet uncertain, information. Born in auspicious circumstances as the son of a rāja, we are told, the child was groomed to be a royal heir, and was provided with a highly sheltered life, complete with every indulgence. Married at the age of sixteen, he fathered a son, Rāhula ("fetter"). Though raised luxuriously, the Prince was nonetheless not content. On rare excursions outside his palace, his discontent was crystallized in "four sights": an old man, a sick man, a corpse, and (in some versions) a yogi in a yellow robe and with shaved head, who had gone forth (DN 14.2.14). The Prince's departure from his palace, to be deeply affected by those sights, and later, his more permanent departures into homelessness and nirvana, are archetypal, yet strange, events.

In Aśvaghoṣa's *Acts of the Buddha*, the first-century epic biography aimed at an aristocratic audience, the Prince's abandonment of his eminent position is made to seem peculiar, because he seemed to have everything to lose and nothing to gain. In his royal isolation, he yearns to emerge from a womb-like existence, and his encounter with reality has the hallmarks of a birth or initiation. When the Prince "*set his heart on an expedition outside*," the father, wishing to extend a protective role, "*forbid the appearance of afflicted common folk on the royal road*" (3.2–4).[15] The departure, somewhat like a rock star's today, is marked by temptations and obstacles from his crowd of admirers.

> ... *The women obtained leave from their elders and went out on the balconies in their desire to see him. / They gathered together in uncontrollable excitement, obstructed by the slipping of their girdle-strings, as they put on their ornaments. ... / They frightened the flocks of birds with the jingling of zones, the tinkling of anklets and the clatter of their steps on the stairs, and reproached each other for jostling. / But some of these magnificent women, though longing made them try to rush, were delayed in their movements by the weight of their chariot-like hips and full breasts.* (3.13–16).

The feel of samsāra is suggested—excitement, desire, jingling and tinkling, sensuous pressing and jostling—which again and again (in life after life) keep us entranced, in a world of unstable agitation. The Prince's departure will thus foreshadow his later departure from the world when he achieves awakening.

At this point, as the Prince emerges outside, he sees an old man, and the chariot driver needs to explain:

> "*Old age it is called, that which has broken him down,—the murderer of beauty, the ruin of vigour, the birthplace of sorrow, the grave of pleasure, the destroyer of memory, the enemy of the senses.*" (3.30)

Relentlessly negative rhetorical figures, telescoped here into a single sentence, intensify old age as life's invincible enemy. They set the scene for, and anticipate, the future Buddha's teaching. The Prince asks urgently, in a noteworthy phrase, "*Will this evil come upon me also?*" (3.32). The tone is fearful and, to a suspicious reader, the young man's motives may seem to be merely self-interested. His question might also be read, just as narrowly, as a royal or aryan wish to be spared what commoners must accept: must even royalty endure such humiliation?

A wider dimension of the situation, however, as the charioteer informs him, is that growing old is the normal human condition.

> "*Inevitably by force of time my long-lived lord will know this length of his days...*". / *Fixing his eye on the old man, [the Prince] sighed deeply and shook his head; and looking on the festive multitude he uttered these words in his perturbation: / "Thus old age strikes down indiscriminately memory and beauty and valour, and yet with such a sight before its eyes the world is not perturbed. / This being so, turn back the horses, charioteer; go quickly home again. For how can I take my pleasure in the garden, when the fear of old age rules my mind?*" (3.33–37)

In seeing with innocent eyes, Gautama defamiliarizes the conditions—suffering and old age—that we take for granted. He is worried and disgusted, wishing to see no more. The poet fills in his canonical sources with details that add a human dimension. The Prince, who would in due course urge that we face up to our condition and understand it, here turns away.

At this moment he is ignorant; and ignorance, as he would allege upon becoming a Buddha, is an ominous link in the chain of conditioned causes. He is ignorant not only of old age but of the fact that it might come upon him too. What also disturbs him is the "festive multitude" paying no attention. Perhaps the rāja's son may be concerned, for reasons of state, with the people under his father's care: can nothing be done for them, to mitigate their unhappy situation? Or more generally, how can they be so callous and indifferent to what affects them all?

In the Pāli version, the *Mahâpadāna Sutta*, Prince Vipassī (an earlier but almost identical Buddha) also finds something wrong: "*What is the matter with this man?*" Told that the man is old, he asks, "*Why is he called an old man?*" There is a certain violence done: would the sight discussed still be the entity, "old man," if not so named? By using the phrase "is called," the text opens up difficult questions. On the one hand, old age and death are entirely matters of naming; on the other hand, they are presumably "unsatisfactory" not only on that account. How, in other words, is the Prince being given more than a language lesson?

This text does not address this issue. The Prince's questions are akin to statements whose answers are already determined and will eventually become part of a catechism. Here they are followed by the same question, to be repeated for all the sights: *"But am I liable to become old, and not exempt from old age?"* (DN 14.2.2). When the Prince goes out on his next excursion, he meets with a second sight, a sick man, but already the response is less personalized: *"Is this evil peculiar to him, or is the danger of disease common to all . . . ?"* (3.43). With this sight and with the third, a corpse, the Prince comes to perceive suffering as an inevitable, ubiquitous condition. The sense that possibly in "my" case there may be an exception is also ubiquitous. He thus goes through, and understands, our deepest, most common human wishes. When he returns to the palace, Gautama recognizes that life inside is no different from life outside, except in being more sheltered—thus deceptive, and even dishonest.

From Blindness to Seeing

The Buddha's story begins with the allegorical fiction that, inside the palace, the Prince fails to notice signs of sickness, disagreement, ageing, or death. His later initiation or loss of innocence is thus a staging of sudden visionary clarity. After having been blinded for so long, he sees clearly for the first time, with new eyes, what others had accustomed themselves to "see" but blindly did not see: old age, sickness, death. What starts as disappointment will turn into a way of life. He has not yet seen the yogi, but his later methods of meditation might be already prefigured, in that he "*took no pleasure in the objects of sense, sounds and the rest* . . ." (3.51).

There seems a doubleness in this situation. On the one hand, Gautama sees clearly the unhappy, yet widely accepted, conditions of human life. On the other hand, as a pampered or hypersensitive young man, he seems unwilling to accept life as it is given. Intriguingly, the common people seem more "Buddhistic," in a way, than the future Buddha. They accept their human plight with equanimity and good cheer. Gautama, by contrast, having been sheltered to an extreme degree, is agitated and devastated, not only by the calamity constituting human life, but by their resignation to it: "*Hardened, I ween, are men's hearts; for they are in good cheer, as they fare along the road*" (3.61). The people's calm acceptance is yet another dimension of suffering which requires further contemplation. The Prince can tolerate neither suffering nor even the tolerance for it! He needs to be taken home, once again, to mull over the whole unsavory situation: "*Charioteer, let our chariot be turned back; . . . it is not the time or place for pleasure-resorts. For how could a man of intelligence be heedless here in the hour of calamity, when once he knows of destruction?*" (3.62).

Crisis Mode

Aśvaghoṣa's poem underscores the primal condition of ignorance that leads to karmically unskillful acts, and that can be overcome only with enlightenment. Gautama's—and later the Buddha's—perception of the human plight is in a "crisis mode." In another excerpt, the Buddha of the *Anguttara Nikāya* recounts that, as a child, "*I was delicate, most delicate, supremely delicate.*" He describes his earlier thinking: "*I thought: 'When an untaught ordinary man, who is subject to ageing, not safe from ageing, sees another who is aged, he is shocked, . . . for he forgets that he himself is no exception. But I too am subject to ageing, not safe from ageing, and so it cannot befit me to be shocked . . . on seeing another who is aged.' When I considered this, the vanity of youth entirely left me*" (AN 3.38).[16] The same remarks are used for the sights of sickness and death, and all three are prominent in the first Noble Truth, to be formulated in proposing an escape from them.

In this story Gautama may seem, to a recent reader, like someone fleeing from a natural disaster, bent on survival. Why the desperation? Has the sheltered, coddled, "supremely delicate" Prince been pampered for too long? The locals of Kapilavatthu considered him to be spoiled, and continued to think so, it has been said, even after he became a Buddha.[17] A more flattering interpretation, still paying heed to the young man's superior status, would take into account that the Sakyas were a proud, warrior-like clan, and that the squalid conditions of ordinary life were not acceptable to this scion of the solar race, and best among humans.[18] In questing for an alternative, he would struggle relentlessly against those conditions.

To many, *carpe diem* ("seize the day") may seem a much more reasonable reaction to that unhappy triad—sickness, ageing, and death—than the long road of noble austerity in the direction of "cessation" (*nirodha*, also *nibbāna* in Pāli or more commonly, *nirvana*). In Pāli texts, the idea of seizing the day is warned against, and deemed a snare: it is attributed to Māra, who tells young people, "*You are in the prime of life . . . . Enjoy natural human pleasures! Do not . . . run after distant things*" (SN 4.3.1).[19] Some recent readers, ignorant of the snare and accustomed to realistic fiction, might be inclined to believe, however, that psychology is at issue. A rejection of *carpe diem* seems strange—and is, indeed, a making strange. What abnormality could have motivated the young man to leave his plush home, not for fun or youthful exploration, but for an austere life of deprivation? And did his lack of a mother play some part? Does his quest, sublimated, stem from something missing?

Family Matters

On the basis of a few scattered hints in the texts, readers can only speculate on what lies behind the fact that Gautama lost his mother at an early age and was raised by an aunt, Mahāpajāpatī the Gotamid. We learn of her when she brings a gift to the Buddha, many years after she raised him. He refuses to accept it, preferring that she give it instead to the sangha rather than to him, adding that more merit will accrue (MN 142.8). The scene is impersonal, and there is little sign of family warmth.

Even more strikingly, on another occasion she approaches to ask if she, and other women with her, could be allowed to ordain. The Buddha was extremely unwilling, and Mahāpajāpatī needs to ask Ānanda to plead on her behalf, which he does by reminding the Buddha how, "*as foster-mother, nurse and giver of milk, she suckled the Blessed One on the death of his mother*" (*Cullavaga* 10.1, in W 444). The Buddha, of course, is aware of this, and he often teaches laypersons that they are deeply indebted to those who raise them, whom they can never repay (AN 2.4, 4.63). Presumably he himself owes a similarly huge debt to Mahāpajāpatī. She was not, however, his real mother, and his reception of her is decidedly unaccommodating. Ānanda tells him, with no direct effect, of having seen her come "*with swollen feet, and covered with dust, sorrowful, sad, and tearful, stand[ing] weeping outside in the entrance porch*" (W 442).

She asks the Buddha three times, and is refused three times, in a negation of the very same words she uses: "*Enough, O Gotamid, do not ask that women retire from the household life to the houseless one, under the Doctrine and Discipline of the Tathāgata.*" Ānanda addresses her request to the Buddha three times, in the same words, and is refused three times, again in the same words. The repeated triplets are conventional, but they have an effect of making the Buddha's refusal seem especially recalcitrant (W 441–443). When the Buddha finally does relent, with the addition of "*eight weighty regulations*" for prospective nuns, repeated and laid out in full, he is regretful at having done so, and makes a prophecy that just as when a sugar cane field is attacked by disease and dies out, so when women are allowed to join the order, "*religion does not long endure*" (W 447).

We might sense an untold story behind these painful exchanges. Why the lack of compassion, why the rejections, why the "weighty" additional rules, since the Buddha teaches that women are as capable as men in attaining the goal (W 444)? Is there some element of family rivalry here and, having come so far, is Gautama reluctant to move backward toward the life, with its substitute mother whom he thought he had abandoned?

The issue need not be so narrowly construed. Where Freud emphasized an obsessive nostalgia tying the subject to a lost object, be it the breast or the mother, Jacques Lacan emphasized the problematic lack of an object, or lack in general, and the subject's unavoidable and problematic dependence on signs.[20] We have already noticed Gautama's affinity with signs, and his quest may have been not only to recover the mother he never knew but also to depart from the scenes of "family romance" which, in his case (with father, stepmother, wife, harem, son, servants), must have seemed complicated, confusing, and even meaningless. Psychoanalytically, the departure may be an example of what Slavoj Žižek, describes as a "desperate attempt, on the part of the perverse subject, to stage [a] symbolic castration—to achieve separation . . . , and thus obtain some space in which one can breathe more freely" (PF 104). As the Prince exclaims, "*the household life is crowded and dusty; life gone forth is wide open, . . . utterly perfect and pure as a polished shell*" (MN 27.12).

According to a recent biographer, Gautama "was a sensitive, habitually introverted intellectual."[21] Highly susceptible to pain, he was prone to find relief in meditation, detachment, and, eventually, nirvana. Not all persons would respond as he did. Even so, ideals of utopia, of heaven, and of escape are everywhere deeply fascinating. Demeaned by suffering and by imposed ideologies, we may harbor something like a death instinct (or "Nirvana principle") whose "ancient goal" is to restore us, in our own ways, to a long-departed, pristine, inanimate state.[22]

Emerging into Homelessness

Here we might recall a well-known Shakespearean figure, also a prince, also shocked with life, who might be compared with Gautama, and whose plight, too, is amenable to psychological theorizing.[23] Triggered by a series of unaccustomed events, Prince Hamlet's disgusted feelings toward his beloved Ophelia, his mother Gertrude, and his discontented ghostly father can be compared to Gautama's feelings about his palace harem, his absent mother, his fetter of a child, his loudly solicitous father. And when Gautama decides to leave home, his women are portrayed rather differently than earlier:

> *[Some of them] looked ugly, lying unconscious like corpses, with their ornaments and garlands cast aside, the fastening knots of their dresses undone, and eyes moveless with their whites showing. / Another lay as if sprawling with intoxication, with her mouth gaping wide, so that the saliva oozed forth, and with her limbs spread out so as to show what should have been hid. Her beauty was gone, her form distorted.* (5.60–61)

The Prince is moved to disgust, remarking moralistically, "*Such is the real nature of woman*" (3.64), much as Hamlet does in his outburst, "*Frailty, thy name is woman!*"[24] Certainly it is convenient for the departing Gautama to be sent on his way by an ungainly sight, but unclear why this is "*the real nature of woman*" any more than was the earlier, more alluring, picture. The traditional reader, though, would have no problem, and would link this scene of women "like corpses" with the practice of meditation on dead bodies thrown together in a common grave, meant to help monks overcome lustful attachments.

In leaving his family and loves, Gautama, though shocked and disgusted, does not act, he pointedly says, out of disappointment or old age. He is in the very prime of youth, his hair still black and his faculties fully functional. As he tells us in *The Noble Search* sutta:

> *"While still young, a black-haired young man endowed with the blessing of youth, in the prime of life, though my mother and father wished otherwise and wept with tearful faces, I shaved off my hair and beard, put on the yellow robe, and went forth from the home life into homelessness."* (MN 26.14)

When he thus makes his departure from home, he emerges from the protective shelter of childhood to embark on a perilous quest-journey. He breaks from his past in a symbolic inversion, a radical change of identity, as in a fairy-tale, from prince to beggar. Householders, or ordinary people, depend on the "five strands of sense pleasure"; monks, by contrast, live homelessly in an abandonment of those strands—that is, in a refusal to be enslaved by the senses. Buddhaghosa, citing a canonical text, says that a space "*enclosed with timbers and creepers and grass and clay*"—a house—is like "*a space enclosed with bones, sinews, flesh and skin*," a material form (*rupa*).[25] The Prince's departure from his cocoon of a home is symbolic, and will provide an exemplary model for future aspirants. The departure has, as Steven Collins points out, three dimensions: physically, an abandonment of household for monastic life; psychologically, an attempt to give up desires and self; ontologically, a leaving of the rebirth cycles (*samsāra*).[26]

Since we are already privy to the story's "happy ending," we can hardly imagine the boldness of the young man's departure. Young, healthy, wealthy, and with a luminous future beckoning, he gave it all up—and without back-tracking! The act could be called an "absolute expenditure,"[27] that is, a breaking from any possible economy (*oikos nomos,* household law). The Prince gives up regal life in exchange for something, perhaps a mere fantasy, which as yet was quite unknown to him.

Two Readings

The recent, or "suspicious" reader, to recapitulate, would view the young man's departure in psychological and political terms. A spoiled young man, the son of a *rāja*, is unfulfilled in his life of luxury, and unhappy with the burdens placed upon him, of becoming a ruling monarch and of looking after his family, including the son named Fetter. His departure from home may stem from a sense that there are better opportunities elsewhere, or that sheer freedom may prove a more challenging option for himself, however senseless it may seem to others. His solitary and arbitrary departure seems risky, but he may be searching unconsciously for an imagined figure (maternal or otherwise), and three of the four sights he saw seemed real and frightening enough for him to flee in terror for his life, in quest for an alternative.

The traditional, or receptively "listening" reader would take exception, almost point for point, to this interpretation. The Great Departure is not arbitrary, since it had been prepared for by solemn vows in a previous life, while his motivation, far from being in any way self-serving, was a brave and heroic effort to help all those who mistakenly believe on some deep level (as many people do) that the misfortunes of old age, serious illness, and death can happen only to others. In contrast with the future Buddha, an ordinary man—everyman—appears in the *Anguttara Nikāya*, and he is unaware of the three signs or "divine messengers," or fails to connect them to himself. King Yama asks the man if he had seen elderly people "*with broken teeth, with grey and scanty hair or none, wrinkled, with blotched limbs*?" The man had seen this, he replies, but did not stop to think that he, too, would some day become like that (AN 3.35).[28] Gautama's realization that these unfortunate states "*will happen to me*" is the first step in his awareness of the vast, inescapable web of suffering and impermanence, urgently demanding a response.

Abandoning Self

Trevor Ling has maintained that the two kinds of kingship predicted for the Buddha-to-be are virtually identical, and that with the institution of the sangha, which required the cooperation of wise local kings and the abandonment of personal matters, the Buddha was attempting to cure the disease of individualism. Although the story of the Buddha may look like a personal salvation story to recent readers, Ling continues, we may be projecting back our ideas to the time of the Buddha. For the Buddha, the "self" did not need to be saved, but on the contrary was the source of suffering, and precisely what we need to be saved from.[29]

Self notions and selfishness, true enough, need to be overcome. Selves, even so, are places of moral decision and responsibility. Certain types of selves—the devoted monk or layperson, the ideal ruler, the world conqueror, the arhat, the Buddha—provided, and still provide, models for aspiration. In keeping with the epic genre, Gautama's birth, deeds, and his passing (personal matters that are also more than personal) gain magnitude by having cosmic repercussions: "*an immeasurable light spread through ten thousand worlds; the blind recovered their sight, as if from a desire to see his glory; the deaf received their hearing; the dumb talked; . . . water burst forth from the earth and flowed in streams; the birds ceased flying through the air . . .*" (W 44). Not merely willful and capricious, the departing young idealist is following, in the context of other Buddhas, a well-known pattern. Even the four sights are staged by the gods ("*they changed one of their number into a decrepit old man,*" etc.), and the young man's future is assisted by a devoted charioteer and an intelligent horse (W 56, 62). At crucial moments—in his fasting and his night of awakening—the gods are unable to be of assistance, and the achievement is his alone. This achievement redounds to the benefit not only of the monks whom the Buddha usually addresses but, with skillful means, to the benefit of as many beings as possible.

The Enormous Quest

Consider again, then, the Buddha's literary identity. The young man seems to have exchanged one kind of nobility, as a royal, for another, as a wanderer or *śramaṇa* (one who strives). Departure from the regal household foreshadows another, greater departure. After great struggle, the archetypal hero returns in triumph to take his honored place in a restored, renewed community. The Buddha, too, returns from years of struggle, spending further years to travel and to disseminate his teachings. But after that, this hero, while leaving relics behind, vanishes from our view, saying a sort of farewell: "*birth is destroyed, the holy life has been lived, . . . there is no more coming back to any state of being*" (MN 39.21). We cannot know what happens to him: this doctrinal point is made insistently (MN 72.16) and is part of his magnitude. He neither exists nor does not, though it still can be said, from the perspective of early followers, that he's a man who will never return.

Precisely his non-return is, of course, supposed to inspire us. But if he is one of a kind, or almost, then can anyone truly walk his path? The question may suggest a certain incomprehensibility (the literary quality of defamiliarization) not only at the story's end but in the search itself—its motives, methods, results, and dissemination. Here, for example, is how the Buddha speaks in the *Noble Search*:

> *"Bhikkus, there are these two kinds of search: the noble search and the ignoble search. And what is the ignoble search? Here someone, himself subject to birth seeks what is also subject to birth; being himself subject to ageing, seeks what is also subject to ageing. . . ."* (MN 26.5)

The passage continues with exactly the same pattern for *death*, *sickness*, *sorrow*, and *defilement*. The addressees are "*bhikkus*," or monks, suggesting that they already have made a strong commitment to following the path. Yet would the logic or rhetoric be quite so familiar and powerful outside the monastic assembly whose ideals are being reinforced?

Oppositional Symmetries

The scheme is highly geometrical: a series of strict parallels set within a structure of bipolar valorizations (noble/ignoble). The noble search predictably matches the ignoble search, with oppositional precision:

> *"And what is the noble search? Here someone, himself subject to birth, ageing, ailment, death, sorrow and defilement, and knowing the danger in [them], seeks the unborn, unageing, unailing, deathless, sorrowless, undefiled, supreme surcease of bondage, which is Nibbāna."* (MN 26.12 N)[30]

We are told that the "objects of attachment" (*upādhi*: the "grounds" or "essentials") in the ignoble search—for example, "*wife and children, bondsmen and bondswomen, goats and sheep*" (MN 26.11 N)—will sooner or later, in their mortality, cause heartache to the extent of our emotional attachment. What the bipolar oppositions exclude, even while providing rhetorical force, are any mixtures or degrees of nobility in those attachments. The prince was resolutely uncompromising in his relinquishments of all so-called privileges in his deceptively noble life.

With the text's stark polarities, we are aware of being in the realm of romance. Romance, Frye tells us, "avoids the ambiguities of ordinary life, where everything is a mixture of good and bad, and where it is difficult to take sides or believe that people are consistent patterns of virtue or vice. The popularity of romance . . . has much to to with its simplifying of moral facts. It relieves us of the strain of trying to be fair-minded."[31] The Prince is on a quest-romance, and his way of thinking largely matches that pattern. At the same time, since Buddhist scriptures claim to be truthful and important, to be myth more than folktale, then the binary oppositions, at least to a recent reader, may require scrutiny.

Is something being occulted by these oppositions in their simplistic, hierarchical, seemingly metaphysical formulations? They cry out for what Derrida calls a double reading: "the opposition of metaphysical concepts (e.g. speech/writing, presence/absence, etc.) is never the confrontation of two terms, but a hierarchy and order of subordination. Deconstruction, . . . through a double gesture, a double science, a double writing—puts into practice a *reversal* of the classical opposition and a general *displacement* . . . [or] *intervening* in the field of oppositions."[32] The "intervening" is sometimes described as a rewriting—that is, an attention to the excluded terms (not a simple reversal of them) so as to provide a fairer hearing, noticing their indispensable place in defining the ideologically "higher" or "nobler" terms.

Notice, by way of an initial intervention, that the text's "ignoble" items include "*wife and children . . . , men and women slaves, goats, sheep, fowl and pigs, elephants, cattle, horses and mares, gold and silver*" (MN 26.6). Most of these items, except for gold and silver, are given a subordinate position in a well-to-do household. The Prince then, in his Noble Quest, may mentally never to have left home: he continues with a disdainful attitude toward the servant class, and what they take care of. In leaving home, has he really stopped being "*tied to these things, infatuated with them*," since he still seems to disdain them? If he has indeed abandoned them, then there might be some redundancy, or futility, in his quest. Or perhaps not quite: he wants, still regally and scornfully, to go even further and to discard what marks all of these "lower" items: birth, ageing, sorrow, sickness, and death (MN 26.5–6). We will need to pay attention to the ways in which the Prince, the self-named Buddha, escapes from none of the latter items, at least not in the most obvious ways. We are asked to accept—though some readers may feel a need to revise, as later traditions did—the ideology of "the deathless," or nirvana.

Plotting Comedy

Gautama's going forth into homelessness, like that of so many conquerors before him, is endowed with value by being long and difficult. In and despite great obstacles, the structure of his quest conforms to the literary genre not only of romance but also of comedy, whose theme is "the integration of society, which takes the form of incorporating a central character into it."[33] With his attainment of enlightenment and his setting up of clerical institutions, the Buddha reformed and re-established the social order. His name and teachings became integral to societies throughout the world.

More specifically, his epic story is plotted as romantic comedy in the senses of Roman New Comedy and Shakespeare. Misperceptions and mispairings are followed, after innumerable twists and turns, by a harmonious series of corrections. In Shakespearian comedies such as *Much Ado About Nothing*, the "right" couples are separated or mismatched, owing to misfortune, parental taboos, unavoidable disguises, and misguided evil-doers. Events are contrived, pretended, or theatrical, and there are false accusations, confusions, mix-ups, and exaggerated exchanges. But in the end, divisive forces are finally defeated, all giving way to proper matches and cosmic harmony.

Likewise, the royal Prince, a Buddha-to-be, is mispaired, first with parents, palace pleasures, wife and son, then with inadequate teachers. He needs to combat not only his family, who resist his departure, but also Māra, the tempter. His identity, as the diligent "ascetic Gautama," is mistaken in exchanges with other ascetics. Along the way, he provides what might be loosely called entertainment, in his miraculous deeds and, as will be noticed later, even in the asceticism itself, which takes him nowhere. His final victory, or "lion's roar," is a self-conquest in a double sense: misunderstandings are clarified and he becomes utterly selfless. The quest-romance of the Prince, the Sun-god or the Awakened One ends, in accord with comic genre, with travails resolved and burdens put down, amidst celestial congratulations: a roar of thunder, an earthquake. In what follows, we examine that happy ending, his awakening, but also the peculiarly violent events preceding and following it.

3

The Buddha Awakening

The *Nikāyas*

Rivalry multiplies mirror images of violence . . . Symbolized reality becomes, paradoxically, the loss of all symbolism . . .

Myths make constant reference to the sacrifical crisis, but do so only to disguise the issue. Myths are the retrospective transfiguration of these crises . . . in light of the cultural order that has arisen from them.

—René Girard, *Violence and the Sacred*

The gist of the Buddha's teachings, and not only of his so-called biography, goes against the grain of routine living. Most of us are hardly able to feel indifferent to "*worldly conditions, [which] keep the world turning around: . . . gain and loss, fame and disrepute, praise and blame, pleasure and pain*" (AN 8.6). Our very humanity is linked to worldly conditions. We may become at times more or less detached but are unlikely to imitate the inanimate elements, as the Buddha recommends.

Those elements play a key role in his teachings. When two monks have an alleged dispute—one is accused of hitting another—they are urged not to respond personally. Sāriputta, the accused, testifies to the Buddha:

> *"Just as, Lord, people throw upon the earth things clean and unclean, dung, spittle, pus and blood, yet for all that the earth has no revulsion, loathing or disgust towards it; even so, Lord, do I dwell with a heart that is like the*

> *earth, vast, exalted and measureless, without hostility and without ill will."* (AN 9.11).

Were Sāriputta instead to make counteraccusations, or indulge in name-calling, he would be on the same level as his accuser (the privilege of name-calling, interestingly, is reserved for the Buddha, who calls the accuser a "*foolish man*"). Sāriputta's magisterial demeanor might make some readers chary of the imagery. Yet here, once again, the advice is to go against the grain: no apologies are required for what was done without ill will. To see things elementally, or as dhammas, is to see them most truly or, in a recurrent phrase, it is to see the world "*as it really is*" (DN 22.17).

Mimetic Desire, Mimetic Violence

The conflict between the two monks, with the Buddha acting as an exemplary third party and judge, disrupts the quietude of monastic life and of its tranquil literary portrayal. The event may seem unusual in such a setting. Yet life, like literature, is filled with rivalry, jealousy, and conflict. We imitate a role model, and in due course we imitate the desire of that model, desiring the same objects. Since those objects are in limited supply (we have only one natural parent of the opposite sex, for example), imitation may lead to conflict and struggle. Such conflict is a major literary theme. Indeed, the basis of literature, in classical aesthetics, is *mimesis*: imitation or representation. The artist struggles to imitate scenes of imitation involving ideals, actions, persons, or other artists.

René Girard has shown that, almost inevitably, "two desires converging on the same object are bound to clash. Thus, mimesis coupled with desire leads automatically to conflict."[1] *Mimetic violence* is an incrementally intensifying eye-for-an-eye, tooth-for-a-tooth blood feud in which each party returns "the same" violence in retaliation. The cycles of violence are difficult, if not impossible, to stop. When such situations arise in early societies, sacrifice is required. A victim is found on the margins of society, and potentially destructive violence is diverted onto that victim, who becomes a scapegoat.[2] Sacred rituals are attempts to control violence, and a *sacrificial crisis*, according to Girard, develops when those rituals of peacemaking are no longer efficacious.

Mimetic desire, that is, desire for the same object that one's model or one's rival desires, is not necessarily conflictive. But many examples of imitation show rivalry and violence to be unavoidable. Gautama came into conflict, to some extent, with his parents and teachers, and later, a teacher himself, he was subject to aggression from his jealous cousin Devadatta. One turn perceived to be aggressive evokes another, and violence can easily escalate, until entire societies are engulfed. A way to avoid mimetic desire is, of course, to renounce desire entirely, turning instead to compassionate generosity. Buddhist "cessation" or "loving kindness" are notable examples. How troubled, though, is the path leading in that direction? What happens to our heroes, as asked earlier, when they are driven by instincts to live and procreate—or, more directly put, what happens to sex and violence? We need not subscribe unreservedly to Girard's theory, but it provides a promising framework for reading Buddhist texts.

Questions of Rivalry

Begin with some queries, already sketched out, and phrased inevitably in the language of our times. How sublimated or nonlibidinal was Gautama's quest for enlightenment, and how competitive was he in the course of distinguishing himself, as he certainly did? How valid is the common stereotype of the Buddha as peaceful, unruffled, and all-compassionate? In social terms, was there a "sacrifical crisis" out of which the Buddhist alternative gained plausibility?

At the time of the Buddha, Brahmin priests followed laborious and exact sequences of sacrificial rituals, often involving animal victims. All was done purportedly to sustain the universe, allowing the Brahmins to consider themselves essential to the world's peace and order. Gautama rejected their claims, and his teachings were individualistic and antiritualistic (DN 5).[3] The Brahmins, in turn, claimed that without them, chaos would ensue, and among the many people who followed and believed them, wars were a frequent occurrence. What Girard calls a sacrificial crisis, the breakdown of a culture into a chaos of indifferentiation, with violence running rampant, could be located with the waning power of the Brahmin class and the rise of the mercantile class, who became the Buddha's followers. The crisis was covered up and purposely forgotten, but there are signs, under partial erasure, of personal and social violence in the Buddha's career.

When Prince Gautama leaves home, for example, he comes into conflict with his regal father. Although parents ideally provide role models for the child, in this instance the young man refuses to follow his models. He gives his charioteer a message: the son will depart "*for the purpose of putting an end to old age and death.*"[4] From a parental viewpoint, the explanation must seem almost insane: irrelevant, headstrong, and violent. From a more cosmic viewpoint, however, prophecies had been made, and the Buddha's epic career, with help from the gods, is inscribed in advance.[5] If we consider the *Mahāpadāna Sutta,* moreover, another role model—the wandering meditator—provides an alternate figure to emulate. Like other Buddhas, Vipassī "*saw a shaven-headed man, one who had gone forth [into homelessness], wearing a yellow robe.*" The Prince decides immediately—as if finally discovering his real desire—to imitate that role model: "*I shall . . . shave off my hair and beard, put on the yellow robes and go forth from the household life into homelessness*" (DN 14.2.14–15).

Once having left home, he encounters other wanderers on the road. He learns about the teachers Ālāra Kālāma and Uddaka Rāmaputta, and he goes to visit them. Will he imitate those teachers, and will violence, even the shadow of violence, be engendered in mimetic rivalry? In the *Noble Search* sutta, Gautama follows the instructions of his teacher, Ālāra Kālāma, and is confident that his abilities are equal. The Pāli text, so prone to repetitions, is excellent in displaying imitation, point by point, on the verge of competitiveness:

> *I considered: "Not only Ālāra Kālāma has faith, energy, mindfulness, concentration, and wisdom. I too have faith, energy, mindfulness, concentration and wisdom."* (MN 26.15)

Acquisitive imitation is sometimes distinguished from aggressive imitation,[6] but here the two are not far apart, and equalizing may be a subsuming, rather than a sharing. Gautama quickly follows, and realizes, Ālāra's teachings. The outcome, the text stresses, is felicitous. Ālāra remarks:

> *"You know the Dhamma that I know and I know that Dhamma that you know. As I am, so are you; as you are, so am I. Come, friend, let us now lead this community together."* (MN 26.15)

This passage, with its repetitious equalizations of "I" and "you," creates a mirror image of the aspirant. Gautama has become identical to his teacher, who offers, quite amicably, to share leadership. How Gautama responds, at this point, is crucial.

Had he accepted the offer, his story would doubtless end right there. He instead rejects claims of equality. He proclaims to his teacher, as he did to his father, that he is still dissatisfied, still prey to *dukkha*. Ālāra's teachings do not lead to the goal that he seems to know in advance: disenchantment, dispassion, cessation, peace, direct knowledge, enlightenment. Gautama triumphs by not compromising: "*Not being satisfied with that Dhamma, I left it and went away*" (MN 26.15). There is no mention of thanks being given, and by Indian standards of the time, his departure may have been discourteous, even insolent.[7] The sullen, ungracious departure may signal repressed violence, hidden under Gautama's bland self-control.

Another teacher, Uddaka Rāmaputta, is found, and the encounter is described in exactly the same words: another equalization is attempted. Oral traditions require formulae for memorization, and repetition has an effect of reinforcement. Each teacher offers something (yogic bases and teaching positions), and both are rejected. Gautama could continue to seek teachers, but mere mimesis is fruitless for him. The result would be similar, and so would the reaction. The text's equalization of the two teachers standardizes them and leaves them more in competition with each other than with Gautama. He may seem to have abandoned them, thus moving beyond imitation and rivalry.

Overcoming the Teachers

We will encounter these two teachers again. After his awakening, the Buddha wonders whom he should teach first. He thinks of Āḷāra Kālāma, who would perhaps learn quickly. But "*then the deities approached me and said: 'Venerable sir, Āḷāra Kālāma has died seven days ago.' And the knowledge and vision arose in me: Āḷāra Kālāma died seven days ago.*'" The same pericope is used with Uddaka Rāmaputta, who died the very night before (MN 26.22).

In the Buddha's story—without doubting the text's historical basis, but simply attending to its literary form—we might notice that his enlightenment has the effect of cancelling out, and negating, his former teachers and rivals. There can be no more chance of their competing with him or of asking him to join or lead their schools. It may be less than coincidental, too, that the Buddha, despite his supernormal powers, was entirely unaware of their demise, and thus is distanced from it. Only after the deities make an announcement does the "knowledge and vision" of their deaths arise in him.

The Buddha is making his first attempt to find followers, yet most readers or commentators pay scant attention to this episode, assuming it merely to show his perseverance. Might the two deaths, though, seeming to happen so inauspiciously at the start of the Buddha's teaching career, have something to do with mimetic rivalry? Rivalry, for example in a duel of honor, a family feud, or a boundary dispute, is likely to end with the death or dishonor of at least one of the rivals. Once Gautama has attained his goal and becomes a "World Conqueror," what happens to his former rivals, his teachers, one of them claiming (mistakenly, Gautama insists) to hold the same title?[8] The Buddha is not a pugnacious hero. Yet it is a peculiarity of the narrative that, with his achieving of enlightenment, both his teachers are disposed of. They both die within the same week!

It is not insignificant that two narrated events come in close succession, even though the text does not make any comment on that succession. But a "simple topographic or sequential juxtaposition," Derrida remarks, "is 'in the text,' it constitutes the text itself and can be *interpreted*, it is *interpretable*. . . . It cannot simply be insignificant."[9] In this case, mimetic violence, leading to sacrificial scapegoating, may be connected with the teachers' deaths. Clearly "something happened," possibly more than coincidentally, to these two rivals who, if they remained alive, might claim to be as "awakened" as he claimed to be—thereby continuing a mimetic crisis. Here then, in the blank space or gap, in the founding moment, of Buddhism—between the Buddha's awakening and the beginning of his teaching—there seems to have been some sort of occulted violence. Our ignorance of the details, moreover, is not irrelevant. Religions, according to Girard, conceal or efface their origins: "violence must remain hidden; misapprehension is indispensable."[10]

The moment under scrutiny is not the first appearance of sacrificial violence. There are a number of other sacrifices in the text—Gautama's leaving home and family; his learning from, and then abandoning, his teachers; his trials of austerity; his rejection of the Brahmins' ways—and these are all types of violence, whether mild or intense. Sacrifice, or scapegoating, protects the community from its own larger, uncontrollable violence, thereby establishing institutional order. But the community retains the possibility of violence and ritual by failing to understand the sacrificial mechanism. It occludes the origin of violence by assigning it to a victim, and so is able to keep up a continual search for new victims[11]—in this case, a line of future Buddhas or of new wayward monks.

Foundations of Buddhism

Such a theory impinges upon received ideas about the "founding myth" of Buddhism. What might that myth be? It has been said to reside in the four sights, especially of the corpse, which confirms the evolving doctrine of suffering and its release; it is also said to reside in the Buddha's awakening, which similarly confirms the evolving teachings; or it could said to reside, according to less conventional speculation, in the opportune deaths of two competititors, just as the newly emerging Buddha is on the threshold of founding what would later become a world religion.

These possibilities are not mutually exclusive, but consider the relative weights of each. The four sights are open to anyone, are ordinary enough, and to most people they are neither startling nor even very interesting. That they are troubling for the Buddha might make them his particular problem more than anyone else's. Again, the night of awakening depicts the private experience of a solitary individual; outsiders, even his contemporaries, are in no position to validate his experience. One can admire the way in which it is formulated, and certainly be persuaded that some sort of "awakening" took place. But we have no way of knowing, aside from Gautama's enthusiastic proclamations, that the experience is an infallible indication of having reached "the deathless" in a permanent escape from suffering.

We can reasonably conjecture, however, following Girard's well-documented hypothesis, that Prince Gautama, a highly visible figure who isolates himself from his community (going into homelessness and practicing austerities), was turning into a victim (dying one last time) for a highly contentious society, giving teachings and founding an instititution (the sangha), thereby bringing some degree of detachment and peace to the world. His emerging religion, like other religions, effaces its violent origins, replacing them with ritual and hierarchy: "violence in every cultural order," Girard claims, "is the true subject of every ritual or institutional structure."[12] Buddhist texts do everything they can to cover up violent origins, and the Buddha announces himself as being totally unable to commit violence. Even so, symptoms of repressed violence appear constantly, if at times surprisingly, in all the scriptures to be examined here.

The demise of his two teachers means that the newly minted Buddha cannot limit his teachings to an already well-disposed audience but must reach out, as indeed he did, more widely. The demise also means that, while competitiveness is crucial to demarking his achievements, his achievements are solitary: they are his alone, and no one can match him. True, yet not entirely so. The ongoing paradox, to be seen repeatedly, is that his followers will have a sense that the Buddha (despite a multitude of other Buddhas) was unique in his great accomplishments, but that those followers, flawed as they are, may with effort be able to accomplish the same.

Ascetic Excess

After studying with his teachers and abandoning them, Gautama's solitary competitiveness continued in six years of austerities. Part of his struggle was a mental discipline of remaining unfazed:

> *"I would make my bed in a charnel ground with the bones of the dead for a pillow. And cowherd boys came up and spat on me, urinated on me, threw dirt at me, and poked sticks into my ears. Yet I do not recall that I ever [knew the arising of] evil thoughts about them."* (MN 12.51)

The tone mingles self-praise, serious illustration, and dry humor. Gautama is treated as a despicable, almost inhuman, object. He goes through a time of testing and purgation, but still retains his eagerness. Where other ascetics would eat a diet of sesamum seeds, he would outdo them by eating only a single seed. The effect of his limited diet is set out in an series of admirably hyperbolic similes:

> *"Because of eating so little my limbs became like the jointed segments of vine stems or bamboo stems. Because of eating so little my backside became like a camel's hoof. . . . Because of eating so little my ribs jutted out as gaunt as the crazy rafters of an old roofless barn. Because of eating so little the gleam of my eyes sank far down in their sockets, looking like a gleam of water that has sunk far down in a deep well. Because of eating so little my scalp shrivelled and withered as a green bitter gourd shrivels and withers in the wind and sun. Because of eating so little my belly skin adhered to my backbone; thus if I touched my belly I encountered my backbone, and if I touched my backbone I encountered my belly skin."* (MN 12.52)

The passage has a structure, each sentence gaining cumulative rhetorical power from the repeated phrase, "Because of eating so little." At the same time, the Buddha seems at ease, looking back at his youthful excesses, recounting them to his disciple Sāriputta as part of a biographical tale, almost a tall tale. The body is part of nature, and its neglect is compared to vine stems, a camel's hoof, a deep well. The tone is instructive yet grimly comic, as if impersonal elements were taking over what to most people is near and dear: their bodies. His scalp is like a green gourd withering in the sun: not the same (it's a human scalp) but not different (it's subject to the elements). The sequence of comparisons seems to intensify, moving from bamboo stems, ribs jutting like roofbeams, to the point where, utterly emaciated, his abdomen and backbone can be touched together. Not yet the exalted Buddha his followers usually prefer to worship, he needed to become a living-dying hyperbole in order to discover the middle way. While the two teachers could attest to his meditational achievements, how could extreme ascetic achievements be assessed? There can be no limit to ascetic feats, except the odd "triumph" of dying.

Someone had to stop Gautama in his violence against himself, or else he would starve. The gods attempt to do so, but he sends them away (MN 36.27); like Franz Kafka's hunger artist, he disdains any possible appearance of imposture. He is stopped only when he decides, by his own experience, that asceticism does not produce higher mental states and would not lead to "*any distinction in knowledge and vision worthy of the noble ones*" (MN 36.30). In phrases like "distinction" and "worthy of the noble ones," the struggle is still mimetic: he is in competition with his ideal and with ideal others. He is in competition even when deciding to leave the field, so as to find a worthier style of emulation.

The Buddhist Aggression of Māra

A similar pattern occurs in his struggles with Māra, which seem deviant and lopsided. Most heroes perform lengthy, violent combat with a strong opponent, and at times the outcome is excitingly in doubt: think of Ariosto's Orlando Furioso fighting in bloody rampage, or Spenser's Red Crosse Knight in combat with Errour. The battle is also furious, though less in doubt, when Indra, in the *Rg Veda*, fights Vrtra the cloud dragon. By contrast, and much to the dismay of those would favor a feisty hero, the Buddha's inability to fight, in this inverted world, is a sign of success. He does not fight in any ordinary sense of the term: "*I do not dispute with the world*," he famously proclaims, "*the world disputes with me*" (SN 22.94).

It is Māra, then, and not the Buddha, who assumes the traditional role of epic warrior. Māra could even be said, perhaps strangely, to do so *for* the Buddha, as his stand-in, and out of concern for him. He may even do so *for* the Buddhist tradition, which needs and deserves warriors! When he sees the Buddha on the night of awakening, seated in meditation, Māra is worried and alarmed, marshalling an enormous army:

> *Sounding the Māra war-cry, [he] drew out for battle. . . . The god Māra, mounting his elephant, . . . caused a thousand arms to appear on his*

> *body, and with these he grasped a variety of weapons. Also in the remainder of that army, no two persons carried the same weapon. . . . The host swept on like a flood to overwhem the Great Being.* (W 76–77)

Their prodigious efforts are in vain. The army weakens as it draws near to the Buddha, and weapons prove ineffective. The Buddha takes his Ten Perfections as a shield. When Māra launches a shower of weapons, including swords, spears, and arrows, they "*flew smoking and flaming through the sky. But on reaching the Future Buddha, they became celestial bouquets of flowers*" (W 78). There is no use in fighting against such an opponent.

On less elaborate occasions, the Buddha has only to recognize and name his adversary ("*I know you, Evil One. . . . You are Māra*"), and Māra is banished (MN 49.6). He does, on occasion, proclaim victory in triumphant verses. And Māra, for his part, does not relent, but constantly reappears as a perfidious enemy:

> *Māra the Evil One . . . manifested himself in the form of a giant king Serpent, and approached the Blessed One. Its body was like a huge boat made from a single tree trunk; its hood, like a large brewer's sieve; its eyes, like the large bronze dishes of Kosala; its tongue darting out from its mouth, like flashes of lightning emitted when the sky thunders; the sound of its breathing in and out, like the sound of a smith's bellows filling with air.* (SN 4.6)

The situation is doubly fictional, presenting a conventional epic monster, but also Māra's show or fabrication. The Blessed One is not impressed and gives no response. He simply, once again, recognizes: "*[he] understood, 'This is Māra, the Evil One.'*" The epic concoction is seen to be such, the images are detected to be merely invented. The Blessed One, advancing a literary counteridentity, recites verses against Mara: "*Though many creatures crawl about, / Many terrors, flies, serpents, / The great sage gone to his empty hut, / Stirs not a hair because of them*" (SN 4.6). "Terrors," even if not theatrical, will neither affect the Blessed One nor disturb his equanimity (MN 4.20).

Gautama is not perturbed, either, by Māra's allegorically named daughters—Tanhā, Aratī, and Ragā. Seductive though they are, they return defeated. Māra, in the absence of a more overt conflict, turns, as epic monsters do, against his own progeny. He upbraids them, in a series of figures, for even having made the attempt:

> *"Fools! You tried to batter a mountain / With the stalks of lotus flowers, / To dig up a mountain with your nails, / To chew iron with you teeth. / As if, having lifted a rock with your head, / You sought a foothold in the abyss; / As if you struck a stump with your breast . . . .*" (SN 4.25)

The images of demonic effort here are mixed—surprisingly—with the Buddha's images: *tanhā*, lotus flowers, and palm stumps are in the language of his greatest insights, and not gaining a foothold is associated with an end to rebirths. Binary oppositions turn out be not quite secure and to have strange affinities. Māra and the Buddha are parts of one another; they have a symbiotic relationship by which each defines the other.

In this way, self and soul, so to speak, carry on a dialogue, and the literary effect of Māra's fatherly reprimand is to reverse roles, and become the Buddha's advocate, both to show frustration at his daughters and to exalt the Buddha. Māra acts out an allegorical part, repeating himself endlessly as the Buddha's counterpart and much-needed counterweight. Māra operates, Trevor Ling says, not only as a demon of popular thought, deceiving and possessing his victims, but also as the embodiment of Buddhist "evil," or *samsāra*: ignorance, pleasure, lust, greed, pride, and death. Māra defends traditional rituals, trying to hinder the Buddha from teaching, and instead advocating the joys of life—love, marriage, possession, excitement, fame, and procreation.[13] Since most people are variably dedicated to such pursuits, Māra could also allegorize the average reader, who could easily enough become the devil's—in this case, Māra's—advocate.

More than that, Māra is part of the Buddhist system: his violence and his daughters' sexuality build up an allegory of the Buddha's repressed but always covert powers—his *virtù* or *viriya*. The struggle with Māra is, in short, the Buddha's struggle with himself. He seems to triumph over Māra by not doing anything, but certain powers remain latent—Māra will return—and are crucial to the Buddha's earthiness, to his remaining life. This is true even during the enlightenment, whose crucial *jhānic* steps are described, in some texts, as a blindfolding of Māra (MN 25.12–20).

Winning Awakening

Enlightenment, or the achievement of nirvana, is recounted as a narrative taking place during three watches of the night, and completed at sunrise. The story of that night, so definitive to Buddhism, is told succinctly and in relatively few canonical texts. The *Fear and Dread Sutta* and the *Greater Discourse to Saccaka* (MN 4, 36) provide the standard formulae, and are offered as direct, first-person narratives.

In both suttas, imitation and mimetic rivalry are prominently displayed. The second text's conversation is started by Saccaka, a clever speaker who "*wants to discredit the Buddha*," and the *Fear and Dread Sutta* begins when a Brahmin (quite possibly also a teacher) raises the question of whether homeless clansmen follow Master Gautama's "*example*," and have him "*as their leader, helper and guide?*" (MN 36.3, 4.2). The Buddha replies positively, and the Brahmin continues by pointing to daunting difficulties: "*remote jungle-thicket resting places . . .*

are hard to endure, seclusion is hard to practice." Gautama entirely agrees, but contrasts himself to "*recluses and brahmins devoid of wisdom*," who will be overcome by fear and dread. With that point, he begins the account of his awakening.

Fear and dread are terrifying aspects of the holy, the taboo, the sublime. On auspicious nights, Gautama dares to dwell in "*awe-inspiring, horrifying abodes*," as if venturing, perhaps trespassing, into forbidden, sacrosanct spaces: "*orchard shrines, woodland shrines, and tree shrines.*" Eerily, even the slightest sounds were terrifying: "*And while I dwelt there, a wild animal would come up to me, or a peacock would knock off a branch, or the wind would rustle the leaves. . . . While I walked, fear and dread came upon me, [but] . . . I subdued [them]*" (MN 4.20). Initations place the archetypal hero in terrifyingly dangerous places, and here the future Buddha, with a great effort of concentration, must subdue fear and dread. By conquering such mental states, Gautama is steadfastly courageous, passing beyond delusion, and tranquilly entering into the jhānic states, which, together with his analytical efforts, are taken to be the conditioned causes for the three knowledges of his enlightenment.

Watching with a Divine Eye

The text splendidly balances the specificity of an "I" narrative with the cosmic scope of supernormal vision. It purports to show how the emerging Buddha's experience is not merely personal and subjective but also objective and universally lawful. In the first watch, when his mind is in the right state:

> "*I directed it to knowledge of the recollection of past lives. I recollected my manifold past lives, that is, one birth, two births, . . . ten births, . . . a hundred thousand births, many aeons of world contraction, . . . world expansion: 'There I was so named, of such a clan, with such an appearance, . . . such my life-term; and passing away from there, I reappeared elsewhere.' . . . Thus with their aspects and particulars I recollected my manifold past lives.*" (MN 4.27)

This is a memory of remembering—indeed, a "mythology of memory."[14] It uses expanding, hyperbolic numerations to link this individual's immediate experience with cosmic aeons. At the moment of death, one is said to recall scenes from one's entire life in an instant. Here Gautama, at the moment of bidding farewell to conditioned existence, is able to to recollect his "manifold past lives."

The passage could just as well be read as an expansion of self. The "I," able to "direct" his mind into areas of cognition, knows itself to have lived countless lives. Like a Spanish picaresque hero living under one master after another, the "I" seems to have survived, passing away from one place, reappearing elsewhere. Or else the passage could be read, on the contrary, as a minimizing or devaluation of self: no "I" or life has much importance, since there are so many of them, and since they are recounted so flatly. The "aspects and particulars" are not particular, and in sheer bulk and number they are standardized, like items in a warehouse.

A drive toward generality, and away from particulars or ego, is continued in the second watch, in which the Buddha describes the workings of karma, not merely in his own case but from a broader visionary perspective:

> *"With the divine eye, which is purified and surpasses the human, I saw beings passing away and reappearing, inferior and superior, fair and ugly, fortunate and unfortunate. I understood how beings pass on according to their actions [karma]."* (MN 4.29)

The quality of lives is conditioned by preceding actions. Better intentions are the conditioned causes of better lives or, in the Buddha's case, a lack of such causes leads to release from all lives. And the third watch, even more universalized, provides the symbolic hallmark of Buddhist teachings—the four Noble Truths, about suffering, its origin, its cessation, and the way (MN 4.31). The insight here climaxes the enlightenment series, along with one last reference to himself: *"I directly knew: 'Birth is destroyed, the holy life has been lived, what had to be done has been done, there is no more coming into any state of being'"* (MN 4.32). This closing formula states with powerful certainty that the awakening had been successful, and that a release from the prison of suffering had indeed been achieved.

We are confronted in this text with visionary poetry, less emotional yet comparable even so to that of St. Teresa of Avila or St. John of the Cross, both also recounting what they vividly remember. The poets act as mediators between wider mysteries and the limited experiences of their readers. Similarly Gautama, with his supernormal divine vision or dharma eye (*dhamma cakkhu*), penetrates into the workings of the universe, transferring his vision into language. His experience lasts several hours, and three times he states "*When my mind was concentrated, . . . I directed it to knowledge of*" each of the three areas he describes: past lives, karmic law, and the destruction of the taints (MN 4. 27, 29, 31). This is a careful systematic investigation, in which he retains extreme lucidity. He is not carried away or "transported" out of himself by those experiences, as in Western mystics, or in Longinus' *On the Sublime*.[15] The Buddha offers a clear, expansive worldview to those who may lack eyes to see it.

Some of Edwin Arnold's most majestic verses in *The Light of Asia* portray, occasionally in epic similes, the achievement of the watches:

> *He saw,*
> *By light which shines beyond our mortal ken,*
> *The line of all his lives in all the worlds;*
> *Far back, and farther back, and farthest yet . . . .*

> *Also, Buddha saw*
> *How new life reaps what the old life did sow;*
> *How where its march breaks off its march begins;*
> *Holding the gain and answering for the loss;*
> *And how in each life good begets more good,*
> *Evil fresh evil. . . .*[16]

Possessed of heightened faculties, and located at a special viewing point, Gautama is privy to dharma, to the cosmos seen in lawfully ordered array: his past lives lined up in great number, karma seen through telescoped expanses of time and space, showing that evil begets evil, and good, good. The third watch, presumably linked to the prior two watches, draws out their implications. Successions of fortunate and unfortunate lives move in ways that are lawlike, yet not necessarily confining or inevitable. For there is a way leading to the cessation of suffering: a place mentioned, yet apart from the karmic objects of his vision.

Readers' Wonderings

If the night of awakening were strictly part of a quest romance, then the discovery of nirvana would be our hero's coming upon some sort of paradise, holy grail, or heaven. In romance fiction, these special places are notoriously delusive (as in the pastoral interludes in Edmund Spenser's *Faerie Queene*); if set in a romance context, we might be mistrustful of Gautama's experience. In romantic comedy, the major figures undergo countless dreamlike metamorphoses. Events in sleeping, dreaming, and magically-induced waking states are comically confused in Shakespeare's *A Midsummer Night's Dream*, though at the end, the characters finally emerge, awake, into a happy consonance. Could we possibly say, similarly, that Prince Gautama, in his night experiences, had a dream, and then awoke to proclaim himself a Buddha? This is quite unlikely, and here his story may depart to some extent from the romance paradigm.

Though hyperbolically vast in scope, the sutta is not dreamlike but rather is highly conscious, seriously objective, and meticulously clear. An effort is made to connect Gautama's cognitions, arising in a step-by-step sequence, with the watches of the night, and he is thus shown to be awake, wide awake, all night long. Further assurances on this point are based on training and confidence in meditative states, and also on an insistence that the concept of awakening is metaphorical: a figurative dimension is crucial, since the experience is not an ordinary, literal awakening from an ordinary, literal, dreamy sleep. If the text's tone moreover is neither ordinary nor oneiric, it is also not, strictly speaking, mystical. The language of mysticism, according to Michel de Certeau, has an element of the ineffable, often veiled in secrecy. Secrecy "designates a play between actors. It circumscribes . . . strategic relations between the one trying to discover the secret and the one keeping it"; moreover, "the secret introduces an erotic element into the field of knowledge. It impassions the discourse of knowledge."[17] We may choose to discern an erotic element, or may read the Buddha's discourse as the disclosure of a secret, but the style is direct and plainspoken. He generally does not keep secrets, but tells, as straightforwardly as possible, what he claims to know.

This much said, however, the Buddha's experience of awakening is necessarily formulated retrospectively. Clarity in the exposition comes later than the experience, which may have been more dreamlike and ineffable than the later reconstruction suggests. The traditional reading is that with "retrocognition," previous lives are confirmed, with "clairvoyance" the law of karma is confirmed, and with "knowledge of the destruction of defiling impulses," the Noble Truths are discerned.[18] But we cannot verify, short of a similar awakening, such claims. Despite the lucidity of Buddhist meditation, linguistic clarity is surely the Buddha's addition, and it cannot adequately represent his experience. For how can a profound, totalizing incident be stated in ordinary, communicable language, drawing on ready-made concepts?

Despite reservations then, we need not assume that Gautama, as he becomes a Buddha, entirely leaves, rather than culminates, a quest romance. As Frye remarks, "the improbable, desiring, erotic, and violent world of romance reminds us that we are not awake when we have abolished the dream world: we are awake only when we have absorbed it again."[19] Perhaps the Buddha's awakening is *both* dreamlike *and* the absorption of his dreams into masterful clarity. However this may be, we are unavoidably outsiders to his experience, and may have found a certain mystery in his wondrous story, which begins in eerie regions of the jungle. The Buddha's night of awakening verges on *hybris*, in the epic violence of cracking open secrets of the universe, and in a similar violence in breaking apart our comfortable ignorance—that is, in disclosing universal facts, supposedly in order to bring us peace of mind.

The Buddha's open-handed manner runs the danger, though, of having said too much, and suspicious readers might have literalistic questions to pose. The passages on past lives, karma, and a release from suffering may seem didactic or ideological, especially when framed by doubts at the start and a conversion at the end. Such readers may not have thought to read the text primarily as literature. Instead, influenced by science, historiography, or the text's own clarity, they try to read the Buddha's account in a sensible, straightforward way, and might sooner or later decide to abstain, as many scholars do, from commenting on the awakening experience. Or else they might be puzzled: how could such a large number of lives possibly be remembered? Gautama would not have the time, unless the process were rapid indeed—which would distort the results. These readers might ask how intentions or actions could be correlated to outcomes, especially in so many cases. Here, too, there would not be enough time, unless by visionary access (and this seems to be the assumption) to a special order of space and time. Last but not least, the idea of an emergency fire exit, or a "way out" of the world, seems unjustified by the data presented. The "divine eye surpassing the human" may surpass certain readers, just as it may inspire others to marvel, and even to convert. It is thus all the more imperative, after the vision, that the self-produced Buddha proclaim his certainty about no more rebirths. But saying so, even in a lion's roar, does not make it so. Feelings of certainty can be mistaken, and often are.

Reading as Literature

A third type of reader, distinct from both the traditionalists and the recent skeptics, might allow that the Buddha did not have exactly "this" experience, but at some point formulated it in such a way so as to make it symbolically accessible to others, and a gateway to his teachings. As the Buddha noticed, names *"have weighted down everything"* (SN 1.7.61), and any verbal report is bound to be a distortion. Such a reader, sympathetic to the experience but wary of names, takes it indirectly or symbolically. Literature, to this kind of reader, is more flexible than either scientific literalists or orthodox dogmatists would permit. Precisely a literary reading precludes doubting at every step of the way, just as it precludes tilting at windmills, as Don Quixote did.

In the end, however, no kind of reader has the upper hand. Our text can be "*a lamp in the dark for those with eyesight to see*" (MN 4.35), but it is not the sun. Mental training, eyesight, and direct experience are required, not reading or common sense. Here especially, differing cultural assumptions may harbor blockages. The uses and validity of supernormal perceptions, with the "divine eye," are not as familiar in the West as in traditional India.[20] The *Fear and Dread Sutta* makes clear that the Buddha's authority, and the text's as well, derive from lengthy mental training to develop mental powers. Anything but mere fantasy or deception, these powers stand behind Gautama's magisterial assertion, "*When my concentrated mind was thus purified, bright, unblemished, rid of imperfection, malleable, wieldy, steady, and attained to imperturbability, I directed it to knowledge of the recollection of past lives*" (MN 4.27). A similar mind state is directed to other knowledges. Anyone wonder struck by such cognitions may find the story filled with freshness and immediacy.

The results, too, are wondrous. Each of the three knowledges is followed by the formula, "*Ignorance was banished and true knowledge arose, darkness was banished and light arose, as happens in one who abides diligent, ardent, and resolute*" (MN 4.18, 30, 33). The movement is out of darkness into light, here with the fine repetition of "arose," as archetypally befits someone traditionally deemed a Sun-god ("*when the sun and moon arise in the world, then there is . . . great light and radiance*"; SN 56.38.8). There is also the implication, in the phrase "as happens in one," that the achievement, difficult though it may be, is open not only to the Buddha. The emulation recommended, far from being mimetic competitiveness, claims to be a new way of moving away from all violence. The *Fear and Dread Sutta* ends with a return to the "*remote jungle thicket*," where the Buddha—now indeed a Buddha, an awakened one—returns, out of "*compassion for future generations*" (MN 4.34–35), to provide them with help and encouragement.

Plot Configurations

The story, seen in retrospect, has a notable structure. The night of awakening, with its three watches, is a narrative that recapitulates and climaxes Gautama's biography. With the first watch, the relatively personal insight into his previous lives might be compared to his early insights into suffering and impermanence. With the second watch—his insight into karmic causation—he moves outward, as in his leaving home and encountering the world. With the third watch of the night—the story's climax—the two narratives converge: by the benefits of yogic training and by his own efforts, he achieves the goal, which is the celebrated end to his story and, except mainly for the years of travel and teaching, to any further stories of self.

The temporal thrust of his awakening plot is intersected, more generally, with a series of spatial perspectives working against linear narrative. Conventional storytelling needs to keep its suspenseful focus—its attachment—on a sequence of developing events. By contrast, the enlightenment narrative, in each of the three watches, is marked by detachments—that is, by huge visionary expanses that slow the story down and make it less and less of a story. Finally, for a while, there is no more story. Gautama has "*laid down the burden, reached the true goal, destroyed the fetters of being, and is completely liberated through final knowledge*" (MN 73.6). With four emphatic verbs, he is divested of the encumbrance of identity—and of storytelling. This is entirely appropriate, since the becoming-Buddha of Gautama is a departure from samsāric life. The Tathāgata triumphs over pain and impermanence, and he "leaves no traces." The disruption of temporal narrative by spatial perspectives culminates in a realization: the mind at its deepest is spatial, and the unconditioned, assuming we can say anything about it, is entirely spatial.

Gautama's story thus becomes the Buddha's story. The plot, in other words, continues, but only after the protagonist overcomes an intense and understandable wish to quit, in all senses of that word. He needs an apparently outside stimulus, the descent of a divinity, to propel him back into the story line, this time as an awakened teacher of gods and humans.

4

Winning Conversions

The *Nikāyas*

> *How is it possible for a cultural text which fulfills a demonstrably ideological function, as a hegemonic work whose formal categories secure the legitimation of . . . domination—how it is possible for such a text to embody a properly Utopian impulse, or to resonate a universal value?*
>
> —Frederic Jameson, *The Political Unconscious*

Is there a contradiction between the universal fact of suffering, and the hero's bringing a definitive, final cure to only the monastic few, who needed to submit to a strict regimen? The laypeople did, to be sure, richly benefit from the Buddha's counsel, and his legacy has endured for centuries. But both he and they believed that the ultimate goal was, in most cases, a faint and distant hope. With his awakening, the Buddha was obliged to take account of this situation and, more generally, of how his own plight might relate to the rest of the world. Here, once again, there seem to be unknowns, or gaps, for a reader to contend with.

According to standard biographies, once he attains enlightenment, the Buddha dwells contentedly for several weeks and sees no particular reason to communicate his achievement. He has reached the goal by his own efforts, mostly in solitude, and he wishes, quite simply, to be left alone. He muses, in a well-known formula, that his insight is subtle and difficult to apprehend. He may have provided a "*lamp in the dark*" for some of his followers (MN 4.35), but to others his Dhamma is "*hard to see.*" The Buddha is vastly superior to those of *"this generation"* still in samsāra, and he is uninclined to return to a world ignorant of its own pain, from which he struggled so mightily to free himself. Even if he were to try to teach, the effort would prove useless, and *"that would be wearying and troublesome for me"* (MN 26.19).

The Buddha's predicament has two aspects. First, he has become almost superhuman and can look down calmly upon the common world of greed, hate, and delusion. But, second, that attitude itself could seem subtly, if momentarily, to put into question his relationship to the world. To many readers (and to the Buddha, too, in other texts), such an attitude may seem marred by a certain disdain or selfishness—familiar traits of the world supposedly left so far behind. It is common enough, after all, to want to be left alone, to put up signs, "Do not disturb," or "No trespassing."

Returning to the World

The mind-reading Brahmā Sahampati, like a *deus ex machina,* at this point suddenly descends. The Buddha is prodded, in a rousing pep talk, to let the world know about his newly discovered escape from suffering. Paradoxically, the Buddha, famous for compassion, is urged to have compassion; the Buddha, famous for his divine eye, is urged to see that some humans might benefit from being taught. Brahmā Sahampati's speech, or call it cheerleading, combines a panegyric with a stirring call to action:

> *"Arise, victorious hero, caravan leader,*
> *Debtless one, and wander in the world.*
> *Let the Blessed One teach the Dhamma,*
> *There are those who will understand."* (MN 26.20)

Neither the panegyric nor the call to action would seem to be strictly necessary. But their literary effect is undeniable, and if risks are involved in showing the Buddha reluctant to teach, there are also compensations. His reluctance allows for rivalry and triumph: Brahmā, the brahmins' highest god, needs to humble himself before the Buddha, begging him to reveal truth to the world.[1]

There seems to be, however, a blank space here. If the Buddha has this particular conflict, allegorically depicted, are there others we can only guess at? Was there perhaps some unstated sense that the awakening was "his thing" only—a private matter of no value to anyone else? The unsatisfactory results Gautama obtained with other teachers suggest that he has gone beyond them. But how can he be sure his awakening is "complete and perfect," as later traditions would insist, rather than a close miss? With Māra perpetually trying to trick him, does the Buddha have his moments of doubt? Will this newfound elation pass, like all else, is he perhaps asking, and has the goal been reached, if no one else can be inspired? Conversely, if it happens that others become inspired, will that prove enlightenment? Is the whole episode, then, complete with the descent of a god, a staging? Is enlightenment a simulacrum or, as the text would have it, the world's only non simulacrum?

Existential moments will be overcome, and listeners usually fill the gap willingly enough. One benefit, too, of the Buddha's possible doubt will be the felicity of a water-lotus simile to the effect that some persons are below, at, or above the water's surface. The simile will justify the reluctance, yet account for the Buddha's need for skillful means and his listeners' (later, his readers') degrees of instructability, and their differences in response (MN 26.21).

Sutta Structures

Once having decided to teach, the Buddha delivers his message to the world, and that message is later conveyed in meticulously constructed forms. The Pāli suttas show a standard pattern. They start with the phrase by a reciter, "*Thus have I heard*," indicating direct oral contact with a legitimate, traditional source, and thereby providing a stamp of authenticity. The text is noted to have arisen in a specific location, in reponse to a specific occasion, and is offered to a specific group. These details have a bearing on the discourse's form and content, requiring that the Buddha size up his audience and use the proper means to reach them. In many suttas, as listeners enter the hall, they pay homage to the Buddha, keeping him on their right side as they move, whereupon they seat themselves to one side.

Eventually a problem or a question is posed and, depending on the situation, the Buddha initiates a discourse, addressing his interlocutors by name, and then telling a story or expounding doctrine. The speaking of the Buddha or one of his representatives is usually dominant, though it is occasionally interspersed with further questions, or with answers to the Buddha's questions. Major themes are repeated exactly, in accord with oral-formulaic conventions. The repetition reinforces a sense that the teachings are thus and not otherwise, that the words signify only in the manner given. Ideological hegemony is reaffirmed, a body of ideas can be memorized, and the sutta ends with the listeners' thankful praise for the discourse, with a statement of benefits received ("*satisfied and delighted in the Blessed One's words*"; MN 81.23), and, at times, with a conversion ("*I would receive the going forth under Master Gotama*"; MN 7.21–22).

The First Sermon

The first sermon, showing many elements of this structure, is recounted at its start by the Buddha, referring to himself in the third person, as the Tathāgata—"one who has become authentic," or "one who has thus (*tathā*) come (*āgata*) or gone (*gata*)."[2]

> *"At Benares, Bhikkhus, in the Deer Park at Isipatana, the Tathāgata, accomplished and fully enlightened, set rolling the matchless Wheel of the Dhamma, which cannot be stopped by any recluse or brahmin or god or Māra or Brahmā or anyone in the world—that is, the announcing, teaching, describing, establishing, revealing, expounding, and exhibiting of the Four Noble Truths."* (MN 141.2)

The unstoppable wheel's motion is enunciated in a plethora of verbs, all with objective force, none of them suggesting anything like inventing or imagining. What the Buddha is thus depicted as offering is factual—the way things actually are, despite our contrary wishes, and despite the doings of Māra or anyone else.

Sacca is an existential rather than merely a propositional truth, and it can mean something real or actual, while *saccakiriyā*, an "asseveration of truth," or a "solemn declaration" is used in the *Jātakas*, according to I. B. Horner, as a "charm or spell uttered for gaining some desired end."[3] A declaration of the truth of suffering could thus be both factual and productive. It is phrased, as in a serious lyric or a catechism, as a question for which answers can be given:

> *"And what, friends, is the noble truth of suffering [dukkha]? Birth is suffering; ageing is suffering; death is suffering; sorrow, lamentation, pain, grief and despair are suffering; not to obtain what one wants is suffering; in short, the five aggregates affected by clinging are suffering"* (MN 141.10).

The repetition of "suffering" makes the main issue seem inescapable and relentless. Except for the last phrase, which uses a doctrinal term, the facts are common and to be encountered everywhere. The hammering insistence on *dukkha* reinforces its ubiquity, connected as it is with basic facts of the life cycle—birth, ageing, death. The Pāli language lacks articles, making for conciseness. The first three items are simple equations, but the fourth phrase combines a series of terms—*soka-parideva-dukkha-domanass-upāyāsā*—as if "grief-lamentation-suffering-unhappiness-misery" were all entangled.[4] Words for entanglement are indeed recurrent: "*this generation . . . is submerged, become like a tangled skein, like a knotted ball of thread, like matted reeds and rushes, and cannot pass beyond the plane of misery, bad destinations, the nether world, samsāra*" (SN 35.229). *Dukkha*, the condition of instability or unrest,[5] is unavoidable, like a serious, chronic disease; and release "*is not to be obtained by wishing*" (MN 141.19). There seems, at this point, no way out—not by fantasy, not by dreaming, not even by suicide. For such is our human condition.

The second truth, too, seems unpleasant, and is connected with the first. Suffering, we are told, comes from its apparent opposite—namely, what we enjoy and delight in:

> *"And what, friends, is the noble truth of the origin of suffering? It is craving [tanhā], which brings renewal of being, is accompanied by delight and lust, and delights in this and that [tatra tatra]; that is, the craving for sensual pleasures, craving for being, and craving for non-being."* (MN 141.21)

The language is deictic, pointing unarguably to the futile repetitiveness of desiring of one object after another. The very experiences that are most pleasing, entrancing, and delightful, the experiences that we welcome and cultivate, those experiences invariably lead to suffering. Bluntly put, "*with the arising of delight, there is the arising of suffering*" (SN 35.88). The result of delight and attachment is the "renewal of being," which will be no different; the cycle is repeated. As with the first truth, each instance in the last phrase, about the kinds of craving, is telescoped, showing mutual entanglement—*kāma-tanhā bhava-tanhā vibhava-tanhā*.[6] Craving, thirst, desire: these are repeatedly proclaimed to be "*the root of suffering*" (SN 42.11). The point is brought home by an example: if one had never seen or heard of a certain beloved person—say, a friend or the friend's mother—there would be little or no grief if something bad happened to that person. "*Before you saw Cirvāsi's mother or heard about her, did you have any desire, attachment of affection for her?*" The answer is negative; but now, having formed an attachment, if a misfortune happened to her, one's life would be upset, and full of "*sorrow, lamentation, pain, displeasure, and despair*" (SN 42.11).

The third truth, though, is extremely promising. The cessation (*nirodha*) of suffering involves the cessation of the conditioned cause: "*the remainderless fading away and ceasing, the giving up, the relinquishing and rejecting of that same craving*" (MN 141.22). Here as elsewhere, oppositions are stark and uncompromising. No ideal middle is mentioned between craving and not craving, although the cooling of certain types of emotion is part of a gradual, disciplined process, a "*fading away*," "*giving up*," "*relinquishing*," and "*letting go*."[7]

Cooling Off

The "secret forces" of sexuality are, in Indian ascetic traditions, to be preserved rather than depleted in what Shakespeare would call "*the expense of spirit in a waste of shame*" ("Sonnet 129"). To avoid such expense, Indian (including Buddhist) texts speak of an extinction, or "rooting out."[8] A price will be paid for such suppression of the instincts, and the return of the repressed is visible in, for example, the *Vinaya*'s extreme concern with any and all sorts of taboo sexual activity.[9] Whether successful or not, though, the effort of practice is to move away from the thirsty mind, relinquishing a tightness in habitual clingings. Taking desires less seriously—that is, witnessing and releasing them—leads to the "*brightly shining mind*," or *nirodha* (AN 1.10).[10] The texts describe *nirodha*, at times equated with nirvana, as the end result of repeated abandonings. The fourth Noble Truth, the eightfold path (a perfecting of view, intention, speech, action, livelihood, effort, mindfulness, and concentration) also requires abandonings, or abstainings.

Right concentration, for example, is a sequence of increasingly subtle withdrawals and reductions:

> *"Here, quite secluded from sensual pleasures, secluded from unwholesome states, a bhikkhu enters upon and abides in the first jhāna, which is accompanied by applied and sustained thought, with rapture and pleasure born of seclusion. . . . With the abandoning of pleasure and pain, and with the previous disappearance of joy and grief, he enters upon and abides in the fourth jhāna, which has neither-pain-nor-pleasure and purity of mindfulness due to equanimity . . ."* (MN 141.31).

Viewed as a journey of abandonings and disappearances, the meditator "enters upon and abides in" a rarified new territory, as an indefatigable explorer arrives finally upon a mountain top, looking "*with eagle eyes . . . / [and] with a wild surmise*"[11] upon some vast, wondrous expanse.

The Fire Sermon

The Buddha needs to convince listeners, not only by showing rewards in higher jhānic states, but also by showing that ordinary life should, if possible, be abandoned or radically modified. The danger of attachment to insubstantial, changing forms is great indeed, and in the fire sermon (thematized in T. S. Eliot's *The Waste Land*), the Buddha makes his celebrated declaration, gathering force with repetitive expansion, that the world is on fire:

> *"All is burning. . . . The eye is burning, forms are burning, eye-consciousness is burning, and whatever feeling arises with eye-contact as condition—that, too, is burning. . . . Burning with the fire of lust, with the fire of hatred, with the fire of delusion; burning with birth, ageing, and death; with sorrow lamentation, pain, displeasure, and despair, I say."* (SN 35.28)

The untrained mind state of worldlings is thus depicted in an extended metaphor of fire as a huge threat. All things are flammable, though in the passage cited, technical terms provide some equanimity to what otherwise might seem like sheer Old Testament outrage. Whatever is burning is in the process of being painfully destroyed and losing whatever value it once had. Fire worship was widespread in India, and the Buddha here challenges the fire ritualists, alarmingly and skillfully overturning their assumptions.[12] Since new fires erupt with each new birth, the fires spead wildly as population increases, along with suffering. By contrast, the positive news, also conveyed with fire symbolism, is that nirvana is a "blowing out" of the fires of passion, hatred, and delusion.

The discourse ends quietly, as if putting out its own fire. And a thousand monks, upon hearing the Buddha speak in this way, are "*liberated from the taints by nonclinging*" (SN 35.28). The excellent and quick results might be explained by earlier training and preparation, but not entirely. Kassapa asks the Buddha why, in earlier times, there were fewer precepts and more monks attained enlightenment. He is told that "*when beings are in decline and the true Dhamma is waning, there are more precepts, and fewer monks attain enlightenment*" (SN 16.13).[13] If there was a decline during the Buddha's lifetime, how much more so after his passing! His charisma had magical effects that were later, and are still today, less available. As Max Weber shows, the passing of a charismatic founding teacher, who had performed miracles and heroic deeds, means that freshness is lost as the teachings become consolidated, canonized, routinized, and institutionalized.[14]

Buddhism as Ideology

The question can be asked, most likely by a recent reader with Weber's thesis in mind, about the ways in which the Buddha's teachings might have been taken before and after the time when "beings are in decline." In speculating on this issue, we will need to consider the Buddha's teaching as a system or philosophy, while the next chapter will consider the teaching as a process or a narrative.

Some such divided consideration is prominent in histories of Buddhism, following up on a distinction between faith-followers and dhamma-followers (SN 25.1) with claims that the Buddha's legacy may be viewed either as a practice or a system—that is, either as a way of living or as a codified set of tenets. We earlier pondered the ideological forces at work in Buddhist India, and might briefly mention how the evolution of monastic institutions is fraught with ideological issues—say, in the Buddha's relations with local kings and local law, in claims that gifts to the sangha bring the most merit, in a frequently negative attitude, when monks are involved, toward family life.[15] Our concern here, however, will not be with ideology in practice, but in the teaching or system itself.[16]

There is a certain structure to ideological formations. For example, despite notions of decline, the movement from direct experience to enlightenment is stated to be, under the right conditions, an almost automatic process. Whoever develops certain mental qualities, called "wings to awakening," will come to the same realization as did the Buddha.[17] The process is typically described as follows:

> "*Seeing thus, a well-taught noble disciple becomes disenchanted . . . . Being disenchanted, he becomes dispassionate. Through dispassion [his mind] is liberated. When it is liberated there comes the knowledge, 'It is liberated.'*"
> (MN 74.12)

There may be some circularity in claiming that "seeing" is what leads to "disenchantment" and "liberation"—or else it would not count as "seeing." A scholar, if not a meditator, may be led to wonder whether in Buddhism the teaching is almost too consistent.

Formulations of the teachings as a system, attempted frequently by Buddhists, are not the most esteemed way to travel the path, since one might then become attached to that system. But as a hermeneutic tool, the teachings are systematic: they are of a single flavor, we are told, and structured by what Thanissaro Bhikkhu calls "feedback loops."[18] They are everywhere arranged in interconnected lists, almost always numbered (four Noble Truths, twelve links, eight stages, and so on). Each list, as Rupert Gethin demonstrates, is a matrix for further lists, so that "the structure of early Buddhist thought . . . is an intricate pattern of lists within lists."[19]

The listings may make the path logically integral, but they are not empirically scientific. As Frank J. Hoffman observes, where scientific hypotheses are modified in light of experimental results, the Buddhist sees what "really is," and this seeing is not provisional or modifiable. Meditators whose insights do not confirm the teachings are told to keep on trying, but the teachings themselves, though adapted to audiences, are not modified. The world when seen with Buddhist eyes is filled with suffering that can, by diligent effort, be overcome: "to see the world *yathā bhūtaṃ* [as it really is] is thus not to see what a video camera would record, but is in part to see in a hopeful manner the possibility of liberation."[20] Thus vision and possible liberation, as in the passage just cited (MN 74.12), are mutually confirming.

The circularity bounds or binds the system, and we will notice points where the system sets out borders or reaches its limits. There are moments, for example, when the system seems at odds with itself: at the end of the path, what happens to whom? As Steven Collins remarks, Buddhism, "despite its being a system which emphasises almost to an exaggerated degree individual responsibility in ethics (through . . . *karma*) and which offers a way to complete salvation (in *nirvana*), there is a radical refusal to speak of a self or permanent person in any theoretical contexts. It is . . . fruitless for a scholar to try to explain . . . what this 'means,' and what such a salvation can be. Rather, he should see Buddhism's ideological stance as a social, intellectual and soteriological strategy."[21] Another scholar, Peter Harvey, disagrees, maintaining that it is indeed possible to give some account of what the doctrines mentioned mean, and how the strategy of salvation works.[22]

As in many texts (including MN 74.12), this debate about a scholar's role may have to do with ways of seeing. Depending on how one sees, Collins rehearses a familiar conundrum: how can we be saved, if there is no visible or tangible "we"? As his phrase "ideological stance" indicates, this question might not be only spiritual or academic but also moral, historical, and political. We may thus wish to view the Buddhist legacy as an ideology marked by a "soteriological strategy" intended to propagate its authority. The fate of that legacy—perhaps related to the "decline" just mentioned, when the goal is less easily attained—is to have become institutionalized, and to have become more, or differently, ideological than when the Buddha was alive.

Ideology Criticism

The issue of ideology was raised at the outset here, in questions about how Buddhist teachings may have been packaged for and by the West. The packaging—a social and literary troping is ambiguously something both added to the product and already structured into it, thus seeming to endow it with a "universal"—not simply a Western or an Eastern—appeal. Questions of doctrinal adaptations or tropes, as ideological tactics, have long been prominent in literary analysis. The ideological forces implicated in literary works have been examined in the writings of, for example, Georg Lukács, Roland Barthes, Edward Said, Frederic Jameson, Terry Eagleton, or Raymond Williams. Such theorists show how literature, a historically conditioned product, is inextricably bound up with ideology. They have generally not dealt with Buddhist literature, but in the wake of their work, one might ponder the relevance of ideologies that shape sacred rhetorical strategies.

How to define ideology? Terry Eagleton characterizes it as "a body of meanings and values encoding certain interests relevant to social power. . . . Ideologies . . . are unifying, action-oriented, . . . legitimating, universalizing and naturalizing."[23] Ideologies are "unifying" in that they attempt partially to homogenize their followers and to resolve conflicts. Consider each of these aspects in Buddhist texts. The Buddha harped on harmonious social interactions, and the teachings are "unifying" in their stress on compassion, and in their high degree of internal unity, or even circularity. The teachings are "action-oriented" in furnishing practical measures, as the arrow parable indicates, for the relief from suffering. The teachings are "legitimating" in showing that the Buddha became established as a master by his skillful means and by the mandates described in many texts.

The "universalizing" and "naturalizing" aspects of ideology go together, and both of them can be used to consolidate power. The first occurs when "values and interests . . . specific to a certain place and time are projected [or extended] as the values and interests of all humanity."[24] Early Buddhism flourished in ancient India, and many of its assumptions (for example, about six realms, supernormal powers, magic, devas, Māra) may seem outdated, and thus are often quietly revised or ignored. More acceptable is the first Noble Truth, which assumes that all humans suffer in similar ways, and that they all wish (if they "see" clearly) to be released from that condition. These assumptions about all humans are usually "naturalized"—that is, taken to be "natural and self-evident," a matter of common sense or, once again, "the way things really are."

The Way Things Really Are

Versions of this phrase, appearing continually in Buddhist texts (MN 12.10–16, DN 2.97, 22.17), may today seem suspect, yet *The Net of Views* (DN 1), with its critical perspective on common views of the time and the pointless debate they engender, fits nicely into the tradition of ideology critique. As Troy Organ remarks, "for Gautama, all knowledge was ideology, that is, all knowledge was held and expressed for certain reasons. His *dharma* was revealed only because it contributed to . . . salvation."[25] The Buddha's open hand suggests that he had no hidden ideological agenda. And the *Net of Views* sutta presumes that once the mind is cleared, as presumably it can be, of prejudices and self-interest, it is then left with no views or, in some texts, with only the "perfected" or "right" view, which turns out—circularly and not surprisingly—to be none other than the Buddhist teachings. In explicating the sutta, Bhikkhu Ñānananda demonstrates how *ditthi* is integral with craving and conceit, proliferating into mental states leading to conflicts in individuals and between societies. It is closely connected with *dukkha*, causing grief and rebirth. The silent sage has no views and is attached neither to false views nor to *sammā ditthi* itself.[26]

False views are not an issue for those who have become detached. It also happens that, in recent times, "false consciousness" is no longer an issue in defining ideology. In Marxist traditions, the term "ideology" was once taken to be "false consciousness" erected as a superstructure, disguising and protecting economic interests. But for contemporary theorists such as Slavoj Žižek, ideology is not simply false consciousness or an illusory representation of reality. Instead, reality itself is already ideology, and its "very existence implies the non-knowledge of its participants." This non-knowledge (which reminds one of *avidya*, ignorance) is symptomatic, and symptoms provide a tool for critique—that is, they are noted as being both "*heterogeneous* to the ideological field and *necessary* for that field to achieve its closure, its accomplished form."[27] Paradoxically, the marginally other, the unfitting, or even the meaningless element in the system is nonetheless *also, at the same time*, necessary and definitive. Thus, for example, the universal term "freedom" is necessary to define democracy but in specific instances becomes heterogeneous or symptomatic: when workers make a "free choice" to sell their labor, they lose freedom, and become a slave to capital.

The Master Signifier

The ideological aspect, to paraphrase Žižek, is the effect of a perspectival error. The key element or master signifier, the "Meaning" that holds all else in place, is also the element that substitutes for a lack, seen erroneously as a plenitude "exempting it from the relational–differential interplay and guaranteeing its homogeneity." Meaning is produced, as Jacques Lacan maintains, retroactively, when floating signifiers become attached, or sewn into place, by a "quilting term." As an example, words like "freedom" and "peace" float through the ideological space until they are quilted into place by a master term, such as "Communism," thereby giving "freedom" or "peace" a (Communist) meaning.[28]

"Freedom" and "peace" can, of course, also be quilted with a Buddhist master term. If we were to look for Buddhist master keys—or what Kenneth Burke calls "god terms"[29]—what would they be? The Buddha often proclaimed, especially in fending off irrelevant questions, that he teaches nothing else than "*suffering [dukkha] and the cessation of suffering*" (MN 22.38; 63.8). We are thus provided with a few quilting terms: *dukkha*, often linked with *avidya* or ignorance, and release, or the goal, namely *nirodha—nibbāna* or *nirvana*.

Viewed from an oblique or defamiliarized perspective, these terms function as place-markers, differences, or supplements, covering up a lack. Systems of signification, as Ferdinand de Saussure famously argues, depend on regularized differences. In language, signifiers (or sound images) are conventionally and arbitrarily connected with signifieds (concepts), thereby producing signs or meanings. Signs are shown, in a theory that interestingly parallels conditioned origination, to be empty, since "language is a system of interdependent terms in which the value of each term derives from the presence of the others"[30] The limits of the signifying system, moreover, cannot themselves be signified, but can only display themselves as an interruption of the signifying process.[31]

Meanings from Gaps

As an example, here is the start of Lewis Carroll's nonsense poem, *Jabberwocky:* "*'Twas brillig, and the slithy toves / Did gyre and gimble in the wabe . . .*"[32] Narrative conventions allow us to imagine that a scene is being set, while the syntax and connecting words allow the nonmeaningful words to be subordinated to a presumed meaning, in approximation to something familiar. Reading, as ever, is a matter of extrapolating, or filling in gaps. Assuming the master key to be standard English, *wabe* is close enough to *waves*, and *slithy* to *slimy* so that they can be brought into approximate signification. *Toves* is like *doves* but the waves, if there are any, may make the word likely to be something more like *turtles*, though it could mean other things. There's alliteration in *gyre and gimble* and an overlap with *gambol*, suggesting that playing is going on. *Brillig* seems further outside the system, and we can only grope around, guessing that it may have to do with the weather, by analogy with *sunny* or *cloudy*. Not wanting elements to remain outside the system (that is, to be merely floating words or nonsense) we draw them in and quilt them, even at the risk of vagueness.

Likewise, to move from the ridiculous to the sacred, if *nirvana* is said to be *cool* and *peaceful*, we extrapolate about it from the more familiar words. Since we need it, or the system does, we don't want to leave *nirvana* entirely outside, though perhaps we should. We can never be sure about insides and outsides, and can never bring it fully in, any more than we can *brillig*. There's some mild consolation to be had in noting that all words are inexact, anyway. Like it or not, the terms holding the Buddhist (or any) system together have "no sense" in themselves. This may not be apparent, since the terms are naturalized—that is, taken for granted as common sense. The terms become foregrounded, though, when other kinds of "common sense" emerge.

Ignorance, for example, akin to common sense, engenders suffering, and is usually listed first in the chain of conditioned origination, with *dukkha* as the starting point, the motivating factor, and the condition to be overcome by leaving home to go into homelessness. *Dukkha* may be translated in several ways (sorrow, grief, unsatisfactoriness, unhappiness, ill, discontent, anguish) and may be considered in several dimensions (as pain, conditioned formations, or impermanence) (SN 4.38.14). Yet for many people, with their common sense, it poses no special problem, as the Prince himself observed of them. In any sense of the term, it is instead merely considered to be a necessary part of the human life cycle, the progression from birth to death, repeated with each generation. The life cycle, with its weddings and new babies, may indeed be willingly, even cheerfully, accepted. If so, ignorance (not primarily assessed as suffering) becomes heterogeneous to the ideology.

There may be instances, then, of heterogeneity. William James has described a "healthy-minded" type of religious sensibility: individuals who enjoy virtually everything, who are perpetually joyful, and who persist in their upbeat mood even amidst handicaps, hardships, and misfortunes. They are aware of the vicissitudes of life, but such persons (among them, Walt Whitman) are prone to enthusiasms over "our oneness with this Infinite Life," and "when unhappiness is offered or proposed to them, positively refuse to feel it, as though it were something mean and wrong."[33] We encounter such figures in the Pāli texts: certain devas and human beings "*are delighted in existence, rejoice in existence. When the dhamma is taught to them, their minds do not enter into it . . . or resolve upon it*" (It 49).[34] We may guess that they would not assent to the noble truth of *dukkha*, and even if told of pleasure's concealed binding powers, they might not be existentially shaken.

Cheerfulness or attachment do not, in themselves, decide the issue. As Walpola Rahula points out, the Buddha was described by people of his time as "ever-smiling," and his followers as jubilant, elated, and peaceful.[35] Those followers may have been of a sunny disposition to begin with, but the implication is that their joy is informed by a dedication to the Buddhist way, and that an "ignorant" joy would not be granted so high an esteem. We may still ask, though, whether a naturally jovial or accepting attitude toward the life cycle is necessarily to be reckoned as "ignorance."

Ignorance and Its Opposite

It can be so reckoned only within the Buddhist system, semiotically cross-hatched in lengthy lists. *Avidya* is a term of importance in the major Indian philosophies, but it is given a "specialized meaning" in Buddhism. When that happens—that is, when the traditional, free-floating term *avidya* is "quilted" by the Buddha—it becomes part of an ideology, and is marked by certain peculiarities. Since it tends to get us entangled with unskillful action, it is more than simply a lack of knowledge; it is an obstacle to the path.[36]

The role of ignorance is stressed in a simile: "*just as all the rafters of a peaked house lead to the roof peak and converge upon the roof peak, and all are removed when the roof peak is removed, so too all unwholesome states . . . converge upon ignorance*" (SN 20.1). Just as the peak, like a keystone, is crucial to maintaining structure of the house (or self), so ignorance keeps us in illusions of strength and permanence. By contrast, when awakening transpires, illusions give way to knowledge, and the peaks and rafters are finally destroyed (*Dhammapada* 11.154). "Ignorance," not easy to describe apart from similes, is a link in the causal cycle of dependent origination. The general formula is: "*with the arising of this, that arises; . . . with the cessation of this, that ceases.*" The "this" and "that" are filled in with the following items in sequence: ignorance, volitional formations, consciousness, mentality-materiality, the six sense bases, contact, feeling, craving, clinging, existence, birth, ageing-death, followed by the cycle repeated or, with the fading and cessation of one of the items (usually ignorance or craving), a cessation of the entire cycle. As an impersonal process, the cycle is an alternative to notions of "soul" or "God." It shows how existence is repeatedly renewed, but also how it can be stopped.[37]

The list of causes, often equated with the Buddhist dhamma itself, is presented with a variable number of links and contents. It could function just as well without "ignorance" as a link: earlier versions of the sequence had fewer links, with "ignorance" omitted or left outside (DN 15.2–3).[38] In the Sermon at Benares, *The Exposition of the Truths* (MN 141), only "thirst" is mentioned as the cause of samsāric entanglement, and liberation is dependent on its removal. The Buddhist way, however, contains a strong cognitive dimension, and "ignorance" later replaced "thirst" as a key term.[39] Yet "ignorance," though it thus becomes prominent, is not defined in the texts except by difference, that is, by lying on the wrong side of a list of polarities: those who are ignorant consider what is impermanent or incomplete to be permanent and complete, etc. Or else "ignorance" means, quite simply, being unaware of the four Noble Truths (SN 6.4, 12.2).

There is a certain circularity, then, which quilts together the Buddhist identity or sign-system. A positive element is set out, involving knowledge, and ignorance must be, by polar opposition (SN 45.159)—a style already noted in the *Noble Quest* sutta—the absence of that element. "Ignorance" is a lack to be filled in by the four Noble Truths, but they would have been unnecessary without that lack. Not viewed as a lack or insufficiency, not defined against a specific "positive" good or knowledge, "ignorance" ceases have a role.

Outside as Inside

Not surprisingly, the other pole to ignorance, final knowledge or nirvana, is equally a null point outside, so to speak, yet also crucially inside, the Buddhist system. Although we are offered the understandable positives of "*happiness*," "*peace*" or "*coolness*," one of the best-known descriptions of cessation or the goal, attributed to the Buddha, is given in the *Udana* 8.3: "*There is a non-born, a not brought-to-being, a not-made, not-formed.*" The text shows an affirmation ("*there is*") followed by a series of negations, and we are told that without nirvana, there would be no escape from the restlessly agitated realm of their opposites, where most of us currently reside.[40]

This binary opposition nirvana-nirodha/suffering-ignorance-samsāra, like the noble/ignoble quest opposition, places the quilting term in a hierarchically superior position (along with the Buddha, his noble truths, and monks), a position far above the common folk (*puthujjana*), who are viewed as impure, clueless, and, of course, lowly. With a deconstructive intervention, however, the binary terms are less clear and separate than the ideology would claim. Nirvana, like Derrida's *différance*, is neither something nor nothing—neither presence nor absence, identity nor difference, life nor death. But deferrals, half-steps, or gradations in nirvana (with or without remainder; before or after death; to be gained by streamwinners, but not yet) suggest impurity or tentativeness, even in the allegedly most sacred and dominant of concepts.

With "nirvana" as a master term, moreover, Buddhist ideology locates itself in a supplementary relation to society. It depends on local contributions and produces advice for laypersons but is also, as Steven Collins notes, outside the social order: the body and procreation are linked with ageing and death, while the Buddhist celibate aspires to "a kind of well-being which will not decay and die, . . . [which] is not physically reproductive."[41] Such an ideology is not only for a minority of ascetics, but also is part of the collective imagination, as in stories of a "golden world" or a utopia. Utopia is often contrasted (misleadingly) with ideology, and set out as an escape from it. Sir Thomas More refers to his *Utopia* as "*a place of felicitie*," while nirvana in Pāli texts is also a good place (*eu-topia*) that is no place (*u-topia*) located outside the space–time realm of conditioned life.[42]

Thomas More was able to satirize his utopian world, whose denizens were ridiculously far from perfect. Not so with nirvana. Words about it are serious, and take the form not of logical arguments or referential statements but of poetic or rhetorical images: fire blowing out, a house being destroyed, a long-lost city, the ocean. Nirvana is marked, too, by paradox: the deceased enlightened ones are happily nowhere, but they have not vanished.[43] We thus confront what

Collins designates as two aporias: "nirvana is without the Aggregate of consciousness and without any feeling of happiness, but to attain it is not to become non-existent, and [is] to accede to the highest bliss."[44] Such felicity is overdetermined, and faced with aporias, we might be well advised, Collins says, to maintain (as the text does) a discreet silence.[45]

Considered ideologically, however, aporetic overdetermination can be accounted for, and is hardly surprising. Ideological quilting points, while firmly in place for devotees, are frail and shaky—consisting as Žižek remarks, of a "symbolic solution to real antagonisms," with the overarching signifier capacious enough to contain a multiplicity of contending meanings. Ideological appeal resides in contrariety, "so that one and the same figure stands for inconsistent 'contents': in ideology one can have one's cake and eat it" (PF 75). Nirvana is just such a cake. Hyperbolic joy, with its ambiguous excess, is a kernel of what Lacan calls *jouissance:* blissful enjoyment, with an erotic tinge—the basis of all desire, however repressed or sublime. *Jouissance* is the impossible place of the sublimated selfless subject, who is always displaced and out of joint, here and not here. This situation cannot be expressed except in silence, or else, perhaps, in rapturous singing.

Singing Nirvana

The early nuns, unburdened, sing of the joys of liberation: "*Home I have left, for I have left my world! / Child I have left, and all my cherished herds! / Lust I have left, and Ill Will, too, is gone, / And Ignorance I have put far from me*" (T 18). As with the Buddha, there is no more fuel to burn: "*I feel a feeling terminating with life*" (MN 140.24). The self has run out of gas and will not be returning, gone where there is no more burning, beyond any possible designation, outside the linguistic system we operate in. Any aggregate is abandoned: the arhat has "*cut it off at the root, made it like a palm stump, done away with it, so that it is no longer subject to future arising*" (MN 72.20).

Why is this particular destiny, attaining nirvana, so highly cherished? Notice the poetic imagery. Figurative castration—a cut off, no-longer-arising palm tree stump—might seem awesome as an image of renunciation or, more generally, as part of an ideology in which it functions as a place-marker in forceful opposition to *avidya* and *dukkha* arising from uncontrolled, proliferating craving. Even, or especially, castration will not matter. Yet the oppositional terms are almost without articulated content: they are thus the most essential, most incontestable, elements of the ideology. Without them, the path and the sangha would be unjustified.

Ideological terms are most powerful when located both outside the system (not describing or accounting for themselves, and thus marked with a charismatic aura) and inside it (crucially engaging with the system). The inside/outside distinction is rarely clear-cut or defensible, but if either sort of term becomes too weak, the ideology becomes unbalanced and less effective. The teachings may then enter into decline, as noted, and they may need to be reformulated for new generations and cultures. Yet, one need not cling to ideologies of a golden age. Just as in the raft parable the teachings can be discarded, so too can any particular ideology be discarded, or at least attempts can be made to transcend it.

Ideology and Utopia

Attempts to go beyond ideology invoke utopia as an oppositional concept. Although "nirvana" and "ignorance" may be taken as part of an ideology, the Buddhist way is not merely an ideology, then, but also—in the sangha, and in the concept of nirvana—a utopia. Where ideology is a strategy of containment and oppression, visions of utopia provide a basis for resistance, and a way out. Frederic Jameson argues that the two are inseparable, citing Ernst Bloch's discovery of utopian impulses even at the debased level of media manipulation and advertising slogans. According to Jameson, the most stringently ideological texts are simultaneously utopian: "all ideology, in the strongest sense . . . is in its very nature Utopian."[46] By that same logic, we cannot always tell when utopian images are being co-opted to advance an ideological agenda. Perhaps that very difficulty—requiring all our resources of belief, practice and faith—makes our encounters with ideologies, including the Buddhist ideology, so challenging.

This point is itself an ideological formulation, and it is not necessarily critical, or even unorthodox. It has been skillfully staked out by the Mahāyāna schools, with their insistence that samsāra is nirvana, with their turnings of the wheel, and a new charisma in bodhisattva figures. Where we have spoken of null terms or place-markers, the texts of Nāgārjuna and of the *prajñāpāramitā* show, in sweeping and detailed ways, that all entities are empty of any abiding essence or identity. This demonstration is held to be totally in tune with the teachings, indeed to be reviving and cleansing them, after centuries of scholastic obfuscation. For now we will defer discussion of those other schools, looking instead more closely at the earlier teachings and at how the Buddha conveyed them.

5

Passing On

The *Nikāyas*

Once out of nature I shall never take
My bodily form from any natural thing,
But such a form as Grecian goldsmiths make
Of hammered gold and gold enamelling . . . .

—William Butler Yeats, *Sailing to Byzantium*

We will speak here of the Buddha's teaching career, of his conveyance of doctrine and practice, and of the circumstances of his passing away. Passing on is the Buddha's work of transmission, and fact of his own dying. His ways of teaching are inseparable from his teachings of the way, from his sense of his dying-in-life, of his detachment, of his being a serious but temporary visitor. He did not wish to be bothered with trivia, including dharmic trivia, and in a common pericope, the Buddha extols a follower who "*practised in accordance with the Dhamma and did not trouble me in the interpretation of the Dhamma*" (MN 145.8). The finest followers simply put the teachings to work, without troubling the teacher with problems of interpretation. The phrase "trouble me" recalls the phrase, soon after the awakening, that any effort at teaching would be "*troublesome for me*" (MN 26.19).

Even so, much of his life was taken up with teaching. He had to deal with the variable powers of "*sacred words*"—hymns, mantras, possibly his own sermons—which disciples but fitfully retained ("*Why is it, good Gotama, . . . that sometimes the sacred words I have long studied are not clear to me?)* (SN 46.55). The Buddha had to contend, as well, not only with followers, possible followers, and challengers, but with political leaders, malefactors, and teachers from other schools. He persistently needed to adapt his techniques to his listeners' situations, making use of skillful means in pointed parables, apt similes, lyrics, dramatic ploys, and even disciplinary measures. Once he dismissed a noisy group, calling them fishmongers, and Brahmā Shahampati needed to intervene yet again with an appeal for compassion (MN 67.4–10). The Buddha's teaching, though adapted to listeners, was demanding, and not to be taken for granted.

Know for Yourselves

One of the best-known illustrations of his pedagogy, ceaselessly cited in the West, is the *Kālāma Sutta*. The Kālāma people, exposed to contradictory tenets, were confused about what to accept or reject. Aware of the Buddha's reputation, they decided to put their problem to him: "*Lord, some ascetics and brahmins . . . explain and elucidate their own doctrines, but disparage, debunk, revile and vilify the doctrines of others. But then some other ascetics and brahmins [do the same]*" (AN 3. 65). The Buddha sympathizes with the Kālāmas' plight, telling them, "*Do not go by oral tradition, by lineage of teaching, by hearsay, by a collection of scriptures, by reasoning . . . by the seeming competence of a speaker, or because you think, 'The ascetic is our teacher.' But when you know for yourselves, 'These things are unwholesome, these things are blamable . . . ,' then you should abandon them*" (AN 3.65). His position is then conveyed in a series of hypothetical questions, giving listeners a chance to respond as they see fit. Unlike other teachers, with their partisan name-calling, the Buddha advises loving kindness as a basis for equanimity and, thus, for clear decision-making. The listeners are soon persuaded, and the sutta displays a harmony of pedagogy, practice, and persuasion.

The ideal teacher, the Kālāmas are told, retains equanimity in times of difficulty. *Sati* (mindfulness) is crucial, even when the teacher's words do not have an effect, or when disciples are obnoxious or fail to understand.[1] That the teacher remain unfazed seems especially urgent, of course, when precisely mindfulness is being taught. Exemplary in this context is *The Foundations of Mindfulness* sutta (in two versions: DN 22, MN 10). Reckoned to be the most important teaching in the Pāli canon, it defines, in practical terms, the Buddhist way.[2] Here the Buddha teaches meditation, expounding the point-by-point method that led him to enlightenment.

Meditation and Power

It may be a sign of our times, however, that meditation is often viewed a technique for gaining power. That power may be used, in turn, for any ends whatsoever: as Žižek remarks, "What if—a horrible thought—the Zen meditation technique is ultimately just that: a spiritual technique, an ethically neutral instrument that can be put to different sociopolitical uses, from the most peaceful to the most destructive?" Meditation, integrated with the martial arts, can serve armies well in times of war, as it did for the Japanese in World War II and earlier.[3] Žižek mentions Zen, but the remarks may be applied more generally to the recent practice of Buddhist meditation, often interpreted as yet another, if difficult, scheme for self-empowerment. We would be mistaken, however, if we exalt the value of meditation at the expense of the big picture, including the workings of power in cosmology, history, and politics. And the opposite mistake has also occurred: even within the monastic tradition, morality, cosmology, and wisdom may be discussed, but formal sitting meditation has often not been practiced, and the relatively recent revival of *vipassanā* is a product of reform movements.[4]

In the Buddha's day, as in later times, formal meditation may have posed obstacles, and *The Foundations of Mindfulness* is structured as something like a sales pitch, with the Buddha promising the highest result, nirvana, within relatively short, if variable, amounts of time. The sutta begins with a large, high-minded statement:

> *This is the direct path [ekāyana: the one way], bhikkhus, for the purification of beings, for the surmounting of sorrow and lamentation, for the disappearance of pain and grief, for the attainment of the true way, for the realisation of Nibbāna—namely, the four foundations of mindfulness.* (MN 10.2)

"*Ekāyana*" is a striking phrase, with its announcement of one single way out of the morass of suffering. The "one way" may also refer to its being followed by one person alone (no practitioner can meditate for another), to its being the way of the One (the Buddha), and to its leading to a single goal.[5] It makes a hyperbolic, almost magical, offering. Is there really only one way to go, or only one basic skill to learn? Is meditation a one-way street, and does it proceed in one single, right direction? All of these meanings are indeed likely. Any sense of hyperbole is counterbalanced, however, by the Buddha's open invitation to try the method for oneself, to come and see (SN 55.1.1). The tone in the cited passage is majestic and elevated in its sweeping scope. At the same time, though not entirely a business offer, it seems meant to elicit a response.

What, then, is the deal? In recommending unruffled attention, the text moves, after its attention-grabbing start, to a more straightforward tone. The sutta is in the tradition of how-to-do-it manuals, not far from the literature of advice in science, in art, or in psychology. The Buddha here makes an analogy to woodworking: "*Just as a skilled turner or his apprentice, when making a long turn, understands: 'I make a long turn'; or, when making a short turn, understands: 'I make a short turn'; so too, breathing in long, a bhikkhu understands, 'I breathe in long. . .'*" and similarly with "*breathing in short . . .*" (MN 10.4). Meditation is an expert technique, and it can be developed, like other skills, to produce tangible results. The process of arising and decay need not be a cause for sorrow: a penetrating perception of that process can allow us to overcome its hurtful power. The Buddha's achievement, it is said, was not only to have developed meditation techniques,[6] but to have shown, by that very fact, his understanding of samsāric conditions, what leads to them (being carelessly swept along), and how they can be overcome (by insightful attention).

Marketing Tactics

Once the Buddha has expounded his method, the sutta returns at the end to his opening promise, repeated in exactly the same words, but this time specifying the lengths of time required for either "*final knowledge*" or "*non-return.*" Those lengths are variable, starting with "*just seven years*" but, in a decrease, "*not even seven, but six*" and then, as in a countdown, five, four, three, two, one, and even less (DN 22.22). Why the rhetoric of diminution? It might be linked to the encouraging, if simplistic, "only one way" trope at the start, and is equally a selling tactic. The diminution trope is commonly used,[7] and here it is meant not only as encouragement but as a bringing closer, a "making present" of the goal, which chimes with the making present called insightful attention.

We do not know what the historical Buddha actually said. But as a literary character he panders, with his diminution trope, to the wishes of his listeners, much as a used-car dealer might offer successively lower and lower prices, so as to retain a prospective buyer's interest. Surprisingly, in light of his many teachings on the dangers of craving and attachment, the Buddha teases listeners in ways similar to lovers' strategems, as when speakers in Robert Browning's poems remark that they need not wait much longer ("*So, I shall see her in three days / And just one night, but nights are short* . . ."), or else the lovers rush across a night landscape, remarking eagerly how the distance to their beloved is diminishing ("*Then a mile of warm sea-scented beach; / Three fields to pass before a farm appears; / A tap at the pane, the quick sharp scratch / And the blue spurt of a lighted match* . . ."").[8] The Buddha's rhetoric, like Browning's, lowers the distance between us and the beloved, showing once again a return of the repressed. The quest seems erotic, although its goal, despite great bliss, is allegedly of a quite different order. As with verbal approximations of nirvana, the Buddha skillfully appeals to what his listeners know best.

Value of Detachment

Contrary to what may be suggested, the dhamma is best taught, we are told, without appeals to desire. It is best taught without reference to persons, and thus without conflict: teaching must embody the Middle Way, "*giving vision, giving knowledge, it leads to peace, to direct knowledge, to enlightenment, to*

Nibbana. . . . One should neither extol nor disparage, but should teach only the Dhamma" (MN 139.3). The pursuit of sensual enjoyment is thus shown to be "*low . . . and unbeneficial*," without implicitly disparaging or praising specific persons or groups. Thus, instead of saying, "*all those engaged in the pursuit . . . of sensual enjoyment have entered upon the wrong way*," one says, more impersonally, that that "*pursuit is a state beset with suffering, vexation, despair*" (MN 139.6–8).

With skillful circumspection, "*sharp speech*" may be helpful: when "*true, correct, and beneficial, one may utter it, knowing the time to do so.*" But the overriding concern, both in the subject matter and in the methods of teaching, is to avoid conflict, thus giving meaning to the injunction "*teach only the Dhamma*": stick only to these teachings, not others, and do not muddy the waters with personal, ego-related issues (thus, traditional Buddhist teachers deliver their sermons from behind a large fan, so as to avoid distractions[9]). Keep personalities out, and the teaching will be more clearly apprehended, and even seem to be taught automatically.

In many cases, however, the teacher's juxtaposing of himself with other persons is a pedagogical tactic, and so we are confronted, once again, with competitive rivalry. Far from avoiding personal comparisons, the Buddha in *The Great Lion's Roar* announces his superiority to all other teachers of his time. He distinguishes himself, he tells the naked ascetic Kassapa, not only in doctrinal teachings but in morality: "*There are some ascetics and Brahmins who preach morality. . . . But as regards the highest Ariyan morality, . . . I do not see any who have surpassed me*" (DN 8.21–22). The Buddha continues with the same formula to proclaim that in austerity, in wisdom, and in liberation, he is the greatest.

We are presumably not to interpret these assertions as exhibitionism; enlightened ones do not compare themselves to others (AN 6.49, SN 1.2.10). Yet that's exactly what the assertions look like. They are enjoyable as tall tales, and certainly the Buddha has bragging rights. Whatever the motives, he plays the familiar role of the *miles gloriosus* who boasts cock-a-hoop, swaggers, and performs astonishing feats. In movies, the skillful cowboy pulls out his six-shooter and lays waste to all opponents. The Buddha, less spectacularly, in something more like a courtroom drama, can and does support his statements of superiority—which are, he suggests, simply matters of fact—when confronted with the disciples of those who derive their knowledge, as he also does, from supernormal vision (MN 136.9). He concedes that they are endowed with a similar vision, but that they fail badly in their interpretations.

An Examining Magistrate

Since correct and incorrect phrasings of the interpretations are laid out side by side, and seem very close, the reader needs to be mindfully attentive. The difference is sometimes in a single word, and often the whole case hangs upon that word. Some recluse or brahmin, we are told, attaining concentration and the divine eye, may be hasty in making inferences:

> *"He says thus: 'Indeed, there are no good actions, there is no result of good conduct; for I saw a person here who abstained from killing living beings . . . and held right view, and I see that on the dissolution of the body, after death, he has reappeared in a state of deprivation, . . . even in hell.' . . . He obstinately adheres to what he himself has known, seen, and discovered, insisting: 'Only this is true, anything else is wrong.'"* (MN 136.12)

The Buddha cites each statement, and then notes whether he grants the point or not. As teacher, the Buddha could be called an interpretive reader or an examining magistrate. He starts from what the other teacher is said to have said, repeats it several times, dividing it into its components. Then, using the exact wording, points out the unwarranted claims. Thus, for example, it is incorrect to use what happens to "*a person who kills*" as the basis for some law about what happens to "*everyone who kills*" (MN 136.13–17).

Conveniently for the policy of nonconflict, the other seers are not present to amend their statements or, if they dared, to apply the same tactics to the Buddha. Perhaps his generalizations, like theirs, were not based on enough samples. The Buddha did not allege that his teachings were derived from a supernatural source, but rather, as suggested in his advice to the Kālāmas, from direct, empirically verifiable, observation.[10] The teachings were inductions from a large number of insights. And yet no induction can ever be complete—especially, it would seem, when "*no beginnings can be found*" to our faring on, or when the world's being infinite or finite is not thought worthy of discussion (DN 1, MN 63.2–4).

In the passage cited, the Buddha seems concerned not only with wrong view but with dogmatism. Yet he himself is not necessarily undogmatic. When he repeatedly "*does not grant*" the other teacher his point, the reason given is, quite simply, that "*the Tathāgata's knowledge of the great exposition of action is otherwise*" (MN 136.14). His knowledge is, in other words, a gold standard against which others are measured, and found wanting. As Sangharakshita observes, dialogues may take place, but without much give and take: the interlocutors "in comparison with the majestic figure of the Buddha, are of pigmy size: they ask questions that are immediately answered, raise problems that are at once resolved, . . . to the rhythm of constant repetitions, like a Bach fugue marching triumphantly, and with absolute assurance, to its predestined conclusion."[11]

Issues of Karma

The topic discussed with such assurance, here and in the preceding sutta, is the teaching on karma. The karma doctrine intersects with Girard's theory of mimetic rivalry: good deeds will produce good results; evil deeds, evil ones. Action is never in vain, since all doings are cosmically interconnected. The person who "*kills living beings and is murderous, bloody-handed, given to blows and violence, merciless to living beings . . . reappears in a state of deprivation, in an unhappy destination, . . . even in hell, . . . [or if] instead comes back to the human state, then wherever he is reborn he is short-lived*" (MN 135.5). The taking of life results in one's life span being taken away. Envy results in being reborn as an uninfluential person, stinginess as a poor person, or generosity as a rich person (MN 135.11–13). Various sorts of behaviors and outcomes form a consistent enough pattern for a general law to be promulgated, which the Buddha articulates without the slightest reservations or uncertainty: "*beings are the owners of their actions; they originate from their actions, are bound to their actions, have their actions as their refuge*" (MN 135.19–20).

So sure is this law that another sutta on karma is entitled *The Incontrovertible Teaching* (MN 60). It is addressed not to monks but to laypersons, and thus it needs to reach a wider, less informed, possibly more uncertain, audience. Laypersons are often unable to cultivate meditation, but instead make merit, giving offerings and trying to behave in karmically favorable ways. The doctrine of karma is thus important for them, and doubtless they wish to hear about it. Here the Buddha examines alternative teachings. There are nihilist recluses and brahmins whose teaching is that "*there is nothing given, nothing offered, nothing sacrificed; no fruit or result of good and bad actions; no this world, no other world; no mother, no father; . . . no virtuous recluses and brahmins who have realised by direct knowledge and declare this world and the other world*" (MN 60.5). They deny, item by item, Buddhist moral teachings. And there are other recluses and brahmins who take, item by item, the opposite position to the deniers. The difference in formulating doctrine matters, because our behavior follows from those views, and wrong views may seem to sanction wrong action.

The Buddha's role is not to argue. Instead he simply states, in each case, what he knows to be the truth: for example, "*since there actually is another world, one who holds the view 'there is no other world' has wrong view*" (MN 60.8,11). Rightness of view, speech, and action are all coordinate in right teaching, and beneficial to all: "*since there actually is another world, one who convinces another that 'there is another world'*" does well (MN 60.11).

A Good Bet

Even if there should be some lack of certainty, it would still be wise to act as though karmic causation were valid. Here we come across a version of Blaise Pascal's wager—namely, to weigh the gain and loss in believing in God: if you win, you win all; if you lose, you lose nothing. The Buddha speculates nontheistically but similarly, with karma as the god-term or quilting point: "*let me assume that there is no other world: still [a] good person is here and now praised by the wise as a virtuous person. . . . [And] if there is another world, then this good person has made a lucky throw on both counts: . . . praised by the wise here and now and . . . after death, he will reappear in a happy destination*" (MN 60.12). There is nothing to lose, then, and much to gain by behaving well. Some may not know or care, though, about any such wager. As the Buddha considers their views and behavior, which reflects their indifference in a world without karmic causation, he invokes the Ganges river banks to vivify a setting:

> *If one were to go along the south bank of the Ganges killing and slaughtering, mutilating and making others mutilate, torturing and making others inflict torture, because of this there would be no evil and no outcome of evil. If one were to go along the north bank of the Ganges giving gifts and making others give gifts, making offerings and making others make offerings, because of this there would be no merit and no outcome of merit.* (MN 60.13)

When evil persons lead others to commit evil, we are confronted with what Girard calls a "sacrificial crisis" in which chaos ensues; karma (or mimetic violence) can work destructively.

Rivers and Families

Much is implied by the setting. The river Ganges is a sacred place, its banks the site of traditional sacrifice and bathing rites, whose efficacy was allegedly trumped by the Buddha's karma teachings. No longer a way to salvation by bathing, a river needs to be crossed, as in the raft parable, whereas both of these doers, whose motives are unstated, remain on the shore. Our karma is what's nearest and dearest, our ongoing character, and what we truly inherit.

Each person's sequence is distinct, and karmic operations give rise to results that can never be brought back to the wrong person, just as each mango develops from one seed and not another seed.[12] The fruition of karma, even so, comes about through interaction with one's environment and one's family: harmful action, according to the *Dhammapada*, can lead to "*physical injury, serious illness, insanity . . . , loss of relations*."[13] Karma and family, then, are rhetorically connected: a cluster of family imagery describes beings who are "*the heirs of their actions, originate from their actions, are bound to their actions.*" Karma is like—and more than—our parents, determining "*wherever [we are] reborn*," along with our characters and moral resemblances (MN 135.4, 14–15).

It is more than family, or perhaps our real family. As Nâgasena declares in *Questions of King Milinda*, when great harm is done, "*neither mother nor father, neither sisters nor brothers*" can help, and "*no other influence can avail . . . [when] karma is working out its inevitable end*" (QM 4.4.3).[14] The working out of a family curse, like the working out of karma, is at the heart of Greek tragedy and gothic fiction. We can count on our actions having consequences, which may well match our deeds.

Sealing the Discourse

The Buddha, in teaching about karma, makes an effort to keep mimetic violence under control, and to that end he uses the imagery of rivers, seeds, and family inheritances. Figurative language brings home the point in ways that an abstract explanation would not. At times the similes may seem excessive, but that is precisely when the greatest attention is required. If we wish, for example, to avoid dangerous karma, we need to guard against sense pleasures, and once again, fire imagery is invoked:

> *"Householder, suppose a man took a blazing grass torch and went against the wind. . . . If that man does not quickly let go of that blazing grass torch, wouldn't [it] burn his . . . body, so that he might incur death or deadly suffering because of that? . . . So, too, householder, a noble disciple considers thus: 'Sensual pleasures have been compared to a grass torch by the Blessed One; they provide much suffering and despair, while the danger in them is great.'"* (MN 54.17)

Here the fact that the Buddha himself constructs the simile gives it an extra seal of authority. As in the allegories he tells and then interprets, he controls the comparison, which is about a lack of control. A final stamp of legitimacy, a sort of imprimatur, is marked on each comparison, warranting its provenance. And that, too, is part of the lesson.

Elsewhere the discourse is ideologically sealed in other ways. The Buddha gives a helpful talk to the painfully sick Anāthapindika, telling him not to cling to anything (MN 143.4–16). Anāthapindika dies thereafter, and reappears in Tushita heaven. Then, when night comes, "*Anāthapindika, now a young god of beautiful appearance, went to the Blessed One, illuminating the whole of Jeta's Grove.*" He utters verses about how humans are purified by "*action, knowledge and Dhamma, / . . . Not by lineage or wealth*" (MN 143.17). The wealthy Anāthapindika achieves blessedness not by his possessions but by living in accord with the teachings. Multiple seals of legitimation are offered: the teaching is confirmed by Anāthapindika's Tushita appearance, by the "young god" reciting Dhamma verses who is recognized (supernormally) as Anāthapindika, and whose verses are sanctioned by the Buddha. He then reports the incident to the monks, who of course approve, adding yet another seal.

A seal for the teachings emerges, even more surprisingly, in the frame narrative to the *Exposition of the Elements*. The Buddha, while travelling in Rājaghata, asks a potter if he could stay for a day in his dwelling. He is welcomed, enters the potter's shop, sits in meditation, and later decides to make conversation with a monk, Pukkusāti, who also is staying there:

> *"Under whom have you gone forth, bhikkhu? Who is your teacher? Whose Dhamma do you profess?"*
>
> *"Friend, there is the recluse Gotama, the son of the Sakyans who went forth from a Sakyan clan. Now a good report of that Blessed Gotama has been spread to this effect: 'That Blessed One is accomplished, fully enlightened . . . teacher of gods and humans . . .'"* (MN 140.5)

Pukkasāti does not recognize that he is speaking with none other than his teacher, whom he had known merely by rumor and verbal formulae, but not in person. The Buddha, for his part, does not disclose his identity but instead launches into a discourse on the elements and on dispassion.

Pukkusāti soon becomes blissfully aware, in listening to the discourse, that "*Indeed the Teacher has come to me! . . . The Fully Enlightened One has come to me!*" (MN 140.33). Like Odysseus and other disguised epic heroes, the Buddha's identity is revealed gradually, as if in a test, to those who truly know him. Here, a delighted recognition vivifies the Buddha's saying that "*he who sees the dhamma sees me*" (SN 22.87). Pukkusāti apologizes profusely for not, at first, having recognized the Buddha, and for having addressed him merely as "friend."

The apology accepted, Pukkusāti asks for ordination, but first he needs to go out and find a proper bowl and robes. Next we are told that "*while the venerable Pukkusāti was searching for a bowl and robes, a stray cow killed him*" (MN 140.34). The abrupt, if not comic, death from "a stray cow" is not explained, but such an episode is relatively unimportant, especially by contrast with the preceding discourse and by contrast with the fact that, as the Buddha confirms when asked, that Pukkusāti "*will attain final Nibbāna*" (MN 140.36).

Refractory Disciples

The teaching does not go quite so smoothly, though it ends well, with other disciples. When the Buddha's disciples pose problems in their attitude, behavior, or understanding, he must resort to creative strategies. When, for example, the Buddha needs to confront Bhaddāli, a refractory, nonobedient monk who "*does not fulfill the training in the Teacher's Dispensation,*" he shames him by indicating how poorly the others in the sangha will regard him (MN 65.9). He gives an example of how an accomplished follower would promptly comply with the Buddha's request "*to be a plank for me to walk across the mud*" (MN 65.11). This situation is hypothetical, but surely it would prove who's master! It is also iconographic: Sumedha, aeons ago, made his vow to attain Buddhahood while lying in the mud (J 19). Lying in the mud, then, may be auspicious, and here command and obedience, as in the military, matter greatly.

With other disciples, the difficulty is doctrinal. Several of them are troubled by "speculative view" questions: is the world eternal or not, infinite or not; is the body separate from the soul or not; does the Tathāgata exist after death or not? The set of questions is standard, and repeated in longer or shorter versions (DN 1.29–37, MN 63.2, 72.3–14); but the Buddha persistently refuses to answer them. Aware of such refusals, the disciple Mālunkyaputta works himself into a frenzy. He is convinced that the Buddha is able to answer but, for some perverse reason, will not do so. Determined to find answers but given none, he threatens to abandon his training (63.2–3).

The Arrow Parable

The Buddha's cool response is a set of a queries. Did he ever agree, when Mālunkyputta joined the order, to provide answers to these questions? Did Mālunkyaputta, in turn, ever agree to lead the holy life on condition that he receive answers? In both cases, Mālunkyaputta concedes that there had been no such agreement. To show what else is at stake, beyond an agreement or contract, the Buddha tells the famous arrow parable, mentioned earlier. The parable embellishes at great length on the wounded man's questions, and all the while, time in the story—and in the telling—is passing by. After extensive questioning, "*all this would still not be known to the man, and meanwhile he would die*" (MN 63.5). The word *die* has multiple overtones: physical death (from the arrow) and, more seriously, death to the holy life, which could not proceed so long as these impractical, attention-diverting questions were being perpetually pondered.

The Buddha quite clearly explains why he refuses to answer the question: "*it does not lead to disenchantment, to dispassion, to cessation, to peace, to direct knowledge, to enlightenment, to Nibbāna*" (MN 63.8). This statement is similar to his reason for abandoning his own teachers, whose teachings did not meet this criterion (MN 26.15–16). Mālunkyaputta and the Buddha thus offer inverted images of one another, but the point, in the end, is the same.

Visible Rewards

Another challenge to the Buddha's pedagogy comes in *The Fruits of the Homeless Life* (DN 2). There King Ajātasattu, troubled in mind for having murdered his father to attain his throne, makes journeys to a number of teachers, with the same question he now asks the Buddha: "*Can you, Lord, point to . . . a reward visible here and now as a fruit of the homeless life?*" (DN 2.14) Every occupation brings with it certain visible rewards or fruits—for example, potters, basket weavers, accountants, all produce tangible products deserving of respect. What, in turn, is the visible reward or "fruit" of the holy life?

The matter of a reward or benefit is still of concern today and can be reformulated for our times.[15] In what ways is the practice worthwhile? Supposing that one makes an effort to follow this way, what benefits will accrue? In order to answer these questions or similar ones of his time, the Buddha deploys an array of teaching skills, and lays out his wares, so to speak, for inspection. The sutta begins with a section on what could be called comparison shopping, in which other teachers' goods are shown to be shoddy and worthless.

It is soon the Buddha's turn to offer a superior alternative. He brings to bear a series of similes, indicating benefits accruing to one whose mind has been freed. Such a person is like a man who took out a loan to develop his business, and who might later "*pay off his old debts, and . . . could support a wife, . . . and he would rejoice and be glad*"; or a sick man who would regain his health, or a prisoner his freedom (DN 2.69–71). In all these cases, and there are others, the similes do the work of bringing out tangible benefits of the holy life.

Every simile, however, is partly inaccurate (it's only a comparison), and the Buddha needs to be more specific about the rewards of meditational states. He speaks of the "*delight and joy born of detachment, [the meditator] so suffuses, drenches, fills and irradiates his body that there is no spot in his entire body that is untouched by this delight and joy born of detachment*" (DN 2.75). The passage may offer a superior alternative to sensual enjoyment, and it uses imagery that listeners or readers can easily understand. That imagery—perhaps necessarily—is sensual: the meditator is "drenched" with "delight and joy." Is the figurative language, as in the *Dhammapada*, doing the work of communication?

Marvelous Hyperboles

The rewards of each jhānic state, still with the formula of how one "suffuses the body" (DN 2.76–79), are followed by a description of supernormal powers (*iddhi*). The first power involves a number of feats, which the Buddha did not recommend putting on display (DN 11.5)[16]—but which he nonetheless lists, as if on verbal display. The skilled meditator applies his mind, and "*being one, he becomes many, being many, he becomes one; he appears and disappears; he passes through . . . mountains unhindered as if through air; he sinks into the ground and emerges from it . . . ; he walks on the water; . . . he flies cross-legged through the sky . . . ; he even touches and strokes with his hand the sun and the moon, mighty and powerful as they are . . .*" (DN 2.87). This is a splendid, astonishing passage, and it seems to belong to a realm of myth or romance where, as we recall, actions are at the limits of desire and all things are possible.[17] Here, in what appears to be a world of myth, the exalted practitioner "touches and strokes . . . the sun and the moon." Commentators have remained silent about the phrase, though Maurice Walshe understandably asserts that it is "not to be taken literally" (DN n 129). In other words, it is done "only" metaphorically.

Once one item in the series starts to seem mythic or metaphoric, so too, as in a falling domino effect, may the others. They are pleasant to imagine and may be inspiringly hyperbolic. But they are also interestingly questionable, and a spectrum of metaphoricity starts to emerge. If the yogi metaphorically touches the sun, then he also metaphorically walks through mountains, though perhaps less amazingly so. And walking on water, which happens frequently in sacred texts, seems the least figurative, and almost banal.

The stress throughout, perhaps as a counterweight, is on good eyesight and clear seeing, "*just as . . . a man with good eyesight*" sees in ordinary life (DN 2.96). Seeing is crucial to the process of liberation, and here the seer sees with supernormal vision, like someone "with good eyesight" who could see to the bottom of a clear pond, noting "*oyster shells and gravel banks*" (DN 2.98). In a pattern to be found elsewhere, figures thus do the work, in this case the work of vision. Having spoken of good eyesight and clearly seen oyster shells, one makes a smooth transition to the fruits of the homeless life, "visible" here and now. The King, however, like most people, has not cultivated a "divine eye." The three knowledges of awakening, like supernormal powers, are as yet beyond his ken—that is, they are precisely *not* visible here and now! The Buddha can take credit, as a craftsman, for being able to endow his vision with verisimilitude, making us think that we see what is, according to literary conventions, visible in a special world, "here and now."

Questions of Survival

We may move now toward the Buddha's end. Having engaged in skillful teaching throughout his life, and having reached the age of 80, he prepares the monks for his departure. In the *Mahāparinibbāna Sutta* the Buddha passes on, again in the double sense of no longer remaining, and of transmitting his final teachings. The text describing the Buddha's death—or more precisely, his "last death"—is framed at its beginning and end with the possibility of violence: King Ajātasattu, whom we just met, is planning an attack on his neighbors, while at the end various tribes contend noisily for the Buddha's relics. Surrounded by chaos in the making, the Buddha's dying endeavor is a struggle for survival, less for himself than for his legacy—his vulnerable sangha.

King Ajātasattu sends a minister to inform the Buddha that he, the King, would like to bring the Vajjians "*to ruin and destruction*" (DN 16.1.2).[18] The message is phrased as the statement of a deed to be carried out, rather than as a request for moral or even tactical advice. Ajātasattu is simply curious to know the Buddha's response. The Buddha obliges, commenting cautiously that "*as long as the Vajjians hold regular and frequent assemblies, they may be expected to prosper and not decline*" (1.4). He also adds that they might be captured, if not by arms, then by something like ideology or propaganda (1.5). As soon as the minister departs, the Buddha, apparently worried and responding to the warlike tenor of the times, calls his monks to a formal meeting in which he lists "*the seven things that are conducive to welfare*" (1.6). He then adds a comprehensive discourse, as if to suggest, in light of possible violence and his own impending death, that the dhamma will protect them.

At about the same time this is spoken, however, several tribes "*were building a fortress in Pātaligāma as a defense against the Vajjians,*" and the Buddha, with his divine eye, can confirm that the devas are taking up residence there (1.26–27). He is concerned, moreover, not only for the monks, but for laypersons, to whom he gives a moral discourse (1.23–25). Can the Buddha, physically sick and weakening, be able to protect his followers from the surrounding, and apparently speading, violence? Will his fledgling sangha survive? It would seem especially urgent, in view of these questions, that the Buddha survive a while longer so as to guide his followers through threatening times. A longer life, he tells Ānanda, is a distinct possibility for those, like himself, who have been devoted to life-extension practices: whoever diligently undertakes them, "*could undoubtedly live for a century, or the remainder of one. The Tathāgata has developed these powers, . . . and could undoubtedly*" live that long (3.3). The Buddha makes this statement, as usual, three times, and it contains, we are later informed, a "*broad hint*" (3.41) that Ānanda missed, as doubtless do most listeners. Ānanda could and should have asked the Buddha to engage in this practice, right now, for the benefit of all.

Ānanda having failed to catch the hint, the Buddha is confronted once again with Māra, and though he is able to defer dying for a time, he concedes to Māra that his passing "*will not be long delayed*" (3.9). The Buddha, in making this concession, admits his mortality. The episode shows that naturalistically the Buddha, as a human being like others, must die. At the same time, however, the text seems to ignore or bypass the more messy physical aspects of dying, and instead shows devotees adorning the body with a sweet, flowery overlay.

The text also implicitly denies the necessity of the Buddha's having to die at that particular time. Ānanda, it reiterates, had failed to undertand the Buddha's broad hint, and the Buddha reprimands him: at a crucial moment, he "*did not beg the Lord*" to live longer (3.4). The implication is that, had Ānanda done so, Māra would not have been able to enter into the vacuum left by failure to make this request. And the subsequent earthquake, when the Buddha "*renounces the life principle,*" would not have occurred (3.7–10). The Buddha is caught, then, between Māra's pressure to die, and Ānanda's dumb silence. The Buddha, a semiotic entity, emits a "*clear sign*" (3.4), but Ānanda fails to recognize the code by which an empowering request must be uttered at the right moment.

Semiotic Failure

The Buddha blames Ānanda for missing "*such a clear hint,*" for not sensing the protocol: "*Ananda, yours is the fault, yours is the failure*" (3.40). In shortening the Buddha's life span, Ānanda accomplishes what Māra wants. Ānanda's mind is said to be "*possessed by Māra*" (3.4), which may or (more probably) may not excuse him. The issue is serious: in the text (or the patchwork of texts)[19] as it survives, the reproach is repeated several times, making it seem harsh. Is the fault entirely Ānanda's? Perhaps the "*broad hint*" was too broad, and was seen as yet another of the Buddha's boastful assertions. The Buddha in any case asks Ānanda, twice, "*Have you faith?*" (3.39, 40), implying that Ānanda may not have fully believed in his life-extension practices. One is reminded of Hamlet's question, also repeated twice, to his obtuse mother: "*Have you eyes?*" In both cases, a lack of insight is taken to indicate moral weakness.

The Buddha, in his irritation, reminds Ānanda of the many places in which he made the hint (3.40–47). The hint was phrased in precisely the same way on every occasion—or at least the text makes no mention of any variation. But why would a skilled teacher fail to note that Ānanda, a slow learner, was not getting the point, and have rephrased the hint—mentioning, for example, that other life-extension practitioners, to be successful, required the help of their assistants? Or why not wait for a time when more monks were present, to witness "the clear sign"? Could the Buddha have been possibly victimized by his own pride, being afraid, perhaps, of losing face? We are unable to answer such questions or to separate the repetitiveness of an oral formulaic text from what might have happened. All we get from the tradition is a virtually cardboard figure caught within a linguistic formalism.

The immediate causes of the Buddha's death—his horrific last supper—are equally opaque. When offered the "*pig's delight*" meal, the Buddha uses his supernormal powers to proclaim, grandly and sweepingly, "*I can see none in this world, with its devas, māras, and Brahmās . . . who, if they were to eat it, could thoroughly digest it except the Tathāgata*" (4.19). The Buddha, who is still prone to mimetic rivalry and boasting (4.26–34), is wrong about this, since he very soon is attacked "*by a severe sickness with bloody diarrhoea, and with sharp pains as if were about to die*" (4.20).

Pharmakon, Pharmakeus

A number of explanations may be given for his eating what he knew in advance to be dangerous food (he may have feared, for example, to offend the host). But the event also shows how the Buddha, who trumpets his triumph over *dukkha* in his discovery of "the deathless" is here manifestly suffering and soon will die. The traditional view is that there are several types of suffering, and that the arhat is not immune to ordinary pain. But here the obvious illness, coming so soon after his boasting, definitely does not look good, and may even suggest that other of his proclamations may also be faulty. This issue is especially pressing, since the Buddha is commonly referred to as a physician or shaman. He can prescribe treatments or medicines for the disease of *dukkha*. In his final days, however, he himself is subject to disease, which his medical and therapeutic insight should, in a case of dietary intake, have prevented.

Plato's Socrates also died of poisoning, though of a different sort. On Derrida's analysis of several Platonic dialogues, a *pharmakon* is both a poison and a remedy, and is prescribed by a *pharmakeus* (magician, shaman, drug expert) to cure or purge diseases.[20] The Buddha as *pharmakeus* is unable to control the powers of the *pharmakon*—in this case, the pork dish that is clearly poisonous, but may also be remedial in producing or purging a scapegoat or *pharmakos*, to use a term closely related to *pharmakeus*.[21]

If, as earlier suggested, the Buddha with his *parinirvana* is acting as a sacrificial victim to bring peace to his troubled community and to his sangha, he is only partly successful (relic wars follow). In the meantime this physician, though discredited (he makes himself sick and is unable to cure himself) offers counter-medicines, or remedies, to his followers. He offers Cunda, for example, a purgative treatment: "*Cunda's remorse should be expelled in this way: 'That is your merit, Cunda, that is your good deed, that the Tathāgata gained final Nibbana after taking his last meal from you!'*" (4.42). In this case, Cunda's *pharmakon*, the poison, was also a remedy, since it allowed for entry into nirvana. But if so, why emphasize that a poison-induced state leads to *parinirvana*, which should have happened anyway, in due course? By being poisoned to death—with no one stopping him from consuming the food he publicly proclaimed to be dangerous—the Buddha may seem to emerge as a sacrificial figure.

Passing Away

Working to some extent against a sacrificial theory, however, is the sense that no ultimate sacrifice transpires: the Buddha does not die, at least not in any common, usual way. A description of his passing is carefully given, in accord with the ideology he founded: he enters into increasingly higher jhānic states, and monks standing by are able to determine which spheres he goes through, and when, "*leaving the fourth jhāna, he Lord finally passed away*" (6.8–9). Thereupon an earthquake, as predicted, occurs. Poems are then recited by Brahmā Sahampati, Sakka, and others, but they do not show much grief, instead reiterating doctrine ("*All beings in the world, all bodies must break up: / Even the Teacher, peerless in the human world, / . . . has passed away*"; 6.10). What might be interpreted as coldness in these utterances, though, is counterbalanced by the weeping and wailing of monks who had "*not yet overcome their passions*," and who are duly chastised for their unseemly displays (6.10–11).

In this account of the Buddha's departure, there is no mention, apart from his initial indigestion, of the physical processes of dying—death signs, decreasing pulse or breath, deteriorating states of the body or corpse. We find instead a strong insistence that this is no ordinary death, and perhaps not a death at all; rather, it is a *parinirvana.* As in many Buddhist traditions, the master's exit from the world cannot be described as "death"; that word is not used.[22] And devotees hide signs of death: they bring perfumes, wreaths, and five hundred sets of garments to cover the body (6.13). The decorating, sweetening, and covering up of the Buddha's body is understandable, especially in a more general context: as a young man, the Prince ran away from home after three sights, one of which was a corpse. He later claimed, in exalted language, at this most sublime moment, to have reached "*the deathless [amata]*" and found the "*supreme security*" (MN 26.12,18). Not surprisingly, the story omits details of what his corpse looked like, and by romance conventions this information is usually not provided.

From the viewpoint of some recent readers, the Buddha dies, just as everyone else does, and his boasting about having attained "the deathless" will have to be taken in a special sense, as an ideological assertion. Since the basic direction of Buddhist ideology is to escape from death, then actual instances of death—most obviously, a corpse in need of funeral rites—are minimized. The corpse (its distorted features, its blood and odors, its color, its bloating, its banality) is the repressed underside of the Buddhist legend, which prefers to tell of saintly corpses that, even after weeks and months, do not decay. There is some wisdom, too, in portraying nirvana as an impenetrable mystery: since most aspects of the Buddha's biography are hyperbolic, why not say, similarly, that he died, but he did not.

Versions of Elegy

Elegies in all traditions also say something to this effect—namely, that the hero is not really dead but only somewhere else. The traditional pastoral elegy in the West displays a double pattern of grief followed by consolation and exaltation. At the end of John Milton's *Lycidas*, the shepherds are told (as Anuruddha tells the monks, though in a different tone), that they need not continue with their lamentations: "*Weep no more, woeful shepherds, weep no more, / For Lycidas, your sorrow is not dead, / Sunk though he be beneath the wat'ry floor . . .*".[23] When loved ones die, we lament for them (and for ourselves without them), but we are prompted to believe, perhaps only in a continuation of what Percy Bysshe Shelley, also in an elegy, calls the "*mad trance*" in which while we continue to decay, while they've moved on, to some better place: "*Peace, peace! He is not dead, he doth not sleep— / He hath awakened from the dream of life.*"[24] At the point of death, the Buddha also speaks of mourning and awakening, compassionately urging his monks not to fear, but simply to do the practice: "*be lamps unto yourselves,*" "*strive for the highest goal, and dwell with your minds tirelessly, zealously devoted to the highest goal*" (2.26, 5.10).

The Work of Mourning

Structures in poetic elegies show elements of the work of mourning—introjection and incorporation. As Maria Torok explains, "while the introjection of desires puts an end to objectal dependency, incorporation of the object creates or reinforces imaginal ties, and hence dependency."[25] The Buddha urges that ties of dependency be cut, but his followers, mourning his departure, often could not do so. When introjection is complete, "the object can descend from its imaginal pedestal"; yet frequently, Torok continues, introjection is incomplete, while an incorporated object, "installed in place of the lost object, . . . continues to recall the fact that some other object was lost."[26] With the death of a public figure, mourning is communal, and unceasing. Any ambivalence toward the Buddha is brought to the surface: the taboos enforced while he lived may now be loosened or freed; thus Subhadda rejoices in the Buddha's passing (6.20).

The most common reaction is to deify the Buddha's image, to transform him, as elegies do, into a divine figure and, if he cannot be literally incorporated (as in the Christian eucharist), then one may acquire material pieces of him—fingernails, bone fragments, ashes—all containing something of his spirit and power. The Buddha's discovery of the deathless is embodied in these undying remains. As John Strong points out, the Buddha's relics were thought to be "alive, own property, perform miracles, inspire devotees," just as the Buddha did.[27] Hagiography is not ended with the Buddha's death, but continues in his relics, which "embody the whole of the Buddha's coming and going, his life-and-death story; they reiterate both his provenance and impermanence. . . . They help legitimate empires here on earth and they further spread the dharma to places the living Buddha never visited. . . . They write new chapters in the Buddha's story."[28] The community thereby palpably retains—introjects and incorporates—the beloved caravan leader.

The Buddha did not seek deification, but urged instead that whoever sees the dhamma "sees me." The huge imaginative effort of identifying his teachings with the Buddha, as so directed, may bring strength: the dhamma's message is of voidness or absence—absence of permanence, absence of soul, absence of comfort or essence. The wandering pilgrims' most proper response to the Buddha and to his relics, it has been said, is of seeking and failing to find.[29] The absence left by his departure had already been inscribed in the teachings, and an honest reading would have anticipated the Buddha's demise, if not the precise endgame.

Signs imply absences, and the newborn marked with signs, who then goes into homelessness, is a wandering sign.

The signs still wander, unsteadily, toward us. The sangha, despite the Buddha's doubts, has survived. And the work of mourning can be extended, as Derrida argues, to include all work: "the work of mourning is not one kind of work among others. It is work itself, work in general, the trait by means of which one ought to reconsider the very concept of production—in what links it to . . . the idealizing iterability of expropriation."[30] More than what can be conveyed by terms such as incorporation and introversion, the work of mourning could thus be in the creation, say, of golden images, as in Yeats's *Sailing to Byzantium*, or in the making of gold-leaved and golden Buddha images. The entire Buddhist tradition could be seen as demanding and loving work: the founder's teaching while he lived, stupa-building, pilgrimages, chanting, merit-making, ordination, prostrations, bodhisattva training, the reworking of doctrines teaching emptiness and the three bodies, the spread of the sangha, commentaries, visualization practices, and, last but not least, the creation of new sacred texts, such as those to be next considered.

6

Right Figures of Speech

The Dhammapada

Name has weighted down everything;
Nothing is more extensive than name.
Name is the one thing that has
All under its control.

—Samyutta Nikāya

What's in a name? That which we call a rose
By any other name would smell as sweet.

—Shakespeare, *Romeo and Juliet*

The Buddha berated monks who eagerly absorbed the "*beautiful words and phrases of poets*," but failed to absorb the words of the Tathāgata (SN 2.20.7). Monks, once ordained, are duty-bound to listen attentively to the teachings. This is not to say that those teachings lack poetry—on the contrary, they are powerfully poetic—or that readers, be they monks or not, are unaffected by the teachings' plentitude of figurative language. Yet if names are tyrannical and weigh down everything, what can be said about the Buddha's own poetry, and his acts of naming? How, or at what point, can one arrive at a free and valid language?

In other words, if all names—words, images, concepts—are merely tokens, what can be the status of the text's own names? Is right naming an ideal, and is it is a possibility for us as well? The Buddha's achievement, after all, was not only enlightenment, but a skillful communication of the teachings. He used explication, exemplification, parable telling, counterquestioning, inspired utterance. In most cases, figures of speech—metaphors, ironies, and especially, similes—are brought into play, so that all listeners might follow. But even coming from the Buddha, are they always examples of "right speech"?

The Rhetoric of Right Speech

Right figures of speech could well be part of "right speech" in the eightfold path, though they are not directly mentioned. Right speech is "*timely, true, gentle, purposeful, and spoken with . . . loving kindness*" (AN 5.198). Figurative speech can meet most of these requirements, but as irony, it might not seem kind, and as figure, its truth cannot readily be assessed. If names are hindrances, and have "*weighted down everything*" (SN 1.7.61), perhaps they have done so unequally, and a middle way must be found to keep watch over figurative language, so it does not become fanciful poetry or misleading naming.

The Buddha is said never to been misled by what are "*merely names, expressions, turns of speech, designations in common use*" (DN 9.53). Does this mean that when speaking, he knows just what to say? In the *Dhammapada*—allegedly the Buddha's words—does the naming never weigh down, are the figures of speech always exactly right? Figurative words, by definition, carry meanings over (metaphor), compare them (simile), rename them (metonymy), or take parts for whole (synecdoche), and so a constant displacing and exchanging takes place. How can such potentially shady dealings be supervised, assuring us that they're all "right"?

They may be right in the sense of "skillful." The Buddha, at times using skillful means, would accept the assumptions of his audience in order to move them in a more profitable direction (for example, when young brahmins were running after a courtesan). At other times, he would need to correct the assumptions made by showing that the question is "*not fitting*," and restating, before answering, a question. At other times, he would teach by asking the interlocutor to do something (find a mustard seed). Or else he would simply tell a pointed story, a parable or an episode from his own life, so as to clarify his message.

He taught his pedagogical methods to his monks, if not explicitly, then by his own example, as a model to be imitated. He authorized and inspired them to go forth, "*for the welfare and happiness of many, out of . . . compassion for the world, for the benefit and welfare and happiness of gods and men.*"[1] The repetitions and parataxis, in this very passage, show a dissemination that is caring and incremental.

Metaphorization

Another example of the Buddha's method is not only when similes are put into play, but when a process of *metaphorization* takes place. Metaphorization is an insistence on what might be called the "higher" or—in Western terms, as in the Bible or in Dante—the "moral" and "spiritual" levels of meaning. In a frequent pattern, a simple or literal question is given a metaphorical answer.

For example, a brahmin asks, "*Is there any single thing of which / You'd approve the killing, Gotama?*" The interlocutor, whose wife Dhanañjāni is a zealous devotee, is displeased at the Buddha and may be trying to trick him, expecting the reply to refer to nefarious evildoers or dangerous animals. Instead, the Buddha's reply is: "*By slaying wrath, you'll live in happiness, / Slaying wrath, you'll have no more need to weep. / Kill the poisoned root of anger, brahmin*" (SN 7.1.1). The metaphorization, not merely ornamental, reinforces ideology, since the metaphors move in a doctrinal direction. Killing, cutting, destroying, rooting out: these are all common, metaphorized (if you wish, sublimated) verbs of aggression. They are countermeasures: "killing" is a figurative violence against the violence in the brahmin's mind. In this case, the metaphorization is successful: the brahmin is converted, and in due course, becomes an arhat.

The immediately subsequent sutta, however, continues the plot in a different key. A fellow clansman, hearing of the first brahmin's conversion, is enraged, and goes to the Buddha to protest. Unlike the first angry brahmin, who asked a polite but pointed question, this brahmin verbally attacks the Buddha, "*overwhelming him with abuse and reproaches.*" Here a different kind of right rhetoric, or right naming, is called for.

> *When he had finished speaking, the Blessed One said to him: "What do you think, brahmin? Do your friends and colleagues, kinsmen and relatives, as well as guests come to visit you?"*
>
> *"Sometimes they come to visit, Master Gotama."*
>
> *"Do you offer them some food or a meal or a snack?"*
>
> *"Sometimes I do, Master Gotama."*
>
> *"But if they do not accept it from you, then to whom does the food belong?"*
>
> *"If they do not accept it from me, then the food still belongs to us."*
>
> *"So too, brahmin, we—who do not abuse anyone, who do not scold anyone, who do not rail against anyone—refuse to accept from you the abuse and scolding and tirade you let loose at us. It still belongs to you, brahmin!"* (SN 7.1.2)

The Buddha at the end of this passage excludes any possibility that the brahmin is mimetically responding to prior personal scoldings and abuse. Then, in verses that follow, the Buddha makes clear that attacks will always be one-sided, that (as with Māra) he does not reciprocate violence: "*Not repaying an angry man with anger, / One wins a battle hard to win*" (SN 7.1.2). The point could not be made without felicitous metaphoric examples: food not accepted, not partaken, not shared. The brahmin, not caring to be left alone with unacceptable food (his anger), sees the point, and he, too, converts.

Personal and Impersonal

The force of metaphorization is often in the direction of humanizing, personalizing, and personifying. In this instance, the Buddha begins by asking, disarmingly, about an opposite, more humane, type of behavior than is currently on display. He asks about the brahmin's habits of offering food to others, and welcoming them. And in the previous instance, "slaying" wrath depends on a personification of wrath, or Wrath, a familiar figure in allegory, and an implicitly ironic personification of the slayer—ironic, since here slaying is virtuous.

The drive toward personalization may be at odds, however, with an antithetical drive toward selflessness or depersonalization (*anattā*). If right figuring is a part of right speech, Buddhist texts must tread a skillful middle way between humane amiability and cool impersonality. The Buddha again and again urges followers to become like the elements—to think, as in the second sermon, "*not me*," "*not mine*." What is conventionally designated as a self are the five impersonal aggregates, interconnected in turn with the twelve impersonal factors in the chain of conditioned origination (SN 12.1.1–3). Nowhere is a self or person to be found, but only an ongoing series of psychophysical processes.

The Buddha's skillful teaching, then, at times personal, is also at times depersonalizing. At one point, he expounds on how there are four nutriments for the maintenance of life: food, contact, volition, and consciousness. A monk then poses the question, "*Venerable sir, who consumes the nutriment consciousness?*" As usual when "who" questions are asked, the question is rejected, and an alternative is proposed:

> *"Not a valid question," the Blessed One replied. "I do not say, 'One consumes.' If I should say, 'One consumes,' in that case this would be a valid question. . . . Since I do not speak thus, if one should ask me, 'Venerable sir, for what is the nutriment consciousness [a condition]?' this would be a valid question."* (SN 12.12.2)

The formulation of a "*valid question*" (right speech, or a naming that weighs down less heavily) constitutes a lesson to be learned, an occasion for reforming thinking.

The subsequent repetition, in the next paragraphs, of a similarly invalid question—that is, the same question for each nutriment, by the same interlocutor—may be disconcerting. The Buddha tries to speak for the monk, tries to put proper words in his mouth, says what the monk should say. Yet this monk, like a Samuel Beckett character, does not learn. He simply repeats by rote the same invalid question for each succeeding nutriment. Could someone go on thus, over and over, making exactly the same mistake? Such a question is itself invalid, since the monk's invalid question is incorporated, and repeated, as part of the lesson.

The effect is that the questioner fades as a person and is made selfless, becoming subordinated to a general tendency and to the lesson being taught. A person, however, or something personal, is rearticulated in other lessons and other texts. Indeed, despite a drive toward selflessness and renunciation, the Buddhist way inspires worldwide popular devotion. How might this have happened?

Beloved Proverbs

A hint may be offered in the *Dhammapada*. As already suggested, figures of speech can humanize the teachings, and this Buddhist poem, one of the best known and most often translated, is highly figurative. It provides a kernel of the teachings in a way that everyone can comprehend. A collection of beloved proverbs and bits of wisdom, it is divided according to topic into twenty-six short sections. Each section and each proverb can be savored on its merits and reflected upon according to readers' temperaments, life situations, and mental conditions. Something is said here, attributed to the Buddha, that even the most wayward of monks might easily listen to, since the *Dhammapada* puts the teachings into brilliant verse.

The sayings are presented in no apparent order. Themes accumulate, not according to an argumentative sequence but rather by the effect of intertwined imagery, or something akin to musical elaborations upon a set of leitmotifs. Each section usually offers negative and positive versions of the sayings, with variations and examples. There may be a few general patterns, as pointed out by Bhikkhu Thanissaro: the text "begins with the duality between heedless and heedful ways of living, and ends with the final attainment of total mastery."[2] According to Indian aesthetics, the text's message comes by means of a heroic "savor" (*rasa*), and with the help of rhetorical tactics—accumulation, ambiguity, encouragement, etymology, examples, implications, praise, prohibitions, rhetorical questions. Great role models, sketched out by this rhetoric, are those who attain the goal, and those who, by following the teachings, gain a better birth.[3]

Centrality of Mind

The *Dhammapada* thus meets the issue of naming, not by making strictly propositional or reportial claims but by figures of speech, by lyrical imagery, by depictions of familiar character types, by time-tested generalizations that delineate a way of life and an ideal of comportment. Its guiding thread comes at the opening.

> *Everything has mind in the lead, has mind in the forefront, is made by mind. If one speaks or acts with a corrupt mind, misery will follow, as the wheel of a cart follows the foot of the ox.* (1.1).[4]

Translations vary: *mano*, here given as "mind," has also been rendered as "heart," "perception," or "thought." In all cases, our mental conditions and figurations play a huge role in the world we encounter and, by encountering, make.

The operation of karma turns on intention, and our mind is integral with what happens. Negative or positive thoughts "about" a situation are actually part of that situation, and vital to what transpires. A common rationale for complaints is "the other": bad circumstances, or someone else's doings. But responses to the same, or similar, circumstances vary: *"'He reviled me; he injured me; he defeated me; he deprived me.' In those who harbor such thoughts, hatred never ceases."* Conversely, those who do not harbor grudges, the next verse states, in them hatred will cease (1.3–4 C m). The two verses are twinned as polarities. The message thus seems simple and didactic. Those who are pure of heart quickly forgive, are neither resentful nor complaining, and that attitude defines the situation. Those who are impure and unforgiving blame everyone, like beings in the hell realms. They suffer more, since they brood on the harm supposedly done to them. They may even calculate some kind of revenge, thus spreading mimetic violence (you hurt me, so I hurt you). And from such instances, a maxim: "*Hate does not cease by hate, but by love. This is an ancient truth*" (1.5). Although hostility may defeat the enemy or satisfy the aggressor, it will not result in love, but at best, a resentful acquiescence that at any moment could, as we hear daily in the news, burst into renewed violence.

The "ancient truth" avoids mimetic violence, and our samsāric world needs to be guarded against it. One might think that the pure of mind (who, in stanza 4, do not bear grudges) would be engaged with the world. But perhaps not immediately, since some degree of distancing is needed. Rather, they cultivate heedfulness, shielding themselves from impurity. Haters, who become resentful, habitually indulge themselves, "*senses uncontrolled, idle and weak, [whom] Māra overcomes, as the wind, a weak tree*" (1.7). The figure is compact: one verb, "overcomes," applies to both the person and the tree. The two are conjoined, illustrating impersonality in both. This is an example of right figurative speech, a merging of the personal (a familiar character-type) and the selfless (wind, tree, overturning) to make a sacred point.

Such a verse, and the other opening verses, offer a delineation of the Buddhist outlook. Training in dispassionate mindfulness will affect our perception of events, and thus our behavior. *Appamāda*, the title of chapter 2, can be translated as "awareness," "heedfulness," "vigilance," "carefulness," or "wakefulness." *Appamāda*, though only a name, has been said to encapsulate the Buddha's teachings.[5] To be mindful is to attune the mind precisely to the Buddhist ideology, that is, to a certain definition of mind, attention, and the value of both. The ideology provides a foundation, too, for a resituating of life and death, in which awareness as nondeath and nonawareness as death, are played upon musically, in a series of repetitions and variations:

Awareness is the path of the deathless,
Unawareness, the path of death.
Those who are aware do not die,
Those who are not aware are as if dead already. (2.1 CP m).

Much is at stake in these binary pairings, which link awareness with immortality, and the lack of it, with death. Is some kind of troping going on, with the obvious unconsciousness of the dead being extended to all kinds of unattentiveness, however lively the accompanying action? The realm of what is commonly supposed to be life at its peak, its fastest, its most thrilling—is also life at its most unaware, even in tense concentration. Lack of attention veers close to death and, as in tragedies or crime films, ends with a pile of bloody corpses. The reckless are deemed "fools," even by one another but here, of course, deplorably so, in counterpoint to those who cultivate mindful attention.

Perilous Flowers

The themes of skillful attention and its lack are reinforced not only by mention of death, but in chapter 4, by the plucking and collecting of flowers. Flowers are entwined with love, desire, and sexuality. Shakespeare's Juliet, even while distrusting names, names a rose. And names of flowers are telling in their associations: Venus flytraps, roses, sunflowers, passion flowers, orchids. With stamens and pistils, they disseminate, cross-pollinate, open up blossoms, and seasonally die, being also allied, in funerals, with death. Flowers would seem far too sensuous for the Buddha's calmly chaste world, except, of course, for the lotus flower. The Buddha is compared to a lotus, and his best followers will be similar: "*a blue, red or white lotus is born in the water, and grows up in the water, but having risen up above the water, it stands unsullied. . . . So, too, the Tathāgata . . . dwells unsullied by the world*" (SN 22.94).

Most flowers are erotic and worldly, and the language of flowers—poetry and rhetoric—are not always to be trusted. The *Dhammapada*, daringly, does not confine itself to lotuses, and uses the word *flower* throughout chapter 4. Indeed, plucking and skillfully collecting flowers is made into an image of the text itself:

Who will conquer this earth and realm of Yama [state of woe] . . . ?
Who will gather the well-taught doctrinal word [dhammapadam sudesitam],
as a skillful expert, a flower? (4.44 CP m)

The questions, since they refer to the *Dhammapada* as a collection or anthology (*anthologos*: a gathering of flowers), also implicate the listener or reader, plucking flowers from the text and, when giving skillful attention, becoming an expert. The next verse thus answers the question:

> *The learner [or pathfollower: sekho] will conquer the earth . . . and gather a well-taught doctrinal word, as a skillful expert, a flower.* (4.45).

Knowing that the world is illusory (foam, a mirage), the learner cuts away the flowery blossoms of Māra. This is no easy task, and the succeeding verse strikes an ominous note:

> *Death carries away someone distracted in gathering flowers, just as a great flood carries away a sleeping village.* (4.47 N m)

An attached or distracted mind, immersed in flower-gathering, is endangered by floral lures, not awake.

Flower-gathering, then, seems an especially "weighted-down" name, or a metaphor with possibly misleading overtones. Finely honed skills may be required of both the path-learner and the reader. Consider, for example, how the following twin verses might be construed:

> *Like a beautiful flower that is colorful but has no fragrance, even well-spoken words are fruitless in one who does not put them into practice.*
>
> *Like a beautiful flower that is both colorful and fragrant, well-spoken words are fruitful in one who puts them into practice.* (4.51–52 C m)

The text praises these flowers for their beauty and color, but gives a higher value to the flower with a fragrant scent.

To all appearances, the metaphor takes over, and is curiously at odds with the teachings. The fragrant flower has an extra dimension of sensual appeal and strictly speaking, should be of lesser value—since it stands in greater opposition, and is more of a danger—to Buddhist practice. It appeals not only to sight but to another cord of sensual pleasure, to "*odours . . . that are desirable, agreeable, likeable, connected with sensual desire*" (SN 23.7). We thus find the *Dhammapada* to be teaching and valuing, despite itself, the exact opposite of well-known Buddhist doctrine. Instead of being wary of sensual entanglement, its metaphors give priority to the flowers and sensual pleasures that stimulate our senses and are most likely to strike our perceptions, disturb mindfulness, and produce attachments.

To some extent, this tendency is pulled back by earlier imagery linking flower-picking with death, but that imagery itself seemed hyperbolic—in other words, it put a huge threat and weight on the mere act of flower-picking. A risk is thus taken, and like the Buddha in his discussion with Dhanañjāni's husband, the text will attempt to metaphorize, or moralize, the image in question:

> *The scent of flowers does not go against the wind; not sandalwood, not aloes wood, not jasmine.*

> *But the scent of the virtuous does go against the wind; the fragrance of righteousness perfumes all directions.* (4.54 C)

The poem uses tempting metaphors, yet it achieves distance by replacing and reworking them. This particular scent, unlike flowery scents, "*goes against the wind*," just as the Buddha's teachings "go against the stream" of ordinary life. The text thus corrects its possible misreadings, its lures and traps, by pointing attentive readers in another direction.

Such readers, however, are relatively few. The text shows the uniqueness of certain followers even as it ends with an image, now revised in value, of flowering:

> *Just as a sweetly fragrant lotus, thrown away on a roadside, may bloom in a heap of rubbish, so also in the midst of ordinary folk, who are blind and like rubbish, a disciple of the Awakened One shines with wisdom.* (4.58–59)

Most blinded ordinary folks will not learn, and will not be able to rise above their samsāric situations. The next chapter, appropriately, describes the fool (*bāla*).

We Fools

There is already some indication, at this point, of who counts as a fool (or childish one). The term could name most people, most of the time. Fools provide a negative counterexample to the Buddha, yet they include most of us.

> *"I have sons, I have wealth"—the fool suffers thinking thus. Even one's self is not one's own; how then sons, how then wealth?* (5.62 C)

One is struck by the term "*suffers*" (*vihaññati*: troubled, vexed, grieved). The phrase performs a turn, or trope, upon the usual feelings of joyful pride that accompany such boasting. It telescopes, in a version of metonymy, the effect (suffering) with the cause (sons, wealth, changing circumstances), concisely merging the three marks of existence (selflessness, impermanence, suffering). It questions conventional ideas about the good fortune of being a proud parent or a property owner. The very phrasing, contesting these ideas, indicates how worry is entangled with pride. One needs to protect what "I have" (or in more accurate trope, what "is not one's own") and pride, like its objects, cannot last.

Most readers are involved in some aspect of having or caring for children, and in some aspect of wealth, whether earning, possessing, losing, needing, or simply worrying. Are we readers or listeners, then, being called fools? Does the name *fool* apply to us? One is reminded of potential quarrels brewing in *Romeo and Juliet*: "*Do you bite your thumb at us, sir?*" someone asks, almost offended. His query prompts the ambiguous response, "*I do bite my thumb, sir*" and, with the question urgently repeated, is told, "*I do not bite my thumb at you, sir, but I bite my thumb, sir.*"[6] Can a gesture possibly be unlinked to either party, and be directed at no one in particular? Similarly, does the *Dhammapada* bite its thumb at us? Can the name *fool* possibly apply to us? If so, we might savor a moment of insult or self-disdain. The usual tactic, especially in reading literature, is to postulate an "other," that is, to imagine that the reference is not to oneself, or only indirectly. The lines may refer, then, to more boastful persons, or persons wealthier than oneself, or persons who favor sons.

The next phrase, a rhetorical question about ownership ("how then sons, how then wealth?"), may both clarify and complicate the situation. We'd be more willing, perhaps, to assent to an abstract doctrine (we don't own ourselves) than to think that our possessions might be threatened. Distancing is possible, and useful, from those who say, "I have sons, I have wealth." We understand full well, for example, though with some amusement, how Shylock, when his daughter elopes and takes his money, can shout out incessantly, "*O my ducats! O my daughter! / . . . Justice! the law! my ducats, and my daughter!*"[7] The "ducats" and "daughter," with their alliteration, are almost equalized—or perhaps the ducats come first, with the eloped daughter also a loss, though of less certain value. A fool, Shylock is tormented and vexed by what he thought he had. He invokes the names "justice" and "law," as if that would somehow rectify matters, allowing him once again, he hopes, to name properly (as property) his possessions. From a perspective of Buddhist right speech, however, such naming would still be neither proper nor skillful.

Wise Ways

One of the defining characteristics of a "fool" is that this person's scope is limited. He or she has frequent regrets for evil deeds, but then later suffers their karmic consequences (5.69). Even in the frequent company of a wise person, the fool still does not learn, "*just as a spoon does not know the taste of soup*" (5.64 N). There is some slender hope that whoever "*realizes his folly, on that account becomes wise*" (5.63). But this does not happen quickly or easily. The next two chapters offer, as against the fool's ways, counterexamples of two beneficial role models: the wise man (*pandita*) and the enlightened person, or arhat. The first is valuable for his teaching and counsel: he admonishes, restrains (6.76–78), and shows the ways in which wisdom is a life's calling, a vocation, a skill:

> *Irrigators channel the water, fletchers straighten their arrows*
> *Carpenters bend wood, the wise tame themselves.* (6.80)

With the arhats who, just so, have tamed themselves, a new metaphor is sounded, which will now become increasingly prominent:

The mindful exert themselves. They do not delight in a house.
Like swans leaving a pond, they abandon their various homes. (7.91 N m)

The swans are not attached, and the house, as noted, is an image of self and comfort. Every aspiring Buddhist contemplative follows the model of Gautama, leaving home, cutting off attachments, and eventually gaining liberation. Flying birds will become admired:

Those no longer dependent, whose realm is empty and signless, their tracks are hard to trace, like that of birds in the sky. (7.93)

The enlightened ones are said to be serenely unhindered and trackless. That image is worth keeping in mind, even if it be unattainable.

Negative images (evil, violence, old age) occur contrapuntally, defining names and reinforcing the oppositions. Similarly, personal models and warnings are counterbalanced with general laws or rules. Chapter 8 states general themes in hyperbolic formulations:

Better than thousands of meaningless sayings is one saying that, when heard, brings peace. (8.100)

The possible exaggeration stretches the mind, and yet draws it back to the assurance of a near redundancy, of certainty, of right naming, of a sense that the "sayings" might be something like these sayings themselves. And so on, for a hundred years as against one moment or one day (8.107–115).

Little Time Remaining

It is natural enough, after such generalities and those in the next two chapters, to relish the more personal imagery of chapter 11 ("*Old Age*"), where most translations employ direct address:

Oh, what laughter and why joy, when constantly burning?
Enveloped in darkness, you do not look for a lamp? (11.146)

An allusion to the Buddha's Fire Sermon is combined with his dying advice to the monks. The questions, not merely rhetorical questions, are possible prods: the situation is urgent, one grows old, time is short, something must be done. The mood is somber, invoking phrases, with variations, from the first Noble Truth:

This body is worn out, a nest of diseases and very frail. This heap of corruption will break to pieces, for life has death as its end.

> *What delight is there seeing these white bones, which are scattered like gourds in autumn?* (11.148–49 N)

The elderly narrator is aware of his condition, and may be practicing mindfulness of death upon "these white bones," scattered as his own soon will be. From the practice, a vision expands very akin to the Buddha's:

> *I have run through the journeyings-on [samsāra] of many births, searching for, but not finding, the housebuilder.*
> *Again and again, birth is painful [dukkha].* (11.153 N m)

The first-person pronoun appears suddenly in the text, and is touchingly appropriate, since conditioned pain is complicitous with the "I" and what it worries about. We don't know, also appropriately, who the "I" is, and to ask would be "not fitting." The "I," a misnomer, is illusory, anonymous, and could be any one of us. Or the "I," as used in moments of triumph, could be the Buddha, more well-spoken than others about the pain running through multiple lives.

Having been associated with pain, the house-as-self imagery reaches a culmination, in words sometimes attributed to the Buddha upon his attainment of enlightenment:

> *Housebuilder, you have been seen. You will not rebuild the house again. All your rafters are broken, your roofbeam destroyed. The mind, set on the destruction of attachments, has attained an end to craving.* (11.154)

The maker of the house is identified, in a synecdoche or personification, with the house. As the Buddha defeats Māra by seeing, naming, and addressing him, here the same acts are enough to destroy. The figure of broken roofbeam and rafters, if violent, is a valedictory to any further violence, to any more mimetic entanglements with life.

The chapter ends with a return to the third person, and a depiction of those who have not followed the Buddha's way and cannot fly:

> *They waste away like old herons in a lake with no fish.* (11.155).

By ending with this depressing image of herons, so opposed to the birds who left their lake (7.91), the chapter shows another side to the situation and, while cautioning readers, realistically admits it as a possibility. The motif will be taken up again, more urgently and yet more promisingly: "*make an island for yourself, strive quickly*" (18.238 N). We are warned, and offered a choice.

Acts of Renaming

The *Dhammapada*, we have been observing, "corrects" common misconceptions or misnamings, figuratively renaming them in a wiser, more realistic light. As earlier noticed, each chapter is named with a one-word title to specify the contents for that chapter. Do the titles name the contents, especially if they do so in surprising ways? In offering instruction, these chapters invite us to discard and then rename or reconstruct our previous conceptions. Even if the names remain, our evaluation of them may, in the process of reading, start to change.

Take for example, chapters 13 to 16, entitled respectively, "*The World*," "*The Awakened One*," "*Happiness*," and "*The Pleasant*" (*Loka; Buddha; Sukha; Piya*). Each topic (as well as those before and after them) works upon the others, and the juxtaposition may have a mutually redefining effect.

The "*World*" chapter urges us to practice diligently, reiterating the motif of the world as "*a bubble*," "*a painted chariot*," "*a mirage*" (13.170–71). This being so—that is, the "*world*" being correctly so named—the wise abandon the world and, in a now familiar image, they fly, as geese do, "*on the path of the sun*" (13.175 N). The "*Awakened One*," in the next chapter, is given his title on account of his huge distance from the earth, and of his affinity with the sun. Possibly in anticipation of what comes next, the Awakened One is described in two ways: first, he or she has rejected sensual pleasures, which provide "*no satisfaction*" and "*are of little taste and painful*," even when they are "*the sensual pleasures of the gods*"; second, since cravings are destroyed, he or she is joyful (14.186–87, 194 N).

The next chapter, on "*happiness*," thus defines the term comparatively, but now with the Awakened One as an implicit measure. "*We live happily [susukham], without hate, amidst the hateful . . . , happily without disease, amidst the diseased*" (15.197–98). Living with the noble ones, and not fools, we have the right model to follow (15.206–208), and happiness can be rightly named. The succeeding chapter, on "*pleasure*," will be affected by these reflections.

"*The pleasant*," as understood by most ordinary folk, is associated, even identified, with happiness. But such a view is quite mistaken. The pleasant, or the dear (16.210 CP), on the contrary, is the condition for misery (*dukkha*), and is not to be encouraged.

> *From affection arises grief. From affection arises fear. . . .*
> *From delight arises grief. From delight arises fear. . . .*
> *From desire arises grief. From desire arises fear. . . .* (16.213–15 CP m)

The pleasant in its myriad forms, then, is connected with grief and fear, and should be renamed or revalued accordingly. Ignorance is sometimes defined, in Buddhist texts, as the topsy-turvy or reversed evaluation of beauty, pleasure, permanence, or stability (we call beautiful what is not beautiful, pleasure what is painful, permanent what is impermanent, stable what is unstable; SN 1.6.4). The ordinary world, seen thus in a reversal of ordinary perceptions, will need to be named differently.

As the process of renaming continues, the text accumulates a store of metaphors to be redeployed in new contexts. The "*fool*," for example, reappears as anyone who choses a dwelling place merely according to the seasons, and like persons engrossed in picking flowers in 4.47, one "*whose mind is obsessed with children and chattels is carried away by death, like a sleeping village by a flood*" (20.286–87 C). The motifs are musically restated and reinvigorated as the piece draws to a close, culminating in the last three chapters, "*Craving*," "*The Bhikkhu*," and "*the Brahmin*." Taken together, these chapters delineate the ideal of renunciation, reiterate the monk's virtues, and redefine the brahmin.

Craving (*tanhā*) is portrayed in the lush imagery of river vegetation and jungle underbrush, with weeds and creepers growing quickly and abundantly. In order that the growth be stopped, we need to dig up and discard all the roots:

> *A tree, though cut down, grows again, if the root is strong and undamaged. Likewise, suffering returns again and again, if latent tendencies to craving are not removed.* (24.338 N m)

The notable phrase is "again and again": *dukkha* regrows from life to life, repeatedly. Samsāric life is depicted as proliferating botanic growth. It also is depicted as agriculture, which requires seasonal and continuously repeated labors of planting, cultivating, and harvesting. Seeds and fields are vast and plentiful, and the growing of good and bad seeds seems unending. Nirvana, by contrast, is entirely apart from karmically vegetal and agricultural scenes.[8]

Figuring the Best

Once having noted the basic scheme, however, we need to be skillful in our figurational reading. For example, whoever lives unskillfully "*digs up his own root*" (18.247). This kind of person is to be separated from the monk who, a few verses later, "*destroys the roots*" of craving (18.250). The image of destroying roots (*mūla*) is used with entirely different valuations. Similarly, though household life is generally dusty and is abandoned by the aspiring monk, we also encounter the monk who "*has gone into an empty house . . . with a tranquil heart*" (25.373 N). The house image, usually reserved for self, now refers to the monk's destination (the house is "empty"). A mindful reader thus will need to rename the figurative name. Such renaming itself may be an act of "right speech," and is akin to what happens in the final chapter.

That chapter, entitled "*The Brahmin*," refers to a figure appearing frequently to question the Buddha's status and teachings, then to be questioned in turn. Here the Buddha is willing to allow brahmins their title. But he purifies the definition (again, as in his dialogue with Dhanañjānī's husband) by relating it to morality and inner development, rather than to traditional rituals or social status. "*He who is free from evil in body, mind and voice, . . . I call a brahmin*" (26.391). Taking on a conventional ascetic appearance is valueless:

> *What is the use to you, o fool, of matted locks, . . . of a garment of goat skins?* (26.394 N).

And after the negatives, a positive naming:

> *Whoever indeed, having cut off every fetter does not tremble, him, gone beyond attachment, . . . I call a brahmin. . . .*
>
> *Whoever is not hostile among the hostile, at rest among those who are violent, not clinging among those who cling, him I call a brahmin. . . .*
>
> *Whoever would utter speech . . . not harsh, [but] informative, pleasant, inoffensive, him I call a brahmin.* (26.397, 406, 408 N m)

Some version of the phrase, "*him I call a brahmin*" is repeated in all concluding twenty-eight verses. It delineates a distinguished way of life, and foregrounds the Buddha's acts of praising and renaming.

The Achievement

The *Dhammapada* thus performs repeated renamings, and its tropings are shown to be "right speech." But what makes right right? To some readers, the proverbs and the concluding repetitions, figuring forth a new ideology of the brahmin, may seem rather too insistent. Is there only one set of boundaries for *sama*—that is, of what is "correct" or "perfect" or "right"? In proposing to deal with perfection, many Mahāyāna texts, like those to be considered next, transgress and efface boundaries. Or should we say, as their advocates claim, that they discover new territories and find new boundaries—ones that are also right and perfect, if not more so?

7

Joyous Negations

The Heart Sutra

Desiring-machines make us an organism; but at the very heart of this production, the body suffers from not having some other sort of organization, or no organization at all: . . . "No mouth. No tongue. No teeth. No larynx. No esophagus. No belly. No anus."

—Gilles Deleuze and Felix Guattari,
Anti-Oedipus: Capitalism and Schizophrenia

The Perfection of Wisdom (*Prajñāpāramitā*) texts, of which the *Hridaya* or *Heart Sutra* is a heartfelt condensation, articulated a number of shifts in Buddhist thinking, taking place around 100 BC to 100 AD. Written, rather than orally transmitted, these texts are vast in length, and make grandiose proclamations. They represent a hyperbolizing of the earlier teachings, which were expanded, taken to their limits, embellished, and sometimes questioned.[1] They offered themselves as new objects of reverence, pleading, as the *Lotus Sutra* does, that they themselves be worshipped. They presented themselves as "the word of the Buddha," who was said never to have died, or to have delayed or hidden his teachings for later turnings of the wheel, and for a more sophisticated audience—namely, these transmitters and worshippers themselves.

Legitimizing Emptiness

One problem, among others, was to allege both that the Mahāyāna teachings were beyond the comprehension of early Buddhists of the so-called lesser vehicle, and that the earlier teachings were nonetheless to be given due credit. The problem would not go away. As Donald Lopez observes, "the issue of the legitimacy of the Mahayana sutras . . . remained a contested one, even a millennium after the rise of the Mahayana." These sutras incorporate earlier figures such as Śāriputra, the Buddha's distinguished disciple, who is given a learner's role, or figures who convert to the later teachings. With such tactics, "revisionist myth is presented as revisionist history."[2]

A kind of revisionism, too, is clear in the *Heart Sutra*. In contrast with the *Dhammapada*, which accidentally hit upon points where the teachings seem contradicted, the *Heart Sutra* is openly subversive, mentioning the major teachings, so as boldly to negate them. As a ritual, it could be a performance of the ending of the raft parable, a discarding of all we cherish—including, especially, Buddhist doctrine itself. The new teachings needed to perform a difficult balancing act, ostensibly both accepting and denying the earlier teachings. That balancing act is part of what makes the *Heart Sutra* so appealing and so powerful an instance of literature as "making strange."

The Sutra has always been popular, and is among the best known of Buddhist scriptures. It is chanted daily throughout East Asia and Tibet, and Westerners with an inclination to practice are likely to have heard or chanted it, possibly in a translation, in temples or retreat centers. It can be cited here, virtually in its entirety.

> *1) Homage to the Perfection of Wisdom, the Lovely, the Holy! Avalokita, the Holy Lord and Bodhisattva, was meditating in the deep course of prajñāpāramitā [the Wisdom which has gone beyond]. As he looked down from on high, he saw that all five aggregates were empty of own-being.*
>
> *2) Here, Śāriputra, emptiness does not differ from form, and form does not differ from emptiness; whatever is form, that is emptiness, whatever is emptiness, that is form. The same is true of feelings, perceptions, impulses, and consciousness. Here, Śāriputra, all dharmas are marked with emptiness; they are neither produced or stopped, nor defiled or immaculate, nor deficient or complete.*
>
> *3) Therefore [tasmac], Śāriputra, in emptiness there is no form, no feeling, no perception, no impulse, no consciousness; no eyes, no ears, no nose, no tongue, no body, no mind; no sight, no sound, no smell, no taste, no touch, no object of mind, no realm of sight, . . . no mind consciousness. There is no ignorance, no extinction of ignorance, . . . no decay and death, no extinction of*

decay and death. There is no suffering, no cause, no cessation, no path, . . . no cognition, no attainment and no non-attainment.

4) Therefore, with nothing to attain, a bodhisattva relies on the perfection of wisdom, and the mind is without hindrance. Without hindrance, there is no fear; he has overcome what can upset, and in the end he attains to nirvana. All buddhas of past, present, and future rely on prajñāpāramitā, and thereby attain unsurpassed and perfect enlightenment.

5) Therefore know the prajñāpāramitā as the great miraculous mantra, the great bright mantra, the supreme mantra, the incomparable mantra, which removes all suffering and is true, not false. And it says, Gate, gate, paragate, parasamgate, bodhi svāhā.[3]

In some English versions (here, in section 3), the negations of the aggregates is followed by hard-stressed, single-syllable rhythm with a battering effect upon the "self," divided as it is doctrinally, into components. The relentless sequence beginning with "no eyes, no ears, no nose, no tongue, no body . . ." annuls for a while—and for as yet unclear transcendental purposes—the dear, familiar world so close to us all. As invocation, the poetry casts a spell in section 5 with the equivalent of a mantra.

Negating the Teachings

The *Heart Sutra* thus pointedly defamiliarizes the everyday world we take for granted, and which we rely upon: our bodies and what they convey. Startlingly, too, it challenges not only the everyday world but, more specifically, the world assumed and set out in basic Buddhist teachings. Anyone with even an inkling of those teachings may be surprised to observe that they are flatly denied and apparently dismissed. The four Noble Truths are negated ("no suffering, no cause, no cessation, no path"), along with the usual purpose and goal in following the path ("no attainment").

The negations are indeed hyperbolic, and we can readily appreciate a recent historian's remark about "how extraordinary these teachings are as religious teachings, and how disturbing they must have seemed to anyone who took them seriously at the time."[4] They are tantamount to killing the Buddha. Even today, these teachings are difficult to grasp—indeed, they oppose all grasping—and difficult to put into practice, since they apparently provide little to do. The items being denied in the *Heart Sutra* are still understood, even while being negated. They are empty not of existence but of inherent self-existence or "*own-being*" (*svabhāva*). Those items are placed at a distance, put under erasure, and thus may seem not so real as something else—which, however, we may somehow have not (yet) fully encountered.

Negations need not, and should not, be a way of escaping into fantasy. Here again we defer to the authority of Lewis Carroll, or his Mouse, when Alice is asked to be properly mindful of the tale (tail) unfolding.

> *"You are not attending!" said the Mouse to Alice, severely. "What are you thinking of?"*
>
> *"I beg your pardon," said Alice very humbly: "you had got to the fifth bend, I think?"*
>
> *"I had* **not!**" *cried the Mouse, sharply and very angrily.*
>
> *"A knot!" said Alice, always ready to make herself useful, and looking anxiously about her. "Oh, do let me help to undo it!"*
>
> *"I shall do nothing of the sort," said the mouse, getting up and walking away.*[5]

Alice asks respectfully about the bends she counts (like dharmas counted in Buddhist abhidhamma lists), but her question is met with a firm "not." Nor is there any need to turn the "not" into a knot, or to try undo it, since that only further enrages the finicky Mouse, who simply departs. The Mouse may fear some damage may befall his tail, and the *Heart Sutra*, similarly, seems fearfully to dispose of bodily parts. But nots have a tale to tell, and negations, as Indian philosophers recognized, are truer than positives. Two cows, according to Dharmakirti, do not truly share any positive thing, but they do share not non-cowness.[6] The *prajñāpāramitā* emptiness teachings, in their lacks or negations, may thus be "truer" than mere assertions.

Those teachings make strange, as literary texts do, what always had been taken for granted. They deploy negations, which earlier were to be found in descriptions of nirvana in the *Udāna*, and extend their applicability. They rework the early metaphor of homelessness and apply it to Buddhist doctrine itself, all the while supposing that such doctrine states, allows, and even extols such an undertaking. The raft in the earlier parable is to be discarded when we reach the farther shore (enlightenment). Yet here we are asked to discard the raft, it seems, before even crossing the stream! We are asked, in something like a leap of faith, simply to dive into the stream—though the stream is no stream, and the faith, no faith.

Desiring Machines

Why so many negations? When Gilles Deleuze and Felix Guattari (in this chapter's epigraph) describe humans as "desiring machines," they use a citation from Samuel Beckett in which one organ after another is gone missing, much as in the *Heart Sutra*'s sequence of negations. They suggest that libinal forces motivate organ negations—in an erotic expansion, liberation, and elation.

Would a body without organs, though, function perfectly—or not at all? Perhaps the process of deleting organs is to be cherished as much as any imagined result: "desiring-machines work only when they break down, and by continually breaking down."[7] Like a worn-out car, the older ideology, encapsulated in standard Buddhist teachings, was sorely in need of lubrication and a tune-up.

Note how this is done. The abidhamma analyses purported to "get behind" everyday appearances to describe the only real things that are: the dharmas making up our world. Abhidhamma scholars had argued, on the basis of early sutras, that reality could be pared down to certain irreducible givens—*dharmas*—which they extensively listed and classified. By contrast, the teachings of emptiness, crucial to the *prajñāpāramitā*, are that so-called *dharmas* are empty of abiding essences, but arise borderlessly from all other factors, in accord with the laws of dependent origination.

In practical abhidhamma, we need to be aware, say, of the *akusala cittas* (unskillful mindstates) of *lobha* (greed), *moha* (ignorance), and *dosa* (aversion), of their respective roots, and of what occasions their arising; such analyses may be taken as the basis for a rigorous practice of mindfulness.[8] If the abidhamma thus makes everyday reality seem strange or guarded—its technical terms are little stepping-stones or resting points in the samsāric stream—then the *prajñāpāramitā* texts perform a further reduction and defamiliarization. The stepping-stones are now gone, and bodies (or rather, no bodies) without organs are interacting energies fluxing and flowing.[9] We are asked to see the world truly, in a dissolving or fluid condition, as if pieces of ice were floating and melting in the moving samsāric stream.

If our seeing of the familiar world be thus subjected to a revision, the result is not nihilistic. In the *prajñāpāramitā* texts, negation and affirmation are often paired: "*Seeing you, one is freed from suffering, / not seeing you, one is also freed.*"[10] Although readers in this genre may come to expect a negation to be coupled with an affirmation, the result is not always reassuring: the tools of thought, as Edward Conze remarks, "take on a radically new character when affirmation and negation are treated as non-different."[11] Even assuming the theory of two truths (of which more will be said), the sheerly negative sequences in the *Heart Sutra* are just as puzzling as the paradox in the passage cited. What lesson is being taught, or what medicine is being given?

A string of denials may go some way toward shocking us, thereby loosening attachments to adhidhammic items, or to any items. Emptiness (*śūnyatā*) functions much as does Derrida's *différance*, in dismantling presumptions about independent or self-present entities.[12] Emptiness (or conditioned interdependence) "is" everywhere, and so nowhere in particular, or nowhere as much as anywhere. Negative language is appropriate and useful, not only for our condition but for a way of bettering that condition. The *prajñāpāramitā*, which hollows out the world, disallowing substantiality, might seem to hollow out, or dismiss, ideology as well. Yet such is not the case; it has an agenda, and indeed has been called a "soteriological philosophy," or "philosophical propaganda."[13]

If a new piece of propaganda, the *Heart Sutra* does not trumpet its radicality; it states, on the contrary, that "all buddhas of past, present and future" have relied on *prajñāpāramitā*. It substitutes, however, for the more familiar articulations of Buddhist teachings, a self-commending magical mantra that concludes the text, and which "removes all suffering." There can be no doubt that this text is an ideological rethinking and revision, both in its denials and substitutions, of earlier Buddhist ideas.

Rivalry as Strong Misreading

A vexed relation between later and earlier texts is well known in literary studies. Harold Bloom has propounded a theory, in *The Anxiety of Influence*, that all great modern poets have needed to struggle with precursor poets (Wordsworth with Milton, Keats with Spenser, Tennyson with Keats) in order to clear imaginative space for themselves. Poets were by vocation diviners and prophets, and they wanted to claim primacy over whomever may have influenced them.

This need for primacy could, and often did, become a mimetic rivalry leading to creativity: "priority in divination is crucial for every poet, lest he dwindle merely into a latecomer."[14] The struggle means that the latecomers (in our instance, the poets of the *prajñāpāramitā*) give, according to Bloom, a "misprision," that is, a misreading or revision of their precursors. The rivalry thus becomes far more than merely mimetic or imitative. A mediocre late poet simply mimes or copies (in a "weak misprision") the precursor, while a great poet (in a "strong misprision") revises radically, and creatively transforms. It is possible but unlikely that some strong "earliest" poet was uninfluenced by predecessors. Whether consciously or not, a certain revision or misprision—which may be called a troping—almost always takes place, and can be mapped out.

Figures of speech, or tropes, are "turnings," substitutions, or twistings from a common or literal meaning, in the interest of vivification or persuasion. Thus, instead of saying, "My mate is attractive," one makes a metaphor and says, more vividly, "My love is a rose." The intensifying trope may seem to elevate or to lower: we can say that a person who begs "prays," or that a person praying "begs."[15] According to Bloom's theory, the later poet takes some part of the earlier poet's text as the common or literal meaning, which is then troped or twisted, in higher or lower ways, into a patently more creative, vivid, and "original" poem.

Troping the Precursors

Similarly, we may view the *Heart Sutra* as a reworking of precursor texts. Poetic texts construct "*revisionary ratios*," or rhetorical re-tropings, which Bloom lists as follows. *Clinamen*, or swerving, is taken from Lucretius to designate how the later poet "swerves away from his precursor, by so reading his precursor's poem so as to execute a *clinamen* in relation to it. This appears as a corrective movement." Another term, *tessera*, meaning a fragment from a larger vessel, is how the poet "antithetically 'completes' his precursor by so reading the parent-poem so as to retain its terms but to mean them in another sense." *Kenosis* is an "emptying out" in a movement of discontinuity with a predecessor; the self is emptied out, but "the precursor is emptied out also." *Demonization* is a "Counter-Sublime in reaction to the precursor's Sublime .... The later poet opens himself to what he believes to be a power in the parent poem that does not belong to the parent proper, but to a range of being just beyond that precursor." Finally, *apophrades* is "a return of the dead," formulated with an uncanny effect, "as though the later poet had written the precursor's characteristic work."[16]

The struggle for textual authority, though differing in ideology from Western struggles of artistic genius, is clearly visible in Mahāyāna texts.[17] The texts, often claiming to be the Buddha's hitherto unrevealed word, praise and accredit themselves. They reformulate or deny all major assertions and ideals, including those regarding the path and goal. They claim all the while to be true—indeed, truer than ever—to the teachings.

There are many ways, more concretely, in which the *Heart Sutra* puts aside the standard terms and scenes of Buddhist discourse. Although the Tibetan translation gives a witnessing role to the Lord Buddha at Vulture Peak, the Sanskrit edition omits these details and starts with the bodhisattva Avalokita who, in a familiar heroic image, "looked down from on high [upon the world]."[18] Avalokita, not the Buddha, is in meditation, which is described, not as one of the jhānic states but as *prajñāpāramitā*, or the Wisdom "gone beyond." He sees not beings but "the five aggregates . . . empty of own-being."

Revisionism in Action

Observe how the text is performing revisionary ratios. Avalokita replaces (swerves from) the Lord, and his meditation is a "Counter-Sublime" (or demonization) in contrast with the earlier Buddha's. The scene is a strong revision of the setting, characters, and content of Gautama's night of enlightenment. In the second watch of the night, we are told in the precursor text, "*I directed [my concentrated mind] to the knowledge of the passing away and reappearance of beings. With the divine eye . . . I saw beings passing away and reappearing*" (MN 4.29). In the light of *śūnyatā*, and according to the *Heart Sutra*, this might not be strictly correct: there are no "beings" to see even, or especially, with a divine eye, and no passing away or reappearing. Such is the beginning of what Avalokita will teach to the Buddha's now less-than-perfect disciple, Śāriputra. The text thereby makes a "completion" and, to some extent, an "antithesis" to the Buddha's vision, which it "empties out" with emptiness itself.

The emptying out, in a succession of negations, has a peculiar, even uncanny, effect in the famous chiasmus, "*Form is emptiness, emptiness is form.*" Form may be interpreted as the interdependent configuration of a named "thing" or "person," but constant dust-to-dust transformation makes form fleeting and insubstantial. On an imaginative level, the two terms are brought together in a certain ghostliness. Forms are hollow, hazy, mirage-like, illusory, and the *Diamond Sutra*, re-troping Pāli texts (for example SN 22.95 or *Dhammapada* 13.170), speaks of "*a bubble. . . , a flash of lightning . . . , a flickering lamp, a phantom.*"[19] We live in a world of specters, then, and are ourselves only spectral—such stuff as dreams are made on.

Form Is Emptiness

One of the burdens of the *Heart Sutra* is to keep us in emptiness, by repeating and extending it. Thus, the first four stanzas—most of the Sutra—provide no shelter. Avalokita's special vision is like an X-ray beam, scanning skeleton bones: the five skandhas in their emptiness of own-being. And the formula about emptiness, seemingly so abstruse, may be usefully instructive. Our fond tendency is to separate form from emptiness, to assume that forms are more or less solid or steady, and thus to give them our allegiance, attachment, and affection. The result, since they are insubstantial and do not stay, is disheartening. In a fondly human way, again, we are tempted to delimit the case, to interpret the curious "here" (*iha*) of section 2 as referring to the world of this text or its ideas, to ordinary life, and, only reluctantly, though the Sutra suggests otherwise, to transcendence. Is there, we might wonder anxiously, some *other* "here"—or "there"?

The Sutra marches steadily and relentlessly in the direction of a negative answer to any such question, reasserting only the emptiness-form chiasmus. "Reality" thus comes to have a chameleon-like elusiveness, like an actor playing multiple roles, appearing as emptiness one moment, form the next, until roles are no longer distinct, or even roles at all. The emptiness-as-form formula in section 2 is not, however, merely about appearances. Form (*rūpa*) is one of the five skandhas making up a person, and the other four are listed as equally empty, followed by a statement that the mark of emptiness (*śūnyatā lākṣana*) justifies the negation not only of all dharmas but of their activities as well. Our familiar world is thus made into a vampire's victim, with all characteristics—our usual life's blood—sucked out ("not produced or stopped"). Nothing can be said about such a world—and the abhidhammists, with their meticulous catalogues of irreducible items, are in effect informed that their life's work has been in vain, and they'd best keep quiet, or find a new line of work.

After having supposedly hollowed out the dharmas, section 3 begins with a strangely arbitrary "*therefore*" to precede a long, impressive list of negations, including the translation's hypnotic, hammer-like stresses in "no eyes, no ears, no nose, no tongue, no body, no mind, no sight, no sound, no smell, no taste. . . ". The nouns here are meant, quite properly, to describe processes, and not entities. They are a recitation of the sense bases, or *āyatana*—eye, ear, nose, tongue, body, mind, each of which arises and passes away (MN 49.50). For each sense base, the Buddha had recommended relinquishment: "*the eye [etc.] is not yours: abandon it*"; it is "*impermanent, . . . suffering, . . . non-self*" (SN 35.138, 140–42). When the path of cessation is cultivated, each of these bases will "*cease completely and without remainder, . . . [and cannot] be discerned*" (SN 35.234).

In processes of cessation, then, the bases may be described negatively, and the pointedly hyperbolic negations of the *Heart Sutra,* figures of emptying, predict and perform an abandoning. The "no" side of these important items imply an ability to let go of them—that is, to inspire and practice, in verbal form, an ongoing cessation. Cessation is not an extinction of the meditator, however, and the *Heart Sutra* poetically enacts the difficult paradoxes of higher jhānic states where, despite the cancellation of our usual waking experience, we are still said to be fully aware.[20] In such a state, "*the monk, paying no attention to any distinguishing signs, enters into and dwells in that concentration of the heart which is without signs*" (SN 40.9).[21]

And so the meditator achieves a "concentration of the heart." Although few practitioners would claim to cognize this signless state, they may have had hints and aspirations. In addition, there may be a huge satisfaction in chanting the list of negations as part of a daily service. We are leaving the intimately familiar world behind, cancelling it out aggressively, though not entirely, since the "*no*"s are placed before a series of familiar items that, in a way, counterbalance them. "No eyes," for example, may mean that none are needed, or that better vision is possible, or more flatly, that "the words do not mean what they say."[22] The Sutra is ironic, or else rather it is giving a brief for the empty side of the picture. The listed items have no "solid" existence, which is not to say none at all.

The negations are joyously appealing for other reasons as well. The word "no" can be used for making prohibitions ("no trespassing," "no smoking," "no parking," etc.) as well as for denials of transgression ("no trespassing took place," etc.). In Freud, denials are admissions or affirmations, and the Sutra's libidinal undercurrent may be a fantasy of power asserted, transgressions indulged, and innocence vindicated. A Tibetan version of the *Heart Sutra* can be staged as a tantric sadhana, that is, as a performance in which the main figures enact the text's ritual in the space of a mandala. It is possible to find, as Donald Lopez does, a scenario of Oedipal rivalry and incest: "the Buddha [given a role in the Tibetan version] unites with the mother [the goddess Prajñāpāramitā] from whom he was born." Śāriputra witnesses a primal scene of parental intercourse, and, in punishment, he is castrated, as symbolized "by . . . his shaven head."[23] Although the Sanskrit version, simpler and shorter than the Tibetan, could not support such a sadhana, it engages in a sort of transgression, already noted, of Buddhist teachings.

Indeed the genius of the *Heart Sutra* is that, even while it claims "emptiness" to be universal, it applies the term "no" to a very specific range of connected items. A pleasant irony (to recall Deleuze and Guattari) is that we are given an eerie double-sense both of moving "beyond" (the usual reading of *pāramitā*) the bodily functions, and yet not doing so, either. The obsessive, emphatic reiteration of "no"—"no eyes, no ears, no nose, no tongue, no body, no mind"—creates a high-energy area, as if someone were at a shooting booth in a county fair, knocking out some row of cardboard ducks one after the other, thereby "transcending" them, or at least gaining a power high. Comfortingly, negations are partial, emptiness is form: they'll all pop up again, so the shooting spree can be re-performed on the next ritual occasion.

Hyperbolic Relinquishments

Prajñāpāramitā texts, including the *Heart Sutra*, are sheer exhortations or incantations, without argumentative reasoning.[24] When emptiness teachings are subjected to analysis, however, certain denials are held to be damaging: Nāgārjuna attacks an opponent who unwisely denies the four Noble Truths.[25] The *Heart Sutra*, by contrast, wildly and exuberantly includes the Noble Truths among its denials. Even they can be discarded, and we ought be generous in doing so! Yet once they have been junked, which is easy enough for a virtuoso like Avalokita, what's next? Where are we now headed? Having burnt our bridges and recycled our rafts, what's the next step?

Here the ideology lends a helping hand. Once again a loosely fitting "therefore" prefaces commendations of the bodhisattva way. There is nothing substantial to grasp at, not even attainment. All that's needed is the wisdom of emptiness. Such wisdom becomes the one thing worth cherishing. The bodhisattva is steady because of having relinquished, in negations, all false comforts, hindrances, and thought constructs. He or she has "no attainments," or "nothing to attain," we are told, and perhaps for that reason "attains nirvana." The word *nirvana* may be useful, since nirvana is often described in mostly negative terms, comparable to those in the Sutra; conversely, the Sutra may have "nirvanized," in a trope of emptying its mentioned elements.

Even so, most traditional Buddhist terms are flatly denied; why not nirvana as well? In the *Ashtasāhasrikā*, another *prajñāpāramitā* text, Subhuti remarks that "*Nirvana . . . is like a magical illusion, is like a dream.*"[26] This sort of comparison, and the Sutra's phrase "nothing to attain," would suggest that nirvana, too, had been sidelined. If so, the closing mantra is puzzling, with its variations, so like nirvana, on "*gone, gone, gone.*" What is to be made of this situation?

Transformations

To claim that all buddhas have used the *prajñāpāramitā* mantra is, surely, a re-visioning in Bloom's sense: a co-opting of the buddhas (who could not, of course, be dismissed as easily as the arhats) according to a new definition of Buddhahood. The bodhisattvas are said to have been untempted by nirvana, since then they would be unable to help others. Instead they attain to "non-abiding" nirvana, an allegedly superior alternative.[27] But there is no explicit sign, in the *Heart Sutra*, of such new definitions. On the contrary, the salvific mantra, here translated, apparently performs the old-style disappearance: "*gone, gone beyond, gone completely.*" After all the talk of negation, the mantra takes action, much like Alice's Mouse, who, tired of discussion, gets up and leaves. Whether or not we know what the mantra means, it works as a magical code, making the path, if there still is one, both easy and obscure.

Commentators have tried, tellingly, to detect some sort of implicit path structure between the lines of the text (which deny a path), but the results, a weak misprision, are less than convincing.[28] Extracting the path may be part of an endeavor to domesticate the text, to stake out a claim for its orthodoxy, so that it then can be read unironically.

A stronger misprision would see the *Heart Sutra* as attempting a number of re-tropings. The long series of negations is strikingly a *kenosis*, an emptying out of the Buddhist world—and a claiming to see it rightly, since that world had always been sheerly semiotic or empty to begin with. The Sutra also performs a *demonization,* or counter-sublime, an opening up to what the parent Buddha would skillfully not admit: the emperor has no clothes. There's no raft, and it would not be needed in any case (one text hints of the parable's "hidden sense"[29]). Instead there may be a "*Fort-da*" game going on, as told by Freud about his grandson. The child plays that his mother is gone (the negations, the mantra) when he throws out a toy on a string, but then later pulls on his string, so that at his wish, the toy (mother-as-mantra) suddenly, joyfully, returns and brings back conventional truth (the ritual ending, daily life resuming).[30]

There is also perhaps an incorporation, the product of mourning (for the departed Buddha) as a version of *apophrades*, a return of the dead—or, in this case, of the Tathāgata's passing itself (*gate, gate*). The later poet, in imaginative solitude, "holds his poem so open again to the precursor's work that at first we might believe that the wheel has come full circle."[31] The "uncanny effect" of such wheel-turning is that the latecomer (here, the *Heart Sutra*) seems to have preceded—that is, to be more scrupulously right than—the predecessor!

A Magical Talisman

The Sutra's reliance on the magical mantra, a talisman, though part of the archetypal hero's equipment,[32] is hyperbolic. It is at any rate far from—and thus, all the more radical a troping of—what the precursor text portays as the Buddha's last sermon. In that text, we recall, the Buddha sets out criteria for doctrinal legimitacy, and then, dying, offers some final advice: "*Ānanda, you should live as lamps [dipa : also islands] unto yourselves, being your own refuge, with no one else as your refuge, . . . contemplating the body as body, earnestly, clearly aware, mindful . . .* "; again, "*All conditioned things are of a nature to decay. Strive on untiringly*" (DN 16.2.26; 16.6.7).

Earlier and later texts come into direct opposition here. The precursor speaks of doctrinal correctness, urging the monks to maintain diligent self-reliance, while the later text, as Edward Conze argues, negates doctrine, neatly removing any motives for striving.[33] If there is no goal to be attained, or if it can be attained magically, why bother to follow the path, especially if there is no path? Why be a solitary lamp or island, striving untiringly, if one mantra can do it all, making your problems be, as an advertisement might say, "gone, gone, gone"? The triumph of the *Heart Sutra* is to make its magical solution seem in keeping with the Buddha's teachings. With its skillful means, one size fits all. The text can be read as an easy means for inept followers, or as an occult message for initiates. Textual emptiness is risky, possibly failing for both audiences,[34] and making the *Heart Sutra* seem, at times, amorphously pleasant but uninstructive.

The trickiest trope of all can be found in a small phrase, quietly modifying the litanies of "no" and "not." The phrase is: "in emptiness" or, in another translation, "given emptiness." Everything is stated or performed under the aegis of emptiness, or on that particular side: *śūnyatā-laksanā* ("with the marks of emptiness") or *śūnyatāyam* ("in emptiness"). We read: "Here, Śāriputra, form is emptiness, and emptiness is form." "Here" (*iha*) is the high or deep level of Avalokita's vision of emptiness, though it might also be read, skeptically, as literature—that is, as the "once upon a time" of this particular scene, of this particular sutra.

Less skeptically, a reader or reciter, if quietly discontent at the many negations, can easily enough change the picture, flipping to the equation's other side: emptiness is also form. As Thich Nhat Hanh reassuringly declares, "Empty of a separate self means full of everything"; thus "form is the wave and emptiness is the water," flowing into and inter-connecting us all.[35] Finally, of course, there's always that mantra, putting a bright flag on our sailboat, the *Heart Sutra*, and sending us onward in the direction of nirvana.

What has happened, however, to the solitary effort urged on his monks by the dying Buddha? Effort may be supposed or included, but happily, as something unstated. Having sweepingly mentioned the way of all buddhas, the Sutra presumably includes all their mindful and compassionate endeavors as well. We need not grasp, then, at the concluding mantra, and "gone beyond" may take multiple forms, suggesting "gone beyond" attachments, but probably not "gone beyond" this world. Thus it would be magic, as in the third Noble Truth, jubilantly proclaiming a way out from the prison of conditioning. An expansiveness of perspective is at work, hyperbolically, in the Sutra's negative-as-positive language in a liberation from everything—indeed, every thing—that is being negated.

The Pertinence of Emptiness

It would be rash to say, as Edward Conze does, that the Perfection of Wisdom sutras "have little significance for our age."[36] On the contrary, contemporary physics and anthropology assume worldviews of interdependence and nonessentialism. Contemporary literature, too, is rife with negations comparable to those in the *Heart Sutra*. Joseph Conrad's *Heart of Darkness*, a counterpart heart work, articulates a notoriously well-known abundance of hyperbolically negative phrases: "*unspeakable rites*," "*dishonouring necessity*," "*inscrutable purpose*," "*impenetrable darkness*," "*without clamour*," "*without glory*," etc. Negations are thus deployed with variations and at greater length than the relatively simple negations of the *Heart Sutra*. And the narrator's hyperbolic negativity tells, far less promisingly than "*gate, gate*," of what will always be beyond human faculties.

The frame narrator in *Heart of Darkness* allegorizes Marlow, the storyteller, as a Buddha: "*with his legs folded before him, he had the pose of a Buddha preaching in European clothes and without a lotus flower. . .*" (9).[37] Conrad thus performs a revisionary troping on the traditional images of buddhas and bodhisattvas, and his story may be construed as a misprision of traditional sermons warning—here, to very slight avail—against the poisons of greed, hatred and delusion ("*imbecile rapacity*," and "*the devil of violence, the devil of greed, and the devil of hot desire*"; 37, 25). Like Kurtz, a nightmarish Māra-like figure whom he ambivalently detests and admires, Marlow may have a mission: "*I had got a heavenly mission*," he jokingly tells his listeners, after he returns from a journey to the East, "*to civilize you*" (10). Yet during and after his sojourn in the heart of darkness, Marlow is callous toward the horrific events in which he is implicated (13, 86, 97). Look closely, and his "*European clothes*" contribute to a sense that he merely has the "*pose*" of a Buddha; earlier, too, his arms are not raised, but "*dropped, the palms outward,* [and he] *resembled an idol*" (9, 4). What can possibly be the sermon of this unlikely Buddha figure?

In emptiness teachings, there are no solid, self-subsisting entities, and all delusions to that effect are undone by the workings of impermanence, causal conditioning, and form-as-emptiness. With its vividly grotesque atmosphere and its dismembered bodies (impaled heads), *Heart of Darkness* provides plentiful lessons in emptiness. The narration, with temporal jumps, multiple tellers, unfinished sentences, and adjectival excess, works to upset conventional ideas of truth or purpose. Crippled by preconceptions about civilized normality, Marlow is unable to absorb what is happening until much later, if ever. Not far into the story, when he learns (falsely, like much else) that he may never be able to encounter his doubtful anti-self—the idolized, madly entrepreneurial Kurtz—Marlow recounts how he was torn by "*a sense of extreme disappointment, as though I had found out I had been striving after something altogether without a substance,*" and later, Kurtz turns out to be "*hollow at the core*" (78–79, 98). Marlow is deeply bothered, then, by the insubstantiality of his nightmare experiences. For the *prajñāpāramitā* writers, by contrast, "*without a substance*" would merely be an accurate phrase for ordinary life, for the path and the goal.

At the end of *Heart of Darkness,* we are again given a Buddha image: "*Marlow ceased, indistinct and apart, in the pose of a meditating Buddha*" (131). He may have preached more than he knows, but the story of Kurtz and Marlow is a failed apocalypse, leaving behind, as we'd been forewarned, "*misty halos [and] . . . moonshine*" (7). Despite appearances, Marlow's moonshine is far from the old perfection of wisdom that is described as "*unthinkable and inconceivable, not something to be done, not something to be undone. . . . It is calmly quiet from the very beginning, because there is no escape, because there is nothing to be accomplished.*"[38]

This latter passage may remind us less of *Heart of Darkness* than of Samuel Beckett's *The Unnamable* once again, or of this staccato passage from *Worstward Ho*, a shorthand version the *prajñāpāramitā*:

> *The dim. The void. Gone too? Back too? No. Say no. Never gone. Never back. Till yes. Till say yes. Gone too.*[39]

The unbelieving speaker is willing, desperately, to say anything, on the off chance that it might have some effect. One is uncertain whether his gamble—"say yes"—could be called a gesture of faith. But Beckett's doubtful text, with its "gone too," suggests that the Sutra could just as easily—without hindrances or "thought coverings"—move in a worse or, if we make a gesture and "say yes," a better direction. The mantra, "*gone beyond*," may suggest a road for us perhaps not taken, but yes, *say yes*, still possible.

Not Relying

To rely on nothing is to achieve great stability. One no longer works from the viewpoint of the "I," with its wants, hopes, hates, fears, or illusions of control. We thus do not try to escape from mundane life, but like bodhisattvas in our own way, continue to live amidst the errors and confusions that surround us. As Zen abbot Obora reads the text,

> *Birth-and-death is Nirvana, so it is not a question of extinction of birth-and-death. . . . There is no Nirvana to be gained; . . . there is nothing to be grasped. Then what to do? For baby Bodhisattvas like us, this is a question which cannot be set aside even for a moment. There is no other way than to discover Bodhi in the passions themselves and experience Nirvana in birth-and-death.*[40]

We live in a boisterous world of birth-and-death, and with all its suffering (no suffering), there is no other world for us. Our task is to discover how emptiness in the mind matches, or becomes, emptiness everywhere.

8

Masters of Emptiness

The Gateless Barrier and Zen Folktales

The crows maintain that a single crow could destroy the heavens. Doubtless that is so, but it proves nothing against the heavens, for the heavens signify simply: the impossibility of crows.

—Franz Kafka, *Reflections on Sin, Pain, Hope and the True Way*

Under the influence of a prodigious expositor, D. T. Suzuki, and of writers such as Jack Kerouac, Gary Snyder, and Allen Ginsberg, Zen became a major cultural presence in the West. The fascination of Chan or Zen was with a certain iconoclasm, with the heightening of varied skills, from archery to motorcycle maintenance, and with Zen masters who were impressively able to conjoin Mahāyāna themes of emptiness, negation, or anticonceptualism with those of Taoism.[1] What else, though, might have made Zen so immensely popular?

Zen Ideology

The power of Zen came partly from propaganda. In a gesture of reverse Orientalism, Asian proponents of Zen took up notions of "direct experience" from such figures as Rudolf Otto or William James, using those notions to convince Westerners that Zen (and only Zen) could provide what was wanted: deep, direct, and life-changing experience, and an alternative way of life.[2] As with perceptions of Buddhist "nihilism" discussed earlier, an attentive reading of Zen texts can help dispel stereotypes or illusions, in this case about mastery, and easy or "natural" ways to gain enlightenment. The issue is complicated, since questions of ideology are prominent not only in Western transmissions and perceptions, but in Chan and Zen in their native settings—in troublesome problems of patriarchy, lineage, discipleship, and hermeneutic skills. At every turn, puzzles arise and demands are made.

In the one of the founding legends of Chan, for example, literary talent is required. In the *Platform Sutra*, the fifth patriarch needed a successor, and proposed that each of his followers compose a verse, with the best poet taking over his post. The head monk, Shen-hsiu, not wanting to disclose his identity, wrote his poem as anonymous graffiti on a corridor wall: "*The body is the Bodhi tree, / The mind is like a clear mirror / At all times we must strive to polish it, / And must not let the dust collect.*" An uneducated monk, Hui-neng, then countered with: "*Bodhi originally has no tree / The mirror also has no stand. / Buddha nature is always clean and pure; / Where is there room for dust?*"[3] These latter verses triumphed, and Hui-neng became sixth patriarch. His poem's negations of a predecessor poem, much like the negations in the *Heart Sutra*, would become a hallmark of the Chan-Zen line. Chan, the new way of Chinese meditation signalled by these verses, would be called "*no thought*" (PS 138), coupled with a rhetoric of minimal expression and extreme terseness. Such discourse was valuable less for its message than for its effects—to catalyze and transform.

Meditation koans, often consisting of dialogues between master and disciple, contain a kernel, or *hua t'ou*, which is the "critical phrase" needed, if it reaches deep enough, to prompt enlightenment. As Robert E. Buswell notes, the simplicity of this "sudden approach" was at first meant to benefit ordinary people in their daily lives; instead of lengthy monastic training over many years and lifetimes, as in Indian Buddhism, in the "sudden" method, even laypersons could be successful in reaching enlightenment.[4] Yet the key to sudden enlightenment—koan study carried into meditation, and into all aspects of daily life—was arduous, plunging disciples into a "Great Doubt" from which escape seemed nearly impossible. Those who could solve the koans, or pass through the barrier, tended to be an élite, and to become élitist. With its "independent transmission," Chan gained prestige and power, but eventually a reversal took place, and it ended up isolated from ordinary people's lives.[5]

Masters Require Reponses

Zen masters, deploying koans, present bewildering imperatives for tangible action. Like the German mystic poet Angelus Silesius (as paraphrased by Derrida), they call for us to "Go there where you cannot go, to the impossible, it is indeed the only way of going and coming."[6] And impossible koans are not just for students or monks, but for us, the audience or readers; as Katsuki Sekida remarks, "all Zen stories are about you, not other people."[7] The need for some kind of response differentiates Zen from the *Heart Sutra*, where we are told neither how to behave nor what to do. By contrast, the koan tradition in Chan or Zen, while similarly dismissive of words and respectful of the *prajñāpāramitā* teachings, is radically performative: the koans are meant to instigate action, rather than to issue statements, even negative ones.

The performative dimension includes ritual recitations of patriarchal lineage, a connection claiming to go all the way back to the Buddha. Emphasis on lineage may have acted as an ideological counterweight to Zen masters' insistence that transmission is empty or is a nontransmission.[8] Those masters sternly denounce mere imitations of Buddhist paradigms, preferring a "direct" performative transmission of the dharma to philosophical talk. The disparagement of canonical texts becomes part of a new canon, and when we move from early Buddhist texts to Zen, a new landscape emerges. Key earlier teachings about karma, samsāra, and the path are marginalized, and instead of a protracted process leading to the goal, Zen practitioners often meet with a surprising, transforming jolt.[9]

In their abrupt discovery of right words and deeds, Zen adepts show the fragility of familiar models of imitation, or mimesis. The Zen disciple cannot obediently follow—that is, "imitate"—the master. The master does not merely ask that disciples do as he does or says, since he rarely provides a clear indication of what he means; nor is following simple, since the teaching is full of traps, double binds, barriers, and impossibilities. We will be discovering new versions, then, of the mimetic violence described earlier. An archetypal pattern, however, still persists: Oedipus, to give a Western example, is the great problem-solver, not only in deciphering the Sphinx's riddle so as to succor his stricken community, but in apprehending how that riddle applies to his own horrendous flesh and blood. Likewise, Zen koans require a period of Great Doubt and the involvement of all one's bones and joints, blood and tears.

Chinese Traditions

The earlier tradition did not ask quite so much of its devotees. In Pāli scriptures, discipleship meant listening carefully, not asking "unfit" questions, and following the eightfold path. The Buddha did not challenge his students to perform double-binds, nor did he resort to a repertory of kicks, shouts, and whacks. Zen adepts, by contrast, are asked not merely to "Come and see," but to "Come and do." How did such revisionings of the Buddhist tradition come about?

In ancient Chinese culture, emphasis was on practical matters, on human interactions, on work and social mobility. Where the Indian tradition valued the solitary yogi achieving awakening, as the Buddha did, a lamp unto himself, the Chan/Zen tradition developed a genre of pithy "encounter dialogues" between masters and disciples, in which one party challenges the other, is given a reponse, and new insights arise.[10] Those dialogues paradoxically block or disrupt communication, spurring disciples to insight, action, and enlightenment.

In encounter dialogues, performative ways put traditional mimetic ideologies into question. Those ideologies had always been problematic to begin with. Mimesis produces a thing's double; if the double is exactly like the "good" model, it is also good (or neutral), and yet may have "evil" effects if we cannot tell the real thing from the copy.[11] Similarly, what if a shamanic trickster or magician (and Zen stories are full of them) does a "good imitation" of an admired model? How will such a trickster be recognized? Mirrors deceive, and the mirror, symbol of the mind's brightness—and of imitation—does not produce anything, though it reflects. Hui-neng, in the *Platform Sutra*, complicates and negates the prior poet's imagery; and although the second formulation is deemed superior, both are judged to have merit, with the verses becoming a key statement of Chan versions of the twofold truth.

Two Truths

According to the two-truths doctrine, conventional truth (used in language) and absolute truth (beyond language or conception) are complementary. The generous doubling given to truth was hermeneutically convenient, and in Chinese practice, according to Bernard Faure, the two truths tended to promote ambiguity and equivocation.[12] Mirror-like doubling is devious, as are metaphors about it. The masters are lineage-holders, yet they enter into dialogues and struggles with "irregular practitioners" who seem uncannily similar to them, or who themselves are masters.[13] Since imitation, as commonly understood, is scorned in Zen, what can be the criterion of authenticity? Can or should the masters be imitated, when their endeavor is to smash referential language, or "mere" imitation?

With mimetic representation disparaged, the koan dialogues yield an obscure conciseness:

> *A monk asked Chao-chou, "What is the meaning of Bodhidharma's coming from the West?"*
>
> *Chao-chou said, "The oak tree is in the courtyard."* (M 37)[14]

A disconnect between question and answer is part of the point, and the case is followed by Mumon's comment that you need to "*see intimately*" into the matter. "Zen deals with facts," D. T. Suzuki proclaims, "and not with their logical, verbal, prejudiced and lame representations."[15] The masters attempt to free us, as the Buddha had also attempted to do, from preconceptions we impose upon the world. How does this happen?

On the one hand, koans need to be seen in intimate ways not only by the collector or editor, but by later masters, and finally by ourselves as well. Robert Aitken and Zenkei Shibayama, in their commentaries, recount legends and private anecdotes associated with the koans. On the other hand, voicing opinions in a Zen context is risky business: personal comments on a koan, however skillful, may propagate the tired concepts that dharma gates are meant to keep out. Yet without some direct involvement with the koans, Great Doubt would not arise, and they would remain untapped and opaque. How to find the right balance?

One way, perhaps, is to juxtapose koans with one another or with other Zen literary genres. Koans may usefully be set alongside other voices or stories. The deployment of countervoices is itself a koan tactic. Koan dialogues can be enacted or answered dialogically; in fact Koans insistently demand some sort of response. And the greater the oddity and multiplicity of aptly responding voices, the more the prior dominant voice—including the patriarchical voice in sutras or koans—is confronted and engaged, developing into dharma combats.

Dharma Combat

A combat element appears prominently in the *Lin chi lu*, a collection of sayings by and about Lin-chi (d. 866), founder of the koan-wielding Linchi, or Rinzai, sect. There we find a constant outpouring of critique, as if all "extraneous" facets of Chan, including hierarchies and rituals, were to be cut away. Lin-chi uses the revisionary trope that Harold Bloom would later call *askesis*—a way of radically simplifying, and getting to the core issue. Lin-chi shows an impatience with sutra-learning that extends to the Buddha, the patriarchs, the disciples, and Chan itself. In one of his teachings, he proclaims, "*Followers of the Way, the really good friend is someone who dares to speak ill of the Buddha, speak ill of the patriarchs, pass judgment on anyone in the world, throw away the Tripitaka. . . .*"[16] The oppositional stance is a clash of heroic warriors: "*If you meet a buddha, kill the buddha. If you meet a patriarch, kill the patriarch.*" The pattern continues with attacks on followers: "*If they come with a raised hand, I hit the raised hand, if they come mouthing something, I hit them in the mouth*" (L 52).

Just as dramatically, there are moments when Lin-chi sees through the "master role" and how it operates. He tells of how Ma-yü asks the master a question: "*Of the eyes of the thousand-armed bodhisattva of compassion, which is the true eye?*" The master simply repeats the question, adding, "*Answer me! Answer me!*" At that point, Ma-yü "*dragged the Master down from the lecture seat and sat in it himself*" (L 12). Mimetic mirroring or rivalry lacks a stable point, and a miming master, it seems, might be replaced by anyone who can gain and retain the high seat. Perhaps the master here cannot perform adequately, but as elsewhere, imitation will not settle the issue. Who is to decide? Who will master the master?

Gates and Barriers

A similarly puzzling and confrontational tone is likely to have popularized the *Gateless Barrier* (Chinese: *Wumen Kuan*; Japanese: *Mumonkan*), a collection of forty-eight koans, or cases, each of them followed by a brief ironic comment and four lines of verse. The editor and commentator, the Chan master Wumen or Mumon, lived from 1183 to 1260, and the text is dated 1228. His acquired name Mumon (which will be used here), meaning of "the gate of No [*wu* or *mu*]," derives from his extensive practice on the first koan, *Mu*. The doorway is open and not open, the gate is no gate, and it is met with from the outset.

Koan practice, and its ideal fruits, have generated immense interest. The *Mumonkan*, which is often translated, can be examined as a literary artifact for its stories (taken from folklore or from monastic events), its drama (in the encounter dialogues), and its poetry (in the koans and commentarial verses). The title, referring to a gate or barrier we need to pass through, can be allied with the Buddha's archetypal journey of discovery as re-enacted in Zen. Joseph Campbell remarks that in rituals of initiation, the hero must confront threshold guardians, who keep watch over established bounds. Only by advancing beyond the liminal threshold can an individual pass into a new realm of experience. Once having done so, the landscape is of "curiously fluid, ambiguous forms," and tough obstacles must be confronted.[17]

In Chan, that landscape is eerily compelling. Gates can be found in Chinese mountain landscapes, as portrayed in scroll paintings. The mountain gate, in this setting, demarcates a liminal entry point into the sacred. As Steven Heine shows, once entered through the gate into the numinous landscape, the pilgrim or master is likely to encounter anomalous spirits, magical animals, or strange practitioners and will need to struggle against them. The Zen master defeats the local spirits—and elsewhere his disciples—by using "no-name" iconoclastic deeds that subvert local or literal icons. Thereafter, those deeds are recounted and transformed in patriarchal legends. Similar deeds are re-enacted, too, with the master's own disciples, and "there is a two-fold structure operating in Zen discourse, or a mixture of mythical and iconoclastic dimensions."[18]

Outrageous Behavior

In mixed discourse, the masters capitalize on ambiguity. Their behavior in the *The Gateless Barrier* involves killing cats, cutting off fingers, forgetting duties, talking to themselves, saying that the Buddha equals a shitstick. Such behavior, as if proving what the masters could get away with, and provoking disapproval in more conservative schools,[19] was partly meant to show the masters' special status. Recent scholars have argued that the masters' social status is more important, indeed, than any message they claim to teach. T. Griffith Foulk asserts that "the voice of awakening is a matter of positioning in a formal ritual or literary structure: whatever the voice of the 'judge' in a dialogue says . . . represents the truth, or the standpoint of awakening. . . . Whoever can work himself (by whatever means) into [that] position . . . will thereafter be judged as a worthy spokesman, regardless of what he says."[20]

This being so, awakening is largely (if not only) a matter of positional power, and whatever the master says, or whatever dialogue transpires, is to be deemed authoritative. Masters of koans display a rhetoric of embodiment: their style of speaking and behaving is supposed to indicate their level of insight. But where style is so important, pretense is always possible. No wonder, then, that Mumon is so quick to consider even the most weighty speeches or dialogues to be farces, comedies, puppet shows, or even dog meat. As he was no doubt aware, the ritualism that made Chan so powerful also detracted from its claims to be spontaneous and iconoclastic. The encounter dialogues, for example, were designed to win imperial patronage and were read out as sermons in a highly formal monastic setting.[21] Subjected to ambiguously ironic analysis, even the words of the patriarchs can be mistaken or misunderstood, and—in a version of Harold Bloom's revisionism—Mumon has an obligation to amplify or modify.

Positional Power

Mumon meets his obligation on the basis of an intimacy with the lineage, and koans gain their force by being attributed to a patriarch. For example, in case 7, an ordinary dialogue about needing to wash up after having had breakfast is to be interpreted as some kind of indirect speech about awakening, since one of the interlocutors is a patriarch.[22] The device of attributing ordinary words to a master, thereby making them less ordinary, is literary and ideological: it is akin to defamiliarization in literary texts, while the presumed "special message" is a secret comprehended only by the masters—who have a lock on power. Chan discourse is ideological in its subordination to a master signifier to which, in this case properly enough, only the masters have access.

To all others, koans are perforce obscure; they are impenetrable to the intellect, like the heavens devoid of crows in Franz Kafka's parable. Many of Kafka's stories and proverbs are Zen-like, as if a question or speculation had been rendered as a fable: (what if) an ordinary businessman wakes up one day as a large beetle, or if a doorkeeper is posted at a place where you must urgently enter, and he is there to deny entry to you?[23] A personal twist is often the clincher: this door has been closed only to *you*, or heavens mean the absence, not merely of things or of life, but of crows in particular (the name "Kafka" means "crow" in a Czech dialect). As in Zen, the struggle is personal and dreamlike; it is blocked and tormented by habitual cravings. Waiting before the door (like being blocked by a gateless barrier) becomes an occasion to strive for the right thing to say—the effective phrase, the turning word—to convince the guard, to try for admittance, or to get free.

By contrast, those who achieve power may no longer need to strive, and are masters of emptiness in several senses: they are duly authorized masters of Buddhist emptiness teachings, and their positions or teachings lack discursive content. They "hold up," uphold, and revise old public records; the koan stories passed down from prior masters. The new master, aware of precedent, is like a presiding magistrate with the power to discern a "clear case" and to mete out thirty blows in instances of transgression or, just as possibly, nontransgression.

The masters, like the judges, clerks, or gatekeepers in Kafka, are supposedly not arbitrary, since koans by definition are *kung an*, or "public records" providing an objective, impartial criterion for both instigating and assessing a disciple's insight. Once a monk achieves *satori*, his mind state can be equated with those of the patriarchs, with whom he becomes eyebrow-to-eyebrow, "*seeing with the same eyes*" (M 1). Enlightenment is passed directly from mind to mind in a "direct transmission," and it cannot be directly taught or expressed in words. Language is repeatedly scorned, along with all imitative behavior.

What, then, can be the status of the patriarch's verses, or of the koans themselves: linguistic dialogues with *hua t'ou* or a "turning word" (*i chüan-yu*) that produces enlightenment? Here we have another instance of the problem raised earlier, regarding the *Dhammapada*, about right speech and rhetorical figures. The problem in Zen is even starker. Koans were assumed to be the direct, undistorted expressions of the enlightened mind from which they emerge; but any such claim is, as Dale Wright points out, in blatant conflict with Zen teachings about language.[24] The conflict is absorbed in a general tolerance, even a flaunting, of contradiction. Koans are nonrepresentational, yet (or thus) they demonstrate, as Buddhist teachings perennially claim to do, the way things really are.

Poetry in Koans

Literature has an uneasy status in this tradition. Chan rejected "words and letters" in favor of direct transmission, yet words, used skillfully and performatively, could be beneficial. Poetry, in particular, could be endowed with authority by depicting awakening. A continual motif in Sung dynasty aesthetics was that a poet, like a Chan master, possessed the dharma eye, and that studying poetry with a true poet was like studying Chan with a master. Poetic genius can never be simply imitated and, as Richard J. Lynn remarks, "the teaching of poetic enlightenment is something beyond the words of any teacher or the scriptures of any dogma."[25] Not all parties at the time, of course, were able to agree about the equation of poetry and Chan: discouraged by some as a diversion, poetry was encouraged by others as showing enlightenment.[26]

This multifaceted situation might have relevance to case 39:

> *A monk once wanted to ask Unmon a question and started to say, "The light serenely shines over the whole universe." Before he had even finished the first line, Unmon suddenly interrupted, "Isn't that the poem of Chosetsu Shusai?" The monk answered, "Yes, it is." Unmon said, "You have missed it!"* (M39 S)

There are many ways in which the monk may have "*missed it*," but the verse here, with phrases like "*the whole universe*," is far from the specificity or suchness of other types of poetry, such as the Japanese poet Bashō's famous haiku:[27]

> *Old pond*
> *Frog jumps in*
> *Water sound.*

Bashō's verse is Zen-like in its immediacy. By contrast, the passage from Chosetsu is conceptual, and it bears no intimate relation to the speaker. The monk is abruptly cut off, and the verse for the koan warns, "*if you open your mouth only a little / Your life is lost!*" (M39 S).

Another poem is cited in case 24, where roles are reversed: the master cites the poem to answer a monk's question.

> *A monk once asked Master Fuketsu, "Both speaking and silence are concerned with ri-bi [equality-difference] relativity. How can we be free and non-transgressing?" Fuketsu said,*
> *"How fondly I remember Konan in March!*
> *The partridges are calling, and the flowers are fragrant."* (M24 S)

The haiku-like verse here is someone's remembrance of a lovely time and place. The monk, with his well-worn philosophical phrases, is met with a particular moment in which his questions are set aside. The response may be compared with the Buddha's resistance to the demands of Mālunkyāputta and others, but here the answer is a cited poem. Master Fuketsu resolves a latent double bind, imposed painfully in other koans: how to speak and yet remain silent. The quotation is "*like lightning*," offering a model and, according to Mumon, a challenge: "*Now set aside the samādhi of words—just give me one phrase!*" The verse commentary recapitulates: "*It was not a verse of elegant tone! / Before speaking, it's already expressed . . .*" (M 24). Such, presumably, in a world left silent, is how poetry may find a place.

Perils of Imitation

Problems of imitation emerge more urgently elsewhere in the *Gateless Barrier*, as in case 3.

> *Master Gutei, whenever he was questioned, just stuck up a finger.*
> *At one time he had a young attendant, whom a visitor asked, "What is the Zen your master is teaching?" The boy also stuck up one finger. Hearing of this, Gutei cut off the boy's finger with a knife. As the boy ran out screaming with pain, Gutei called to him. When the boy turned his head, Gutei stuck up his finger. The boy was suddenly enlightened.* (M 3 S)

The koan has a folkloric dimension in which "teaching him a lesson" provides the pretext, with violence to be expected. The master is like a frightful shaman who bestows boons at a terrible price, or even like the wolf who consumes Little Red Riding Hood. Cruelty in the koan is supposedly compensated by the happy result (and Little Red Riding Hood, in the Grimms' version, gets out from the wolf's belly[28]). On a doctrinal level, symbolic castration is equated with renunciation, or the excision of delusive attachments.

The boy's finger is cut off, he is enlightened, but we are not told what else happens. When we see him last, screaming with pain, the master still holds up a finger to him (almost as if obscenely giving him the finger). The boy in another version, seeing his master raise the finger, again tries to do the same, but now has no finger! And so the boy becomes enlightened.[29] Becoming enlightened is what matters; all else is secondary. If the boy had lost a finger without gaining enlightenment, the master would be a bully or a criminal, and there'd be a far different lesson taught. In one version of this case, the boy's enlightenment is accompanied by the realization "*that simple imitation is insufficient.*"[30] Imitation is thus contrasted with a deeper, more intuitive knowledge.

Politics of Koans

That deeper knowledge and a gaining of *satori* require certain precipitating incidents and long-cultivated skills in koan response. As Foulk contends, "The accepted proof of *satori* is a set of literary and rhetorical skills that take many years to acquire."[31] Years of koan study, however, may be detrimental to the spontaneous or "surprise" aspect of koan encounters.[32] After studying and comparing hundreds of koans, a skilled monk, like a skilled chess-player, knows what moves are best. One may sense this situation in case 40:

> *Pai-chang wanted to choose a founding teacher for Mount Ta-kuei. He invited all his monks to make a presentation, saying, "The outstanding one*

will be sent." Then he took a water bottle and set it on the floor and said, "Don't call this a water bottle. What would you call it?"

The head monk said, "It can't be called a wooden clog."

Pai-chang then asked Keui-shan [the cook] his opinion. Kuei-shan kicked over the water bottle and walked out.

Pai-chang laughed and said, "The head monk loses." Keui-shan thereupon was made the founding teacher at Mount Ta-kuei. (M 40)

The head monk tacitly assumes that words represent or mirror things, and that a wooden clog could not be represented by "water bottle." Kuei-shan's action, by contrast, is "very Zen," and it clearly trumps the head monk's mere shifting about of words. The kick is an admirably disdainful negation of the phrase "water bottle," and his walking out (like Alice's Mouse, who also walks out) is a dismissal of the whole discussion.

Might the kick and walk to some extent, though, have been calculated? The action is skilled, and might be compared to a basketball player's slam dunk, or to a tennis player's winning drop shot. In most cases, inspired tactics usually presume not only talent or a lucky break, but strategic insight and intensive training. In Zen, as in athletics (where Zen is sometimes deployed), the champion practitioner is rewarded with a high rank. What is intriguing about case 40, as we learn from a study of the older records from which it derives, is that the retiring master Pai-chang had already decided, with the help of his geomancer, that Kuei-shan would be the next successor.[33] The felicitous kick provided a perfect pretext for promotion. And there are certain details adding to the literary or didactic value of the story, even while providing legitimacy to the system: Kuei-shan did not particularly want the job, while the head monk had ambitiously coveted it. Such information might have been deleted to make the story more purely a matter of Zen insight, but they suggest ideological matters lying behind some of the happenings.

Here, as with the *Lin chi lu*, a study of the older texts opens a larger context, often clarifying crucial details surrounding the arcane sayings and bizarre doings in koan exchanges. Collections like the *Gateless Barrier* derive their materials from pre-Buddhist folklore collections showing rites and exorcisms, from hagiographical dialogues in "transmission of the lamp" stories showing how insight is transmitted from one master to the next, and from anthologies of "recorded sayings" of the old masters. The *Transmission of the Lamp* collected by Tao-yüan (dated 1044) and the *Blue Cliff Record* (dated 1163) contain more archaic, fuller, and often different, versions of material used in later, more minimalist, collections such the *Gateless Barrier*. Koans recount or allude to well-known stories or legends, and a distinction is sometimes made between "literary" and "nonliterary" koans. In Ta-hui's "nonliterary" Zen, mentioned earlier, the *hua t'ou* is minimally linguistic, even meaningless, functioning only as a prompter.[34] By contrast, "literary" Zen (*wen-tzu Chan*)—to be found in the *Blue Cliff Record* and the *Transmission of the Lamp*—offers refined poetry and encourages imaginative exploration.

Magical Passwords to Enlightenment

In the *Blue Cliff Record*, an uncovering of the mythic and literary roots of koan stories acts to elucidate and to demystify them. Steven Heine remarks that conventional scholarship has paid much attention to the paradoxical language in koans, while ignoring the koans' roots in folklore, dreams, and magic.[35] If his observations be any barometer, the academic study of koans may be moving from an equivalent in literary studies of the New Criticism (with its focus on paradox, irony, and ambiguity) to an equivalent of archetypal criticism (with a focus on recurring patterns of ritual and magic). Interestingly, the archetypal approach, which many have claimed to be mystifying and conventional, may function on the contrary as ideology exposure, pointing to the shamanic rites, magical tricks, and patriarchal power play that are cloaked and opposed by the baffling obscurity, however necessary and essential, of the koans in their most memorable versions.

Of the three texts just mentioned, the *Gateless Barrier* is the best known, owing perhaps to the very conciseness that makes it arcane. There might be a sort of "koan mystique" that attracts us, but also keeps us at bay. We seem to be missing something—that is, the text in its mysteriousness alludes to, or condenses, long-lost myths and dreams. Thus we may wish to focus especially on the folktale-based or dream-like koans in the *Gateless Barrier*, and examine differing versions of the koans in fables and stories elsewhere.

Dreams and Magic

Dream stories are highly relevant. The process of resolving koans resembles that of a "*mute person who has had a dream*" and is about to wake up, while a dreamt sermon displays great skill (M 1, 25). Endowed with ambiguous meaning—and exposing Chan's usual claims to be unmediated, and to be distinct from popular folklore—dreamwork both intensifies and contests satori.[36] Many koans (and their commentaries) are implicitly dream-like. We are placed in a nightmare scenario, hanging by the teeth in a life-or-death situation, unsure of any way out. Pressures rise all around, and the situation can only be resolved within the dream, but also—snap!—by waking up. The sudden transformations of waking up, as in fairy-tales, folktales, or nightmares, are not realistically mimetic. They elevate master and magician to some higher level, enabling them to make miraculous, even enlightening, connections, as in a fingersnap.

Magic, and a dream-logic of sudden transformation, are visible in a folktale-based koan coming early in the *Gateless Barrier*. The well-known fox koan

(M 2) is filled with folkloric elements: an old man (who is a fox in disguise) listens daily to Master Pai-chang's sermons. He comes up one day to recount his story (within the story) set in a far distant past. He had been a head priest at the same monastery, and had given a false answer in an encounter dialogue:

> ... *Pai-Chang asked him, "Who are you, standing here before me?"*
> *The old man replied, "I am not a human being. In the far distant past, in the time of Kāśyapa Buddha, I was head priest at this mountain. One day a monk asked me, 'Does an enlightened person fall under the law of cause and effect, or not?' I replied, 'Such a person does not fall under the law of cause and effect.' With this I was reborn five hundred times as a fox. Please say a turning word for me, and release me from the body of a fox."*
> ... *Pai-Chang said, "Such a person does not evade the law of cause and effect."*
> *Hearing this, the old man immediately was enlightened. Making his bows he said, "I am released from the body of a fox. The body is on the other side of this mountain.... Please perform my funeral as for a priest.* (M 2)

The tone is set by phrases locating the action "in the far distant past" when "one day" he was asked a dharma question. The old man's transformation reinforces a sense that doctrine is decisive, not merely as a matter of intellectual assent or correct formulation, but of one's larger natural identity. As elsewhere in the collection, sudden enlightenment is catalyzed by a sharp phrase, which surprisingly transforms the interlocutor. The magic password opens up the situation, brings things together, solves a dharmic question, provokes disenchantment.

Breaking the Spell

The task of releasing can only be done by a master, and his power is akin to those spell-breaking skills possessed by the deities in Ovid, or by heroes in fairytales and epics. A dwarf in Grimms' fairytale "The Queen Bee" is given the task of discovering "*the youngest and the best of the king's three daughters, ... all of [them] beautiful, and all exactly alike.*" How to decide what to do, when persons, things, or events seem exactly alike? This is a frequent problem in koans (M 11, 26). Here, the dwarf uses a skillful ruse, and after some time, "*the spell was broken, and all who were turned into stones awoke and took their proper forms.*"[37]

The old man in the koan is a fox, and he wishes to be released. It is a great misfortune to transform into an animal, as when Odysseus's men, in Homer's *Odyssey*, are turned into swine by the sorceress Circe, with her potent drugs. The wily Odysseus wishes to free his followers from her spell, and Hermes assists by giving him a potent countermedicine, so that in saving them, he himself is not turned into a swine. Odysseus is thereafter unaffected by Circe's potions. And he is able to convince her, with diplomatic tactics, to transform his men back into their normal forms.[38]

In the *Gateless Barrier*, the turning word, like a strong medicine or potion, seems to have magical effects. But Odysseus's own skill is also relevant, just as the issue here is more than a question of magic. Master Pai-chang's sentence about karma has a striking outcome, but is that outcome miraculously magical, or is it itself causally karmic? Controversy has long surrounded the ways in which *nirodha* takes place: how does a karmically conditioned path give way, at some advanced point, to a gap? In or before this gap—karmically conditioned yet loosely so, since the links of conditioned origination are gradually being weakened—"magical" events may be inserted into the story, perhaps by virtue of poetic license, if not by virtue of supernormal or shamanic powers.

Folklore and Magic

Folkloric legend and doctrine thus intensify and magnify each other, and we are asked to expand our sensibilities in the direction of what Giambattista Vico has called the wisdom of the ancients. The earliest peoples were "*all robust sense and vigorous imagination, . . . born of their ignorance of causes, for ignorance, the mother of wonder, made everything wonderful.*"[39] The fox koan, too, turns on an ignorance of causality, and fabulistic mergings are in keeping with the master-turned-fox's ways of imagining. The metamorphosed master lived many "*blessed happy lives as a fox*" (M2 S). This seems quite natural, as does the even greater happiness of being transformed back into human form.

The koan, then, does not abandon mythical ways. Pai-chang, by exorcising the man-fox, fulfills the role of a heroic savior—a position, Heine points out, entirely in keeping with his reputation as a moralist and strict disciplinarian. The turning word that produces enlightenment is similar to the magical formulae used in fairy-tales to break spells or to rectify unfortunate transformations. Chan asserts its identity, however, at the end of the koan, when the disciple Huang Po asks skeptically, "*What if he had given the right answer each time . . . ?*" Pai-chang tells him to come closer for an answer; Huang Po does so, and he then quickly slaps Pai-chang. This happy act could be taken to indicate that earlier questions and answers about karmic causation are not entirely the issue. It might also be taken to indicate that exorcism is not enough to solve Chan problems, and that the koan story is different from "mere" folklore.

Parallel Zen Stories

Folkloric precedence cannot always help in unraveling koans, nor does it do so in the fox koan. But we find telling prototypes to encounter dialogues in the

Transmission of the Lamp, depicting masters and students graciously exchanging poetic verses (*gāthā*), some of them koans, in appreciative tribute and mutual inspiration. The verses, if offered by disciples, are judged as indicating levels of awakening. In one case, a master rejects earlier versions of a poem, which may have too imitatively followed the ancient masters. The disciple Hsiang-yen, asked to speak more directly from experience, composes a second poem ("*My poverty of last year was not real poverty. / This year it is want indeed*"), which is deemed inadequate, since it is only the "*Ch'an of Tathāgata*," but not yet of the patriarchs (TL 189). The disciple's third effort (one line saying "*I look at you with twinkling eye*") is finally accepted (TL 190), and Hsiang-yen can become a lineage holder. He has learned the rhetoric of enlightenment, which is assumed to be, since his master approves, a fully adequate sign of it.

The atmosphere in the *Transmission of the Lamp* seems relatively relaxed in comparison with a high-tension koan—for example, case 5 in the *Gateless Barrier*, where we are presented with a hypothetical double bind:

> *The priest Hsiang-yen said, "It is as though you were up in a tree, hanging from a branch with your teeth. Your hands and feet can't touch any branch. Someone appears beneath the tree and asks, 'What is the meaning of Bodhidharma's coming from the West?' If you do not answer, you evade your responsibility. If you do answer, you lose your life. What do you do?"* (M 5)

The stakes seem clear. There will be negative consequences if "you" do not have the power to deal with this intricate state of affairs. And there is no easy way out. Any question about Bodhidharma, the Patriarch who brought Buddhism to China, is especially imperative. Presumably, if the bypasser merely wanted to know the time of day, or what's for dinner, there'd be no problem. One would remain silent, teeth firmly gripped around that branch.

Koan Blocking

The situation is much like a joke: "What did *x* say to *y* when doing *z* . . . ?" One confesses to being stumped, and then awaits the punch line. If the joke is good, a laugh ensues. This koan, though, is no joke. We're unlikely to guess an answer or to see any punch line, though *satori* experiences are somewhat like "getting" a joke (*koan*, in one of its meanings, is "to see the point"). Just as jokes can't be explained, or else they're no longer funny, so koans, despite multileveled commentaries accompanying them, can never be entirely unraveled. Many koan dialogues, like this one, are left partially incomplete: a dialogue cannot transpire if one of the parties does not understand. The purpose of koans is to bar entry or block our way—and they succeed best when the listeners, or some of them, fail to understand.

The koan continues:

> *Even if your eloquence flows like a river, it is all in vain. Even if you can expound cogently upon the whole body of Buddhist lierature, that too is useless. . . . If you can't respond you must wait and ask Maitreya about it.*

There's little consolation to be had in a wait for Maitreya, the future Buddha. But waiting is part of the issue: the karmically challenged must remain, amidst their Great Doubt, in suspension. A final segment adds yet another perspective, also offered with ironized compassion, in which the later master pretends to berate the earlier master for talking venomous nonsense.

The koan points to something about clinging and letting go, and about the value of remaining suspended, even when an urgent decision is required. For more on the issue, we may look to a similar but more accessible Zen parable:

> *Buddha told a parable in a sutra.*
>
> *A man traveling across a field encountered a tiger. He fled, the tiger after him. Coming to a precipice, he caught hold of the root of wild vine and swung himself down over the edge. The tiger sniffed at him from above. Trembling, the man looked down to where, far below, another tiger was waiting to eat him. Only the vine sustained him.*
>
> *Two mice, one white and one black, little by little started to gnaw away the vine. The man saw a luscious strawberry near him. Grasping the vine with one hand, he plucked the strawberry with the other. How sweet it tasted!*[40]

We are left hanging in a life-and-death situation, as in action movies when the protagonist is hanging suspensefully from the ledge of a high building, or from a rickety fire escape way above the street. Here, a tiger is below, while the mice are nibbling at the tenuous vine. Life hangs in the balance, and we assume that no one in this situation, however prone to *carpe diem*, would grab a bite to eat. But then again, is the situation—or any situation—really so urgent? Mumon's dangling person, true, has less of a choice, and this parable does not make "the same point" as case 5. But it may have to suffice, and could even allow a pondering of the deeper situation, while we're waiting around for help from Maitreya.

Multiple Voices

In Zen, though, we rarely are allowed to wait for long, and encounter dialogues show an interruption of confident voices in sutras, in poems, or in stories. On this point, the work of Mikhail Bakhtin is pertinent. Bakhtin makes a distinction between *monologic speech*, which is closed and single-voiced, and *dialogic speech* or *heteroglossia*, which is multivoiced, living, and open. The monologic voice, the word of the fathers, is spoken from public loudspeakers or royal thrones, and is meant to make a society uniform and respectful, precluding the possibility of dissent.[41] With dialogism and multivocality, by contrast, differing voices are heard, presenting a challenge to monologistic, authoritarian, or patriarchal governance.

The word of the patriarchs may have a double valence. On the one hand, it may be thought of as the language of earlier texts, vigorously rejected in Chan's best-known definition of itself as a "*a special transmission outside the tradition, . . . not established upon words and phrases*" (M 6). On the other hand, it may refer precisely to koans, which excerpt the sayings of the masters, and which are "held up" for admiration and for public judgments. Koans are usually dialogic: they are often composed of encounter dialogues, and of further dialogues or commentaries upon these. Yet they are also in a sense monologic, since they are beyond intellect and are not to be discussed or understood in common, or reasonable, terms.

The very idea of "communication" in a Zen context is problematic: the masters do not care to be simply "understood" or even empathized with—at least not immediately. Their role, as the title *Gateless Barrier* indicates, is to find barriers. If everyone knew what the masters meant, or even what they were driving at, they would hardly be performing well, and might be less esteemed! The structural arrangement, however, in the *Gateless Barrier* (case, comment, verse) allows a place not only for the ancient encounter dialogues but often for contrarian invective. The text thus preserves patriarchal ideology in showing Mumon's admiration of the koans and his masterful insights about them; yet the same insights ironically revise the predecessors.

Zen masters, old and new, attempt to communicate on some deep level, but they express themselves peculiarly. We might venture to hypothesize, elaborating on Bakhtin, an "opaque dialogism": the masters invite or demand a response, but almost any verbal reply—and at times, even the very attempt to reply—is curtly cut off, or when a dialogue transpires, it is still opaque to others, and provides a stimulus for further investigation (M 1, 15, 22).

Encounter dialogues do not require the original participants, or even any participants at all. They may be rehearsed in solitude, as in case 12:

> *The priest Jui-yen called "Master!" to himself every day and answered himself "Yes!"*
> *Then he would say "Be aware!" and reply "Yes!"*
> *"Don't be deceived by others!"*
> *"No, no!"* (M 12)

The master, somewhat eccentrically, is talking to himself encouragingly. We are privy, it seems, to Master Jui-yen attempting to stay on guard and to build up a certain kind of self-image. He seems disarmingly naïve with his two selves in constant dialogue, curiously like Marcel's grandmother, in Proust's *Swann's Way*, who reminds herself to say she "*never slept a wink.*"[42] Master Jui-yen, like the grandmother, provokes amused and ironically disparaging analysis. "*Old [Jui yen] himself sells and himself buys. He has a lot of masks of goblins and demons to play with . . . . If you would imitate [him], your understanding is that of a fox*" (M 12 S). With goblins and demons being played with, he seems to mirror an irregular practitioner, or a thaumaturge. We dare not try, in turn, to imitate him. The fox is merely clever, and this comment resonates with koan 2, in which a fox body is imprisoning. The self-to-self dialogue is more than psychological self-mirroring, since "Master" may be an impersonal ideal (M 12 S). It bears affinities to folklore and to medieval Western literary dialogues of self and soul. Master Jui-yen is both speaker and respondent, thereby retaining control; his dialogism is thus only partial.

Hearing the Founding Legend

A much sharper juxtaposition of perspectives, a parody of monologism, is to be found in case 6, where the Buddha is presented in his legendary founding of the tradition.

> *Long ago, when the World-Honored One [the Buddha] was at Mount Grdhrakūta to give a talk, he held up a flower before the assemblage. At this, all remained silent. The Venerable Kasho [Mahākāśyapa] alone broke into a smile. The World-Honored One said, "I have the all-pervading True Dharma, incomparable Nirvana, exquisite teaching of formless form. It does not rely on letters, and is transmitted outside scriptures. I now hand it to Maha Kasho."* (M 6S)

Much as a master may hold up a staff (or a cat), here the Buddha holds up a flower, and the action is met with silence. Kasho smiles knowingly, and is presented with the flower, thereby joining the display. The scene is exquisitely lyrical, and Zen devotees regularly recall it. Yet Shakyamuni Buddha's Mahāyāna-like announcement of his achievement, invoking "the all-pervading True Dharma," may be a bit too explicit, while the flower offering, by contrast, may be all too tenuous. Is the Buddha's founding gesture to be achieved with no more than an announcement, a flower, and a certain smile?

The koan is double-voiced, not only in the case statement but, more radically, in the prose comment.

> *Yellow-faced Gotama is certainly outrageous. He turns the noble into the lowly, sells dog-flesh advertised as sheep's head. . . . At that time, if everyone*

> *in the assemblage had smiled, to whom would the True Dharma be handed? Or again, if Kasho had not smiled, would [it] have been transmitted? If you say that the True Dharma can be transmitted, the yellow-faced old man with his loud voice deceived the simple villagers. If you say that it cannot be transmitted, then why was Kasho alone approved?* (M 6 S)

The double-voicing shows, in effect, how a reverence for tradition and lineage may come into conflict with demystifying insight. The ambiguously subversive queries present new riddles, and seem excusably deflating or nicely cynical. The grandiose "World-Honored One" suddenly becomes a deceitful hawker of dog meat. What if the smiles, Mumon asks, had been differently allocated: could the transmission have transpired?

The Buddha's transmission "does not rely on letters," yet like a suspicion-casting dumb-show in Shakespeare, also with cynical commentary,[43] it still uses exchanged signs (a flower and smiles) along with speech and gestures. Might there be some oddity in claiming to have "the True Dharma," even while supposedly dismissing the earlier, open-handed ways of conveying or representing it? Here the mixing of voices of different tones and accents, which Bakhtin calls heteroglossia,[44] puts into question the seemingly authoritative first voice. The sneering tone undercuts the pretenses of no less eminent a figure than "the World-Honored One." An assuming of different voices allows Mumon to mock, with playful ambiguity, the very basis of Chan authority as "mind-to-mind" transmission.

Special Transmission, or Not

The voices may speak for two attitudes. Albert Welter demonstrates that in the Sung dynasty there were two viewpoints, one proposing that Chan was in harmony with the traditional scriptural teachings, the other that it was unique as a "special transmission" without words or explanations, passed down by the Buddha, through the patriarchs, from mind to mind.[45] The advocates of "special transmission" required an exemplary story to substantiate their position, and Mahākāśyapa's flower-meriting smile gratified the tastes of the local literari, eventually becoming enshrined as a founding legend. That legend, lacking scriptural or historical basis, could seem compelling only if it started with a fiction about Shakyamuni Buddha, who otherwise (in most koans) is not given much attention. Although the interpretation of Chan as a special transmission was not universally accepted, it gained popularity, and even a sort of legitimacy.[46]

The basis of the Chan-Zen transmission, then, is partly literary, and Mumon's sarcasm at the fabrication shows his ambivalence. A lack of historicity does not mean that the dharma cannot be conveyed in a mind-to-mind way, yet there may be some fakery going on, and mixed voices bring out the uncertain situation, with all its virtues and defects. In the concluding verse, "*Mahākāśyapa breaks into a smile*"—but with so much hedging and satire, it could be any sort of smile.

In the varied voices of case 6, the authoritative official line is, to paraphrase Bakhtin, parodied, refined, and reaccentuated, surrounded by other possibilities and contexts.[47] Authoritative discourse, attributed to someone else, is distanced or displaced, and, at times, even dialogism may seem off target. How does Mumon "comment" on his ancestors? Consider case 34: "*Nan-ch'uan said, 'Mind is not Buddha; wisdom is not the Tao.'*" Mumon remarks: "*I must say that Nan-ch'uan got old and knew no shame. He opened his stinking mouth a bit and revealed the family disgrace. Only a few can acknowledge his kindness.*" The reaction, though familiar, seems excessive: the case, a reversal of the usual stuff of many other koans, is not especially startling.

Might there be a bit of amiable trickery running alongside the insight here? As in a dream, family secrets are learned, and a great deal is read into something little appreciated. Shame, secrecy, kindness, disgrace, and humor all are brought together. Irony is interfused everywhere, but like Master Jui-yen who calls out "master," we still hear mostly Mumon; the commentary and verse, in their pleasant sarcasm, are unmistakably his. We are left with a milder heteroglossia than that of earlier, less riddling texts.

More Diversifying Voices

Te-shan is subjected to mild parody in the *Gateless Barrier* (M 13, 28), but in *The Blue Cliff Record* parody had been sharper, as a multivoiced conflict between great masters of two differing Zen traditions. A new possible master, Te-shan, arrives to challenge the resident master. He inspects the scene, and starts by walking around like a casual invader, not bothering to stow his bag, and indifferent to decorum. As a primary rival, he may have ambitions to displace the old master, or else to start his own sect.

Main Case (with capping phrases by Yüan-wu)

Te-shan came to see Kuei-shan.

Look at him carrying a load on his shoulder. That wild fox spirit!

He carried his bundle into the Dharma Hall.

This can't help but cause people to doubt him. He has already suffered his first defeat.

Then he crossed from the east side to the west side, and again from the west side to the east side.

He possesses the power of Zen, but what good does it do him?

He looked around and said, "No one is here. There's nothing here," and then he left.

> Give him thirty blows of the staff! His spirit reaches up to the heavens, but only a real lion can roar like a lion.
>
> [Hsüeh-tou comments: "He checked things out!"]
>
> What a mistake, after all.[40]

In this excerpt, everything that Te-shan does, described in a cool, third-person voice, is subjected to Yüan-wu's mockery, further complicated by the perspective of Hsüeh-tou. The differing voices are here set in differing fonts, and the capping phrases intervene disparagingly on the straightforward account. In their relative anonymity, the phrases are like those of a very picky chorus in Greek tragedy—disagreeing, warning, wondering, finding fault with every phrase, taking issue with the drift of the action, and informing us of the assumed motivation, or of what's "really" going on.

The ridicule provides a very different take on the action and, by coming later, it assumes ascendancy. We also have the sense that the observer, who shows such a keen interest in Te-shan, may be an amused but less-than-impartial onlooker. With these various voices as a background, the story unfolds, and a confrontation takes place:

> *Te-shan held up his teaching mat and said, "Teacher."*
>
> Switching heads and changing faces, he stirs up the waves even though there is no wind.
>
> *Kuei-shan reached for his fly-whisk.*
>
> See what kind of person he is, setting his strategy in motion even while remaining in his tent. No one can stop him from cutting off the tongues of everyone in the world.
>
> *Te-shan cried out, shook out his sleeves, and abruptly left.*

We discern, amidst the interwoven, chorus-like voices, a shadowy archetypal struggle going on between the two masters. No encounter dialogue transpires, but Te-shan makes a challenge. Keui-shan draws out his fly-whisk (weapon and symbol of authority), has the power to cut off tongues, but is unable to prevent Te-shan from leaving. Later on, Kuei-shan asks after the newcomer, surmising that he will "*dwell on the summit of a peak all by himself.*" This provokes a comment:

> Keui-shan draws his bow after the thief has already gone. No patchrobed monk in all the world will be able to follow after Te-shan.
>
> [Hsüeh-tou added the comment, "He adds frost to snow."]
>
> What a mistake, after all.

This episode adds to the legendary stature of Keui-shan, who kicked over the water bottle, and to Te-shan, who set fire to his *Diamond Sutra* notes (M 40, 28).

We could well be in the realm of epic, and the version cited may be derived from a longer work of such genre. The intense dialogism, while not enough to allow a crashing of barriers, may be a training in koan practice, and it retains a reader's rapt attention to the plot. We are not certain here of who won or lost, but a great battle seems barely to have been avoided.

Places for Compassion

Part of the Zen master's task is to put disciples to the test, and make them uncomfortable. The method is a radical "making strange," in which neither words nor silence are adequate. Words or habitual behavior provide no refuge, and the follower is violated in order to be awakened. We may feel, however, amidst so much stress on a tough conciseness, that Buddhism's great theme of compassion has, in the *Gateless Barrier* and at times in other Zen texts, been overshadowed. In a paradox earlier observed, the way of Chan, supposedly open and helpful to all, may have ended up being open and helpful to very few.

This is not to slight the masters' benevolent inventiveness. The koan stories collected recount, for example, Nan-ch'üan's "*great kindness . . . little appreciated*" or Hui-neng's concern, "*like a kindly grandmother who peels a fresh lychee, removes the seed and puts it into your mouth*" (M 34, 23). Humorous irony is so pervasive, however, that Mumon's admiration here may seem ironic as well. We may need to look elsewhere, as in the Buddha's last jātaka or the work of Shantideva, for a more outgoing treatment of the bodhisattva way.

9

Extreme Giving

The Vessantara Jātaka and Shantideva's *A Guide to the Bodhisattva Way of Life*

There are moments when we behold your very compassion with indescribable anxiety. . . . You want, if possible—and there is no more insane "if possible"—to abolish suffering. And we? It really seems as if we would rather have it higher and worse than ever. . . . The discipline of suffering, of great suffering—do you not know that only this discipline has created every elevation of humanity so far?

—Friedrich Nietzsche, *Beyond Good and Evil*

With its exaltation of perfect generosity, the *Vessantara Jātaka* celebrates the greatness of the Buddha's penultimate life. And with its praise of compassion, Shantideva's *A Guide to the Bodhisattva Way of Life*—the *Bodhicaryāvatāra*—celebrates the awakening of generous loving kindness.

Epic Intentions

In traditional sagas, the motivations for action include courage, audacity, ingenuity, and a loyalty to family, tribe, and nation. The central figure, with disdain and fury, does battle against enemies. Patience and charity, not prominent among the lauded virtues, appear only in the form of brave endurance, resistance to temptation, and assistance to wounded companions. Amidst this background of Greek or Indian epics, the story Buddha's story moves against the current. When confronted with verbal and physical aggression, the Buddha does not experience hatred or the impulse for violence. And he instructs his followers how to respond if they come under attack: "*Our minds will remain unaffected, and we shall utter no evil words; we shall abide compassionate for their welfare, with a mind of loving kindness, without inner hate*" (MN 21.11). Unlike craving, which grasps for happiness in a limited object or person, and which is fearful of loss, loving kindness is unlimited in quantity, and unseeking of selfish gain.

Unconditional love or generosity recall a heroism akin to *agape* (a great love for all), in contrast with *eros* (sexual love) and *philia* (friendship). *Mettā* is closely linked with other divine abidings or *Brahmavihāra*: compassion, gladness or sympathetic joy, and equanimity. Those abidings, working together as a way to overcome suffering, are each a "*liberation of mind*" (SN 9.20.4). The path of the divine abidings is a pathos: the patience of saints, the passion of Jesus, the passive resistance of Mahatma Ghandi. They are a way, if implemented, to end cycles of mimetic violence.

The divine abidings are visible in early Buddhist texts, and were used in meditation practices to promote the factors of awakening.[1] But in the earlier tradition, they are not foregrounded. Important in meditation, they are not sufficient to take one to the goal, but only to rebirth in the Brahma realms; they may be conjoined to enlightenment as a bonus, not as a cause.[2] For those who follow mindfulness teachings, compassion and well-wishing are mental states to be observed, like other mental states, in their arising and passing away. These states are comforting and skillful, but traditionalist teachers warn against becoming attached to them.[3] Mindful attention does not detract, however, from their joyful importance, and jātakas about the perfection of generosity (*dāna*), including the *Vessantara Jātaka*, may be viewed as major precursors to Shantideva's work.

Giving Away Everything

The *Vessantara Jātaka* is a folk epic narrated in part by "the Teacher"—the Buddha—at Kapilavatthu, his native place. He performs spectacular miracles in order to get the listeners' (his relatives') respectful attention, thereby setting the tone: this moral tale is filled with family drama, magical deeds, fairy-tale wishes, assisting deities, numerology, cosmic reverberations, and lush nature poetry. It moves at a leisurely pace, with the plot following a familiar pattern of kingship, exile and return. This particular jātaka is a favorite in Buddhist countries, partly because it plays on the terror we as children may harbor that our parents might for some reason (or no reason) turn us over to a stranger.

Most listeners cannot imagine nirvana, but the *Vessantara Jātaka*, by hyperbolizing generosity to an unimaginable extent, provides an alternative instance of sheer marvel. Instead of some invisible or internal transformation, audiences can clearly witness series of actions that they themselves would never do, but which are performed without a second thought for consequences. Vessantara, or the Great Being, gives away not only his wealth, but his own flesh and blood—thus moving freakishly, and entertainingly, beyond the bounds of common sense.

His kingdom's most prized treasure, a fabulous adored elephant, is bedecked with gems and ornaments of great value, listed in lavish detail. When brahmins from a drought-stricken nearby community arrive to visit, they ask for this precious elephant, which the young Vessantara immediately donates. As he does so, the entire earth quakes—"*a terrifying thing, something to make your hair stand on end*" (489).[4] Local residents, however, enraged at his having given the elephant away, protest to the king who, fearing that they might kill his son, agrees to exile him. Vessantara, however, cannot understand: "*Why are the people wroth with me? for no offense I see*" (492). Incomprehension reigns on both sides. Vessantara's extreme generosity is beyond the ken of most ordinary folk, while he, obviously to them, does not know the value of this wonderful elephant.

Having been banished from his kingdom, the Great Being feels no restraint. Once on the road, he meets up with brahmins, covetous as usual, now asking for his jewelery, his steeds, and, finally, his carriage—all of which he gladly gives them. Vessantara (foreshadowing Gautama) willingly undergoes a relentless fairy-tale reduction, from king to pauper. With fewer and fewer possessions, there is no more that the brahmins can ask for—except, of course, his family. And here the story reaches its crux: is the Great Being capable of giving away what should be most precious to him—his children?

Jūjaka the brahmin comes to ask courteously for Vessantara's children. The Great Being, on hearing the request, relinquishes them with great joy. He even offers to have them washed and dressed to be made ready, but Jūjaka prefers that the mother (who is away, and may return) not be present for these preparations. The children try to run away, but Vessantara brings them back, insisting that they leave with Jūjaka: "*Come, my dear[s] . . . , fulfil my perfection. Consecrate my heart; do what I say*" (546 CG). The phrase "my perfection" may suggest an element of selfishness, yet an earthquake attests to the value of Vessantara's act.

The children weep as they depart, bidding farewell to their father, asking him to send love to their mother. Vessantara has no qualms: he will attain "*omniscience*," which to him is more valuable than children. Meanwhile Jūjaka, as he makes off with them, binds and beats the children. Vessantara is perturbed at the sight, and plangently laments (548, 551). He even considers killing Jūjaka, but restrains his impulses.

Meanwhile Maddī the mother is returning, but the gods, to shield her from pain, delay her. When finally she does reach home, the children are nowhere to be seen, and Vessantara, sitting idly by, offers no help. Instead, using skillful means, he makes a "*feigned accusation*," blaming her and casting aspersions: "*Maddī, you are beautiful and attractive .... Who knows what you have been doing. You left early; why do you return so late?*" (562 CG). She explains that she was hindered, and immediately goes on a desperate search, looking everywhere, and when her frenzied worry reaches a peak, she collapses. Vessantara, moved, finally divulges what he has done. She asks, sensibly enough, why he had let her "*go weeping about all night, without saying a word?*" He replies that he did not wish to cause her pain, tells her not to worry—and perhaps surprisingly, she immediately agrees that he did the right thing (567). What happens next, though, is that he gives her away, too!

Some versions of the tale end here, when Vessantara, like a monk, has given away everything. In this version, though, a turning point comes when the friendly god Sakka offers assistance: "*I will take the form of a brahmin, and beg for Maddī. Thus ... I shall make it impossible that she should be given to anyone else, and then I will give her back*" (568). The disguise works, and as usual, a hair-raising earthquake provides approval of this course of action. Sakka thereupon returns Maddī to Vessantara, who has passed his final test and, as a reward, is allowed eight wishes. His first wish, notably, is not to carry on as a recluse, but to return home: "*May my father be glad to see me, ... [and] call me to take my seat*" (572 CG). The fairy-tale quality of this story is heightened towards the end, with the hero's homecoming.

Wishes Come True

The story proceeds in a pleasantly wish-fulfilling mode—the karmic return on this Great Being's generosity. The children, we learn, are relieved of their hard times under Jūjaka when, by "*divine prompting*," he takes them home to their grandparents, one of whom, Vessantara's father, had dreamt of their return (573–74 CG). Guided by the children, the parents are eventually located. A great reunion ensues, in which sixty-thousand people all faint from joy, and "*the mountains roared, the earth quaked, the great ocean heaved*" (586 CG). On an archetypal level, Vessantara had undergone exile as a discipline of suffering, and now deserves his long-awaited rulership. But what would make the people, who had asked for his banishment on account of his generosity, now change their minds? His penchant for giving having been proven beyond all doubt, he should be less qualified, not more so, for prudent kingship. What is to prevent this new king from giving away, bit by bit, the entire kingdom?

The story's direction, by now firmly established, avoids any such questions. An elephant is decorated, and when the family returns to Jetuttara, the city is "*full of dancing and singing*" (592 CG). With his impeccable intentions, no evil can befall this "*great king*," who sets prisoners free and wants to give jewels away, with the god obligingly showering down jewels upon his kingdom (593). So ends a perfectly generous story.

Vessantara as Hero

The tale is gripping and satisfying, moving archetypally in an outward and returning direction, kingship lost and regained with the fulfillment of perfection. But the hero's behavior goes so much against the grain that one is left to wonder about what kind of model he can provide. Interpretations of the life of Vessantara, like that of Gautama which follows it, may be divided along the lines of our distinction between recent and traditional readers. A recent reader may take Vessantara to be an aberration, an ogre who talks priggishly about "his" wonderful perfection, even while putting his wife and children at the disposal of any person who asks for them. The story piques our interest by daring to offer a folk hero, a Great Being, a saintly fool, who also seems a monstrosity or a pathological case. This Great Being could not be recommended as a babysitter! His story is grotesque and almost a parody of its own ideal—a person of great compassion, wanting to give to all, may produce (were it not for the happy ending) more suffering than he relieves.

A more traditional reader, though, might recall the *Questions of King Milinda*, when the King asks, "*Venerable Nâgasena, do all the bodhisattvas give away their wives and children, or was it only Vessantara the king who did so?*" Nâgasena's answer is that "*all of them do so, not Vessantara only*" (QM 4.8.1). All bodhisattvas, in other words, let go of what is most precious, and precisely what is nearest and dearest. Such is the great renunciation extolled by the Buddha in the *Noble Quest* sutta, with its relinquishing of cattle, elephants, slaves, gold, spouses, and, indeed, offspring—all those items that bind us, and that we would do well to become detached from (MN 26.7–11).

The gods of all the worlds, Nâgasena says, unite in praise of Vessantara's gift of generosity, whose glory "*has been handed down by successive tradition—till now, today, it has reached to this meeting of ours, at which we are sitting . . . , disparaging and casting a slur on that gift*" (QM 4.8.2). We are not of a stature to sit in judgment over Vessantara, nor can there ever be an excess of giving. As for suffering as a byproduct, King Milinda raises another question: "*he who gives gifts in such a way as to bring sorrow upon others—does that giving of his bring forth fruit in happiness, does it lead to rebirth in states of bliss?*" The answer is a resounding "*Yes, O king*"—it does indeed, despite contrary appearances, bring forth happiness (QM 4.8.3).

The outcome of this discussion is that the Great Being seems to have transcended us in his virtue, and he almost resides in another world. The Jātaka tales suggest that devotees could learn from the bodhisattva's example, but his achievements, in Vessantara's case, seem superhuman. Anyone questing for a more accessible model may thus need to look to the Mahāyāna sutras, where the bodhisattva path became a way of life more within the purview of ordinary laypersons.[5]

New Ideals

In ways available to all, and more strongly than in the *Vessantara Jātaka*, compassion requires offerings of empathy, and Shantideva's *Bodhicaryāvatāra*, though it does not directly mention Vessantara, modifies traditional positions. More is required than cutting off flesh or giving away things or people. The *Bodhicaryāvatāra* recommends a training in generous mental states: work is to be done "*to relieve creatures of their sorrows*" (1.8).[6] Compassion will be expressed concretely, in actual donations, only when the bodhisattva's training is well underway—that is, in some distant future time.[7] And other revisions are also notable: the *Bodhicaryāvatāra* makes a connection, not as explicitly made before, between the process of awakening and the development of compassion. The bodhisattva ideal was a protest against the earlier arhat ideal, which seemed to abandon those in need of help, as the *Dhammapada* does in advising, "*Don't give up your own welfare / For the sake of others' welfare, however great*" (12.166).[8]

The bodhisattva way, by contrast, made the welfare of others a crucial presupposition. Such a way, with its debated origins, it is said to have arisen on a wave of Hindu devotionalism, or *bhakti*—intense feelings and rituals expressing passionate worship of familiar saintly figures.[9] Over the course of several centuries (from the second century BC to the seventh century AD), the bodhisattvas, at first deemed inferior to the buddhas, gradually came to be viewed as their equals. In time, the path of the bodhisattva warrior became a privileged, and especially demanding, option for superior monks and some laypersons. The appeal of the bodhisattva way, according to Jan Nattier, was "the glory of striving for the highest achievement" among Buddhists, much as Olympic athletes "go for the gold" or the Marine Corps recruits "the few, the proud, the brave." Those who followed the bodhisattva way were thought to be special persons, part of an élite corps, and they contributed to a growing, widely shared, cultural ideal.[10]

The bodhisattva path takes root with an arousal of *bodhicitta*, or the mental state of aspiring to achieve perfect awakening for all sentient beings. Aspirants take a vow to strive for this goal. For them, bodhicitta is a force or urge that completely transforms them, so that they are reborn into "the family of Buddhas." An endeavor of selflessly doing good for others is part of the heroic archetype. The strong maverick, whether Prometheus, Jesus, Robin Hood, or Superman, gives aid to the victimized and oppressed, defeats the wicked, and ends in triumph. The bodhisattva warrior also engages in struggles, but is intent, as in Shantideva's text, in beginning with mental rather than physical tasks—in this case, by entering into the path of enlightenment.

A Mahāyāna Confession

The *Bodhicaryāvatāra* outlines a method of awakening, set out in part as a spiritual autobiography, and it may constitute a Buddhist counterpart to St. Augustine's *Confessions.* With its personal tone, and its evocation of virtues, Shantideva's work is surely relevant to our times. It provides an antidote to recent ideologies of entitlement and offers a key to the best of Buddhist motivations. The text is not only a "guide" or "entrance" to the bodhisattva way, with an enumeration of stages; it is also an implied narrative of the poet's hesitant, troubled progress in the direction of buddhahood. The presumed author, Shantideva, was an eighth-century Indian monk writing for other monks, and some sections present formidable philosophical expositions. But much of the *Bodhicaryāvatāra* offers proverbial advice and could be considered a Mahāyāna complement to the *Dhammapada.*

The first-person narrator, here to be referred to as the poet, begins by deprecating himself: "*What I have to say has all been said before, / And I am destitute of learning and of skill with words. / I therefore have no thought that this might be of benefit to others*" (1.2 P). The humility topos is frequent in literature, usually as a self-serving protective device.[11] The Shantideva poet claims no inventiveness for himself, and no skill in composition. Certainly his poem is not entirely original: it includes familiar traditional teachings, moving from an opening praise of bodhicitta to separate chapters on the perfections of awareness, patience, energy, concentration, and wisdom. But we need not believe, in light of the enchanting lyricism, that he lacks "skill with words."

The Precious Jewel

The poet cares profoundly about how the spirit of bodhicitta may arise in an ordinary person like himself, who makes no claim (but can only aspire) to be a full-fledged bodhisattva. He does not attempt to explain this arising naturalistically, but refers to it as a kind of miracle, or a magical jewel. Magicians or shamans, the Buddha included,[12] were highly respected from earliest times, and now an aspirational and petitionary prayer, as if made in a shamanic mindstate, is answered. The answer emerges as part of a story line in which the unassuming author, anxious and needing protection, finds a way of power—a "jewel"—with the ability to relieve all suffering. This precious jewel of bodhicitta, possibly an allusion to Vessantara's jewel (QM 4.1.40–41), is a talisman or mojo and, like the mantra in the *Heart Sutra,* it is said to work wonders.

The opening chapters depict the need to seek refuge from the impermanence of samsāric life:

> *You who are accustomed to travelling abroad among the trading towns of the realms of rebirth, grasp tightly this gem that is the Awakening Mind.* (1.11)

The gem is beyond price, in stark contrast to the place where it is found, recalling the lotus growing out of rubbish in the *Dhammapada* (4.58–59). At this point the poet sees himself, too, to be rubbishy. The text varies in tone between extreme praise of bodhicitta and an extreme sense of vulnerability, wickedness, and weakness.

The self is fragile and unstable, but this gem may be something, blessedly, to hold on to. The defiled human form can be transformed "*into the precious image of the Buddha-gem. Grasp tightly to the quicksilver elixir known as the Awakening Mind, which must be thoroughly worked*" (1.9–10). In alchemy, quicksilver is transmuted into a gem of higher value, and here the metaphor is itself a transmutation. Grasping tightly to an elixir or a jewel—grasping, indeed, to anything—is understandable in a world of ignorance, but in Buddhist teachings, it is a source of misery. The transformed grasping in this case, though, is a mental activity becoming a liberation, or the very opposite of grasping.

Once in possession of this jewel, the bearer "*immediately escapes great dangers*" (1.13). Any extremity in this claim is toned down by a distinction between two kinds of bodhicitta: first, "*bodhicitta in intention,*" which is aspirational (like wanting to travel); second, "*active bodhicitta,*" which is a performance of it (like traveling). The first kind of bodhicitta does have benefits, and it "*bears rich fruit,*" but the second kind, presumably attained with buddhahood, gives rise to a "*ceaseless stream of merit*" (1.15–19P). If the poet can arouse aspirational bodhicitta in himself and others, he will have gone very far indeed, since aspirations and intentions are the beginning of action.

The Fragile Self

Most of us, trying to free ourselves from suffering, only become more entangled in it. The jewel of bodhicitta, by contrast, "*satisfies with every happiness . . . [and] drives off delusion*" (1.28–30). Like the mantra concluding the *Heart Sutra*, a magical result seems to be offered; yet the magic here is not instantaneous. We need a developing awareness, purification, and training. In his confession in chapter 2, the poet is terrified to see himself as "*a brief and passing thing.*" He worries that "*my life is slipping by, slipping by*" (2.39P). In his anguish, he feels "*naked, helpless, unprotected*" and appeals for help: "*Who can save me, who can now protect me?*" (2.46, 45P). With a sense of inadequacy and bitter self-disdain, the Shantideva poet, like St. Augustine, cries out poignantly for divine assistance.[13] He pleads to Manjushri and Avalokita, among others. But while Augustine's *Confessions* in its entirety is addressed to God, the poet here invokes divinities as part of a liturgical process, and his misdeeds are stated in vague terms applicable to almost anyone (2.28–41), rather than in Augustine's lurid autobiographical detail. Perhaps more explicitly than Augustine, the poet is speaking not only for himself but for others; he is teaching others, and enacting a prayer for them.

The invocation to the bodhisattvas seems to have been effective. In chapter 3, he behaves as if the force of bodhicitta has been transmitted, so that he is now able to convey it to others. He seems close to having gained some degree of aspirational bodhicitta, and he engages in a prayer explicitly "*for those who grope, bewildered, in the dark of suffering!*" (3.5P). The prayer is, of course, performative, and thus may also have some element of active bodhicitta, especially since it moves beyond his immediate circle of listeners.

Gift of Bodhicitta

He feels able to make enormous wishes for others, and he starts to enter, prayerfully, into the Bodhisattva way:

> *[May I be] medicine for the sick. May I be both the doctor and their nurse, until the sickness does not recur.*
>
> *May I avert the pain of hunger and thirst with showers of food and drink. May I become both drink and food. . . .*
>
> *. . . For embodied beings may I be the wish-fulfilling jewel, the pot of plenty, the spell that always works, the potent healing herb, the magical tree. . . .* (3.7–8, 19)

One is astounded at the magnificence of these wishes. They are the gift of giving, emerging as a lightning flash, a kind of miracle, a blessing from the buddhas. And a movement from eloquent wishing to a direct performative address dramatizes bodhicitta in action: "*Today I summon the world to Buddhahood and to worldly happiness meanwhile*" (3.33). In holding out this jewel to all beings, the poet is like the Buddha presenting his monks with "one way" of release from conditioned existence. The Buddha of the Pāli scriptures, however, did not expect much from ordinary people, and he advised monks, we recall, to be lamps or islands unto themselves.

Shantideva's advice resonates, by contrast, in a subtle reversal of the Buddha's advice, when the poet offers himself (in the Tibetan version) as a lamp or island for all those who need one:

May I be an isle for those who yearn for landfall,
And a lamp for those who long for light;
For those who need a resting place, a bed;
For all those who need a servant, may I be their slave (3.19 P).

The bodhisattvic "self" is expanded to the point where islands or lamps are for all and any. The self cares about others more than about itself, and the "I" is used, paradoxically perhaps, to underline this very point.

The Great Vow

A version of the Bodhisattva Vow is stated as part of the poet's hyperbolic good wishes: *"For every thing that lives, / As far as are the limits of the sky, / May I provide their livelihood and nourishment / Until they pass beyond the bonds of suffering"* (3.22). The first-person pronoun for the vow includes the poet; in reciting the verses, he participates in the vow and assents to it. A good deal of preparatory ritual has been devoted to cultivating bodhicitta, and traditionally the Vow is renewed in daily recitation.

The very need for vow-making, though, suggests that customary lassitude or self-interest may intervene as hindrances. Our usual psychology runs along the lines of Freud's warnings against ostensible motivations for so-called universal love, or an undiscriminating helpfulness toward strangers.[14] Deviations from an instinctual need for self-interested survival come with a price, and Shantideva's text, for all its sublime glorification of extreme giving, shows, in the poet's hesitations, that ancient survival instincts may be at work. Instincts may have to do with his revisions of earlier teachings in a need to invoke protector deities, and in his wishing every being, until buddhahood is reached, "*every earthly joy!*" (3.34P).

The poet seems to be encouraging and persuading himself, and perhaps the recited words of the vow, a familiar ritual formula, may not be enough to truly bind. He appears to falter: "*I myself have weighted and pondered it, / So why should I now doubt and hesitate?*" (4.3P) The question is to be construed as a rhetorical question, yet there are overtones that it is nonrhetorical as well. The poet feels incompetent or unworthy and, thus, on some level, unwilling to undertake this great calling. He questions his earlier hyperboles and wonders if, having spoken so extravagantly, he can keep his word.

In asking such questions, this author acts as more than a conventional poet. A poet is said to create a self-contained world and despite, or on account of, making fictions, cannot lie: "*he nothing affirms and therefore never lieth.*"[15] By contrast, Shantideva's poet, as part of his poetic world, and beyond it, is making affirmations that he intends to make good on, and he will be worse than a liar if he fails to deliver. That may all be part of the story. Yet even if the entire scene of wishing or promising is imaginary, the imagining mind is, for him, to be held accountable: "*How can I expect a happy destiny / If from my heart I summon / Wandering beings to the highest bliss, / But then deceive and let them down?*" (4.6 P).

We recall the irrevocability of promises aeons before the future Buddha's birth, and just before the Buddha's death. Here a promise—a version of the Bodhisattva Vow to save all sentient beings—is of inestimable consequence. A promise, an intention of giving, is itself a giving: a promise is given. And a subplot of transformation (in a concern about promising) discloses the fitful growth of a giving spirit. The process moves in jerks and swings, "*now under the sway of errors, now under the sway of the Awakening Mind, it takes a long time to gain ground [bhumi]*" (4.11). He has a window of opportunity in which to make something of himself on the bodhisattva road (4.15).

Taking Responsibility

Having gone so admirably far in his devotion, the poet still wavers and draws back from his first generous impulse.

> *At that time I was intoxicated, speaking without realizing my own limitations. After that I can never turn back from destroying the defilements.* (4.42)

To be "intoxicated" can hardly be proper, except metaphorically, to someone following the middle way. The fourth chapter's title, *Apramāda bodhicitta* (recalling perhaps the *Dhammapada*'s second chapter, *Appamāda-vaggo*), may be translated as "vigilance," "awareness," or "conscientiousness" about *bodhicitta*. The opposite is *pramāda*, or something like intoxication: carelessness, a lack of mindfulness. Appropriately yet perhaps comically, he's got himself moving, and can no longer backtrack. If he did, in his ignorance, make the vow, then he is now, in the light of awareness, compelled to follow through. A sober poet is questioning and retreating, in the interests of modest realism, from his earlier hyperbolic speech acts. Yet he is firm in his belief that, in an interdependent world, if he breaks the promise, an endless number of sentient beings will be affected (4.10).

Amidst these various retreats and advances, we sense why the "I" is so prominent: it is a locus of promises made. In the earlier Buddhist tradition, the "I" was to be minimized, and monks, though ordained as renunciates, took no vows: the act of going into homelessness was taken to mean that right behavior would follow.[16] In Christianity, Jesus goes further and rails against all vows or oaths: "*Do not swear at all, either by heaven . . . or by the earth . . . . Let what you say be simply 'Yes' or 'No'; anything more than than comes from evil [the evil one]*" (Matthew 5:33–37).[17] For the aspiring bodhisattva, however, the great vow is to be an ideal or motivation, rather than a source of trouble. Sentient beings are numberless, so the promise is never fulfilled but is always on the way, in action. The burden is never to be put down (as in the early formula for reaching the goal), since giving is never finished but always giving further. And that's its unending loveliness.

The way is not easy: the poet is both inspired and intimidated by the bodhisattva ideal. That ideal produces an awkward combination of tender-minded caring and tough-minded warrior virtues. There is a tension and a hesitating, on the poet's part, between these two roles. Each stance may be a compensation for the other, and neither alternative emerges fully or wholeheartedly: his story shows him neither in acts of giving nor in acts of visible bravery. Frequently he takes on the pose of a proud monk dealing out proverbial advice, but then he collapses into self-disdain or, taking an opposite tack, breaks into sublime, sublimated lyricism about the joys of assisting those in distress. He moves thus through unstable cycles of depression and elated generosity.

The mind's greatest threat, then, is the mind itself. The mind may take on many forms, and can be compared to a stealthy band (*sangha*) of thieves. There is honor, so the saying goes, even among thieves, and the word *sangha* is also the band or order of Buddhist followers—one of the three refuges. Here lack of awareness is "*a thief*," and the defilements are sneakily sangha-like, a "*band of robbers . . . seek[ing] out a point of access. When it has found one, it plunders and destroys life in a good realm*" (4.27–28). The image has a double propriety: we are unaware of the thief's entry into our dwelling, and what he proceeds to steal is awareness. The thieving image recurs:

> *The crane, the cat, or the thief achieves his intended goal by moving quietly and gently. The aspirant should move in such a way at all times.* (5.73)

Is the aspirant, then, somehow like a thief? Any struggle is devious, since the mind's supposed opposite, a quietly intent thief, is much like the mind's watchman on guard.

Subtle Revisions

Transformations are taking place, though, and the alertness being commended in chapters 4 to 6 is a subtle variation on the *Four Foundations of Mindfulness*. There the mind's attention was directed to the body, feelings, mind, and mind objects. Here in chapter 6, which is about perfecting patience or forebearance, the mind is attentive especially to feelings—of anger or hatred in particular. The bodhisattva ideal of compassion depends on an alertness to the arising of anger. Aeons of practice in patience can be destroyed "*in a single flash of anger. / [Thus] there is no evil equal to hatred, and no spiritual practice equal to forebearance . . .*" (6.1–2). The prominence of a mindfulness concerning anger, or hate, rather than all four foundations, produces a certain shaking up of other elements in the earlier Buddhist system.

The key term, for example, of the first Noble Truth—*dukkha*, or suffering—is no longer monolithically negative, but instead may have a positive value:

> *The virtue of suffering has no rival, since, from the shock it causes, intoxication falls away and there arises compassion for those in cyclic existence, a fear of evil, and a longing for the Conquerer* (6.21).

A sea change has taken place, but where revisionary ratios are obvious in the *Heart Sutra*, here in the *Bodhicaryāvatāra* they perform their work more subtly. By regarding suffering as an invitation to patience, the speaker alters its texture, since suffering, no longer a reason to exit conditioned existence, is tolerated as a benefit for oneself and others.

By zeroing in on hatred, rather than *tanhā*, as suffering's negative cause, the second Noble Truth—again, subtly—is also put in the shade. More positively but still in a revision, "*Were all embodied beings to have their wish fulfilled, no one would suffer. No one wishes for suffering*" (6.34). According to traditional Buddhist teachings, wishes or desires, even when fulfilled, lead endlessly to further desires, and thus to renewed suffering. Here the cessation of anger—not of wishes, nor of *tanhā*—is to be cultivated: "*to resist anger is [not] inappropriate: . . . since there is dependent origination, there can be the cessation of suffering*" (6.32). Anger, more than other defilements, is implicitly identified with suffering, and anger is to be brought to cessation.

Rejecting Anger

Having pointed to anger as a prime villain, the chapter on perfecting patience is devoted to ways of putting a dampener on hostility. It offers a version of what in our times, for business or medical reasons rather than sacred ones, is called "stress reduction" or "anger management." Shantideva's text, emerging from a far different cultural milieu, features a furious attack on fury, in a series of paradoxical figures showing a hatred of hatred (6.41). Hatred involves suffering: a hate-filled mind "*neither enjoys pleasure or delight, nor goes to sleep nor feels secure*" (6.3). What is to be done about this condition, so adverse to the development of bodhicitta?

The narrator employs any and all tactics to reject anger in any form. He demonstrates, using depersonalization, that anger at others' behavior is unjustified, since their behavior arises out of conditioned causes. One would not be angry at a fire for producing heat, or the sky for being filled with clouds (6.22, 39, 40P). Likewise, the undesirable behavior of others (including their anger) arises out of conditions which "*once assembled, have no thought / that now they will give rise to some result*" (6.26 P). People who are angry "take things personally."

Yet the angering cause is impersonal, and seen this way, the anger—itself a result of impersonal causes—becomes unwarranted.

At times we become angered at recalcitrant things—a jar that cannot be opened, or a mechanism that breaks down. But humans, with their intentionality, make better targets, and mimetic violence can be expected almost inevitably. All the more reason to avoid anger: it feeds the fires, and is an unskillful response. We're not to accuse or attack people for their behavior, including their angry behavior. Yet we need not hesitate to blame or chastize ourselves: "*Why did you behave before in such a way that others now trouble you in this way?*" (6.68). Others are not to be blamed—but why then does he blame himself?

The poet's intense, self-disciplinary rage against himself is phrased in first- or second-person pronouns (6.74–103). The pronouns may to some extent be distanced, as in "*all you*" of a certain type (5.23P). But the extreme pathos of the confessing "I" in the second chapter establishes an intimately personal tone setting out faults, and that tone continues in his rage against rage. The situation may arouse suspicions. Although we are grateful and intrigued by this poet-monk's personal honesty in laying bare—indeed broadcasting—his shortcomings and hesitations, we may also have reservations. The poet's working himself, even allegorically, into a frenzy of anger against anger discloses what might be called poor linguistic body-language. The poet hardly provides an example of patient equanimity, which he recommends in the same way that Charles Dickens's Uriah Heep recommends humility.

With a personal area that is negatively self-regarding—that is, disdainful and self-concerned—the praise of bodhicitta may seem peculiar: the poet makes a gigantic exception, in his own case, to his insistence that all are equally to be relieved of suffering (8.90). The poet's point may be that energies of anger, in being directed against himself, are shunted away from others. But he is just as much a person as anyone else! His nasty superego, scolding and screaming, seems out of control, and we will soon enough encounter the return of the repressed—for example, in meditations on the corpses of erstwhile lovers, or in exclusions of those who have no chance of attaining bodhicitta, and who will surely be consigned, as he fears he himself will be, to the lower realms.

Motives for Compassion

There may be, then, something other than love mixed up with extreme benevolence; the ideology of "universal love" or of "love thy neighbor" has, in our epoch, been put sharply into question. In this chapter's epigraph, proposed as a heteroglossic countervoice, Nietzsche suggests that habitual compassion or pity (*Mitleid*) may be damaging to the strong virtues needed for greatness in any field of human endeavor. With its direct address to a familiar "you," the passage is cast in implicitly dialogical terms. The speaker has for some time known the addressee, whose habitual compassion causes "indescribable anxiety"—indescribable perhaps, because that anxiety is not itself compassion, or not of the same kind: "*our[s] is . . . higher and more foresighted,*" and belongs to a larger clash of perspectives.[18] "We" propose, as the addressee does not, to make suffering "worse and higher," and part of a discipline whose value has already been proven by great accomplishments. The monk's own austere discipline is part of his suffering and his accomplishment. But any assessment of accomplishment is arguable, and so the dialogue will continue.

To be more particular, though, compassion is not necessarily the motive for altruistic acts. In helping others, we can feel more powerful or more fortunate than they are, and may have hopes for ensuing praise. Or when we unhesitatingly jump into the water to save a stranger from drowning, that person's suffering might offend (*beleidigt*) us: "it would make us aware of our impotence, or perhaps our cowardice, if we did not go to assist. . . Or it can have a painful effect upon us simply as a token of human vulnerability and fragility in general."[19] Our benevolent action "sets a limit to an injustice (the discharge of indignation is refreshing)," and in general, "we never do anything of this kind out of *one* motive."[20] In Shantideva's case, the ideology simplifies motivations for altruism.

The implicit claim of the bodhisattva way is that it follows no economy, that it is a giving without the slightest wish or expectation of reward. Such a claim deserves scrutiny. The Bodhisattva Vow is phrased in the first-person singular, and Shantideva's quasi-autobiographical text is replete with first-person reflections. The "I" making vows and prayers is performing a self-aggrandizement that can be ignored or excused only by being carried far beyond the usual boundaries. There must be a sublime satisfaction and a release from petty hates, in vows and visions of universal compassion. In a moment of ecstasy, the poet spikes himself up from depressing self-disdain to make an exalted heroic proclamation: "*This world is . . . incapable to accomplishing its own benefit. Therefore I must do it for them*" (7.50).

This sounds impressive, and differs in tone from the early Buddha's simple bragging. Yet the poet's focus on self, as suggested, arises not only from a conflicted divine pride but from a transformed, if not strangely distorted, survival instinct. All species intinctively struggle for existence, fighting against predators or fleeing in terror from them.[21] The lion capturing a deer tears flesh, but is unlikely to tear its own flesh. Jātaka stories, by contrast, display the saint freakishly giving up flesh,[22] and the *Bodhicaryāvatāra* asks us to be able to give up our flesh (7.26P). Such self-sacrifice, though an empowerment, is an extreme defamiliarization.

The poet is not presented as sacrificing flesh, and more may be at stake than physical survival. One must make an effort to make the most of one's short lifetime so as to be of service to others. If life is squandered in unskillful behavior, "*what greater folly could there ever be?*" (4.23P). Although in context, the worry is about being sent to hell as a karmic outcome of one's evil, there is also a sense that the chance to offer compassionate action is invaluable, and should never be carelessly wasted.

Watching Corpses

A bodhisattva aspirant thus does not respond to the whims and demands of any complaining fool. The poet's so-called friends may get in the way, indeed, of his aspirations: "*a beneficial word, and they resent it, / While all they do is turn me from the good.*" They cannot be helped, and he keeps them at a courteous distance (8.10–11, 15P). The poet-monk soon departs from his mercurial companions with the comment, "*no one shares our fate, and none our suffering. / So what are they to me, such 'friends' and all their hindrances?*" (8.32P). Is not the burden of this text, however, to argue the opposite—that our sufferings and fates are shared and intertwined?

One answer is that the bodhisattva way is a serious calling (with "avoidances" practiced in the *sudurajayā bhūmi*), and no time is to be dissipated in idle pursuits (5.54). Instead the poet trains himself in an awareness that he (and his false friends) will become like the corpses he observes: "*This form of mine, this very flesh, / Is soon to give out such a stench / That even jackals won't come close . . .*" (8.30P). Flesh, again pivotal, is devalued in its decay, and the insight is a place of overlap for worldly and Buddhist versions of *carpe diem*. Here are the remains of a woman who was once perhaps the poet's beloved: "*She is nothing but bones. . . . Why do you not willingly cuddle them and feel bliss? / You saw that face before; you tried to lift it up when it was lowered in modesty . . . / Now that face is stripped by vultures . . .*" (8.43–45). The corpse is repulsive: rotten, foul and stinking, full of excrement. Does the exposure of a woman in so ungainly a state (as in Aśvaghoṣa's biography, when the Prince leaves his harem) tell the whole truth? The poet is using familiar skillful means: when the erstwhile hedonist or lover catches a glimpse of the beloved person, now horribly deformed and dead, there will be less desire to form new attachments.

Perhaps so, but the opposite also may happen! A long tradition of *carpe diem* poetry is devoted to making the most of any lovely day, because all too soon we decline into senility and death. Seventeenth-century poets such as Robert Herrick, in *To the Virgins, to Make Much of Time*, and Andrew Marvell, in *To his Coy Mistress*, are leaders in this line. A few centuries later, Charles Baudelaire's poem *A Carrion [Une Charogne]* offers an even more graphic vision: the poet is walking with his beloved, when they come across a rotting female corpse in an obscene posture—stinking, oozing, and maggot-filled. Baudelaire is nonetheless able to address conventional Petrarchan epithets ("*Star of my eyes, sun of my being, . . . queen of graces*") to his beloved who is alive, suggesting that they should love each other all the more, and that he deserves gratitude, again by a conventional conceit, for having immortalized her in his poem.[23]

The *Bodhicaryāvatāra* poet thinks rather differently, and from equalizations of corpses and myself (I will one day be like these corpses), he returns to justifications for an equalization of self and other: "*All equally experience suffering and happiness. I should look after them as I do myself*" (8.90). There is a democracy of suffering, and "*I should dispel the suffering of others because it is suffering like my own suffering. . . . What is so special about me?*" (8.94–95). This magnanimous "like my own," is itself an act of compassionate generosity, while the rhetorical question nicely sublimates self-disdain. The poet attempts to undercut any sense of privilege but is not primarily concerned, as many are in recent times, with the sufferings of class, race, or gender. From the nondualistic perspective of bodhicitta, there is no difference between my suffering and anyone else's, and all pain is to be alleviated.

Although all are equalized by suffering, in his next chapter, he posits an inequality: there are two kinds of persons, "*ordinary folk*" and "*meditative thinkers.*" The meditators are more correct than ordinary folk, and some meditators are "*higher*" than others. Ordinary folk are deceived into taking illusory appearances for reality, whereas the highest of meditators, likely to be bodhisattvas and presumably with access to absolute truth, are not deceived (9.1–5P).

Bodhisattva Ideology

Clearly an ideology is being set up or reinforced, with master terms held in place by the superior wisdom of the contemplatives. Here as always, there may be different ways of responding. Many readers will accept the ideology of insightful altruism with few reservations, and without access to higher meditative insights. Other readers, though, may be less enthuasiastic. They might point out that do-gooders of the world have in recent centuries been suspected, as in Nathaniel Hawthorne's *The Scarlet Letter*, of hiding a resentful or self-indulgent side as the repressed inversion of their supposed virtue. From such a viewpoint, the "I" in Shantideva may seem to have glorified himself in eagerly humble helpfulness, and is open to suspicions of hidden arrogance, and even masochism, as when he fantasizes about giving his body to sentient beings, asking them to "*continually beat it, insult it, and splatter it with filth*" (3.12).

Motives for goodness, then, may surely be questioned, and within the tradition, expositors distinguish between differing intentions or "scopes" in undertaking the path of awakening.[24] If readers have reservations about the ideologies of giving, possibly the text has them as well, since, as the Dalai Lama has noted, it is the poet's inner dialogue.[25] Shantideva's misgivings, in such dialogue, and in a first-person narrative, make the poem poignantly intimate: the speaker communicates how a glimpse of *bodhicitta* arises in a person otherwise making no special claims for himself. This, in turn, suggests that it may be a possibility for all.

That suggestion is not a simple one, however, and we may note, as earlier with the terms *ignorance* and *nirvana*, how an ideology is at work. Consider the following passage:

> *No sufferings belong to anyone. They must be warded off simply because they are suffering. . . .*
>
> *If one asks why suffering should be prevented, no one disputes that!* (8.102–103)

The dominant term is undisputed or obvious, giving coherence to the others. Shantideva's speaker assumes, as the Buddha did, that suffering must be attended to, and that details about what may have caused it in any particular case (so goes the arrow parable) are irrelevant. The unquestioned assumption—that suffering is to be relieved—is a null point giving boundaries to the system. Although many readers would immediately subscribe to this assumption, others would just as immediately dispute it. Some sufferings are to be welcomed, the latter might say, for character-building or as rightly deserved punishments meted out to hardened criminals. They might also point out the value of *Schadenfreude*—joy in another's pain. For many persons, habitually enjoying themselves as they torment others, the relief of suffering can wait, perhaps indefinitely!

A specifically bodhisattvic ideology, by contrast, where sadomasochism is ruled out, would go as follows:

> *All those who suffer in the world do so because of their desire for their own happiness. All those happy in the world are so because of their desire for the happiness of others.*
>
> *Why say more?* . . . (8.129–30)

This maxim sounds splendid. It is edifying, and might be viewed as a valuable guide to right behavior: one is unlikely to get into trouble if others' interests are primary. Yet our wishes for the happiness of others may surely at times cause us suffering, as in the *Vessantara Jātaka*, when those others are wounded, gone, or deeply unhappy. The passage's concluding rhetorical question—"Why say more?"—proposes that the statement is self-evident, and that no more need be said. The master term is "the happiness of others" as opposed to "the happiness of oneself." It is quilted into the system's most prominent place, and it is not defined or filled in, but acts as a placemarker. "Happiness" is assumed self-evidently to follow from our desire for the happiness of others rather than of ourselves. The master signifier is an enthymeme, that is, the loose premise in a rhetorical, as opposed to a logical, demonstration.[26] The movement of rhetoric,

Richard Weaver points out, "cannot finally be justified logically. It can only be valued analogically with reference to some supreme image."[27]

The audience in this case, valuing the bodhisattva as a supreme image, already agrees with the altruistic Vow, and the speaker can work from this body of agreement. To a large extent, Shantideva, addressing monks, is speaking to the already converted; there is no wondering about distinctions between altruism and self-concern. The assumption, in the maxim cited, is a foundation for further discussion, but itself is not to be discussed. That assumption, moreover, helps define an entire structure of interconnected binary oppositions: "*fiendish*" vs. "*divine*"; "*bad rebirth, inferiority and stupidity*" vs. "*good rebirth, honour and intelligence*"; "*fool*" vs. "*sage*" (8.125, 127, 130). All rewards go to those who accept this scheme, while for others "*Buddhahood is certainly impossible*" (8.131).

These dualistic gestures classify persons according to strict oppositions, and some persons are denied Buddhahood. Such gestures might seem odd, especially amidst so much praise for nondual insight and endless generosity. To be sure, an élite corps needs high standards, and only a small minority ("a few good men") can become bodhisattvas. But more needs to be said about the issue of exclusion, and possibly the ninth chapter, on the perfection of wisdom or understanding (*prajñā*), may be seen in this light. That chapter furthers the text's ideology by setting Mādhyamaka emptiness teachings alongside others, and finding those others to be inadequate.

Once that is done, the poet concludes with a dedication of merit in chapter 10 that differs from earlier dedications. He may be depicting a progression from intentional to active bodhicitta (1.15–17P). The first generated a set of unforgettable hyperbolic wishes, cited earlier, for the well-being of all those in cyclic existence (3.7–21). With the second awakening, the hyperboles are even more extensive and limitless. The *Bodhicaryāvatāra* thus develops from one set of hyperboles at the start, in which the "I" offers himself as an aid to all in need, and another, more sublime set, in which the "I" is partly suspended, and well-wishing is performed for all types of beings in the cosmos (10.4–50). In both sets of hyperboles, the imagination envisages the achievement of a bodhisattva, and a utopia emerging from those wishes. The wishes are literary in constructing their own world, and defamiliarizing—challenging or quietly revolutionizing—the ordinary prosaic world.

This poet acts as Percy Bysshe Shelley's ideal poets might do, in their position as "*unacknowledged legislators of the world.*"[28] Such legislators' efforts inspire in us an ideal of the Bodhisattva figure who, far from behaving in exclusionary or tribal ways, challenges in effect not only the samsāric world but the entire cosmology: "*May the regions of hell become glades of delight, with lakes scented by a profusion of lotuses, splendid and delightful . . .*" (10.7). Hell, by this action, would no longer be unpleasant, or serve its usual functions. The hungry ghosts need not remain hungry: "*may [they] be fed, may they be bathed, may they always be refreshed . . .*" (10.18). The suffering of conditioned existence—sickness, old age, death—need no longer be obstacles: "*may all beings have immeasurable life. May they always live happily*"; "*may no being suffer, nor be wicked, nor diseased, neither contemptible nor despised . . .*" (10.33, 41).

Here, as elsewhere, traditional doctrines are revised. Although wishes following good deeds, as in the Vessantara story, will be rewarded, the Buddha had warned sternly that an escape from suffering is not to be had merely by wishing (MN 141.19). Much as Shantideva's text subtly modifies the first Noble Truth about suffering, so it also modifies the second. *Tanhā*, or craving, is a mode of intense wishing that perpetuates suffering, but here the wishing is directed not toward selfish grasping but rather toward the welfare of others.

Utopian Subversiveness

The warnings cited earlier against compassion—that it is likely to be harmful rather than beneficial—come from another epoch and culture. Even Shantideva's most ardent admirers wonder, however, about the poet's reckless wish magically to remove all suffering: "the sheer strength and impartiality of Shantideva's compassion seem to be a subversion of the universal order. . . . Where is the justice in it?"[29] The poet's will-to-power emerges in his reformatory zeal: "*May the blind see forms, may the deaf always hear*" (10.18–19). Presenting himself as being addicted to compassion, he imaginarily descends into the hell realms not, as Dante does, to witness divine justice (or karma) at work, but to free those in hell from their woes (10.16). He thus reasserts, at the end of the his work, an imagined heroic role for his oft-despised self: he has much to do "*by the power of my skillful deeds*" (10.10), and he concludes with a prayer of well-wishing for himself, to empower future endeavors: "*As long as . . . the world abides, so long may I abide, destroying the sufferings of the world*" (10.55).

With its Pure Land vision of a place free from all pains and problems, the *Bodhicaryāvatāra*, unlike the work of recent "engaged Buddhism," remains entirely aspirational, eschewing the problems of actual people struggling with life, and laying out an inspired ideal—or what Sir Philip Sidney calls poetry's "*golden world*."[30] Despite glorious intentions and imaginary benevolent exploits, no actual deeds are portrayed, and the Shantideva poet differs temperamentally from the legendary Vimalakirti, who teaches dharma in the streets, in the schools, in the markets, in the temples, and even in the brothels.[31] The introspective Shantideva poet, by contrast, may be of little practical help to the world's ongoing efforts of assisting those in need. Yet he has provided an extensive set of excellent reasons to do so.

The Poet's Offering

In the text's concluding dedicatory verses, there is not even any mention of whether wishes will be fulfilled. His vision is a wished-for beginning for new ways of living. Once again, as so often in sacred writing, we are tested by hyperbole, by a plenitude of generosity. In religious hyperbole, to recall Stephen Webb, we are asked "to imagine more than we know, say more than we dare to believe, . . . hope more broadly than the facts will allow."[32] In disrupting the limited thinking of conventional piety, the poet opens up new horizons. The speaker's imagined acts of salvation, however subversive, are offered because all suffering needs relief. This idea may seem hyperbolic to some, but it helps locate the poem's force.

Shantideva speaks of his work of giving "*aid and benefit*" to others, and of a "*task*" that is intoxicating (8.94P, 7.62–63), but without any detail. There is, however, one activity for which the Shantideva poet might take credit: the *Bodhicaryāvatāra* itself. In the concluding chapter of merit dedication, he refers to his task as showing an entry into the Bodhisattva way (10.1). His work, in the double sense of mission and text, is his way of serving others. He writes a poem, thereby calling upon whatever latent bodhicitta we may possess, and encouraging its cultivation. Readers may vary in their devotion to compassion, or in their valorizations of it. But if they be inspired by this poet's aspiration or by Vessantara's giving, they will find ways—and those ways are manifold—to work for the benefit of others.

10

Final Emergency Reading

The Tibetan Book of the Dead

A work about death modulates readily, if eerily, into a work about literature. For death inhabits texts.

—Walter J. Ong, *Interfaces of the Word*

Death is a displaced name for a linguistic predicament.

—Paul de Man, *The Rhetoric of Romanticism*

A major religious endeavor is to prepare for death, and to encounter it. The *Tibetan Book of the Dead*, among the best known Buddhist texts in the West, works toward this end. It is a ritualized guidebook to the afterlife, or to the period between one life and another. Composed for newly dead persons, sections of it are to be read loudly into their ears. The text is a final emergency reading, identifying postmortem phases, compassionately telling the dead persons not to be afraid, and providing them with abundant prayers and formulae. It pleads that they take a courageous, concentrated attitude—recognizing all horrors as coming from their own minds—and, if possible, thereby avoiding rebirth.

The text speaks to us too, not only the newly dead, about the mystery of death. With great confidence, it gives its answer to age-old enigmas. What happens to us in the process of death, if it is a process? Is dying simply an finishing point, or is more to follow? In encountering the mystery of death, what other mysteries might there be? And how can we gird ourselves, and others, for this great event? These are worrying questions. We see others dying and are in horrified anguish for them. We are also in anguish for ourselves, when serious illness strikes, and the time of death approaches.

Examining Dying

Long before our hour arrives, we may feel something of the terrible disquiet of Leo Tolstoy's Ivan Ilych, and recent times, with global technologies of war and terror, are hardly auspicious for wise final departures. Even amidst incessant killing in our news media, the dying and dead nearest to us are relegated to hospital wards, and then primped up for funerals. Turning away if possible from unpleasant details, we take recourse in religious mythology to embody our worst fears and deepest wishes. Our curiosity to know what "really" happens, in and beyond this mythology, often remains unsatisfied.

The last few decades have thus seen a proliferation of studies about dying, mourning, death, near-death, and past lives, with the *Tibetan Book of the Dead* taking a leading place in the field. First published in English in 1927, it was culled from a Tibetan collection on the subject, then translated and retranslated into many languages. The *Bardo Thödol*, as it is entitled in Tibetan—or *Great Liberation through Hearing in the In-between State*—with its apparently esoteric rites, mysterious deities, and arcane symbolism, apparently offers a more convincing picture of the postmortem world than can be found elsewhere.

The exotic features of the text have meant that it comes to the West swaddled in explanatory paraphernalia. The earliest version, translated by Lama Kazi Dawa-Samdup, features illustrations, prefaces, forewords, a psychological commentary, an essay, and a long introduction followed by copious notes and an appendix. These extras engender a potent brew, making the book seem accessible yet intriguingly arcane. The *Bardo Thödöl*, or *The Tibetan Book of the Dead*, was thus appropriately decked out for Western consumption.[1] More specifically, the text was said to be "scientific"—an eye-catching term. The first editor, W. Y. Evans-Wentz, declared that Western scientists "seem to be approaching [a point] on the path of scientific progress, where . . . East and West appear to be destined to meet . . .".[2] Scientific investigation will confirm, in other words, the ancient mysteries.

A comparable claim would be made years later by Robert Thurman, in the introduction to his translation: whereas astronauts walk on the moon, Tibetan lamas could be called "psychonauts," since they journey across the frontiers of death into the in-between realm, passing "through the dissolution process, [their minds detached] from the gross physical body, and [using] a magic body to travel to other universes."[3] Presumably, just as astronauts send back scientific information about the moon, so psychonauts send back information about the world of death. This sounds like science fiction, but may have some basis.

A body of testimony exists regarding previous lives, and many of the experiences investigated by medical researchers in recent decades include accounts, by supposedly dead or almost-dead persons, about a benevolent white light, intense emotions, perceptions of the world left behind, and, in some instances, nightmarish scenarios.[4] The experiences, often radically transformative, are called near-death experiences, and those who have them return to everyday life.

Why "near-death," though, and not simply "death" experiences? In a post-Kantian environment many are inclined to believe that, like things-in-themselves, "death itself" is unknowable or noumenal. It is supposedly another realm, cut off from life and, as the saying goes, "dead men tell no tales." A patient's time of death is currently measured, among other ways, by flat lining on an electroencephalogram monitor.[5] But patients have been known to recuperate long after that. Possibly death, as Nietzsche cautions, is more ambiguous and more continuous with life than we usually assume: "Let us beware of saying that death is opposed to life. The living is merely a type of what is dead, and a very rare type."[6] An organic process goes on, like the growth and falling of leaves, and the terms "death" or "life" are merely convenient fictions. "It is a mistake," Zen Master Dōgen says, "to suppose that life turns into death."[7] That "mistake" is common enough, though, and given the obscurity of these matters, the best accounts of death are visionary or literary. Their value is in allowing us to imagine some defamiliarized yet archetypal scene—be it heavenly, hellish, or neither.

Advising the Dead

The *Bardo Thödol* differs from Western death stories in that much of it is addressed not to readers but, oddly enough, to the corpse. Sections of the text are to be read out by the deceased's guru or dharma friend, in a loud voice, and following instructions provided, close to the dead body.

> *In the case of a dharma brother, one should call him by name and say these words: "O child of awakened family, that which is called death has now arrived, so you should adopt this attitude: 'I have arrived at the time of death, so now . . . I will adopt only the attitude of the enlightened state of mind . . .'"* (36).[8]

The text thus read out orally goes on to teach vividly about the dangers of craving, and the misfortune of rebirth, suggesting that tantric yoga practices may be useful to the deceased, as well as to us, the not-yet dead. The physical process of dying is described as a gradual separation back into the four elements, and the mind is likely to be terrified and confused, unless trained in clarity (a point made, too, in the *Gateless Barrier*, M.35).

A work about death, Walter J. Ong has noted, often turns out to be literary. Here the text can be read as a fictional narrative, perhaps more readily than as a teaching, since one may wonder about its authority. Chögyam Trungpa allows, in the introduction to his edition of the *Bardo Thödol*, that the text may seem, to some, "like the study of a myth" (3). For traditional followers, however, its status derives from being a *gTer ma*, or hidden treasure text, secreted by a prophetic Tibetan sage—in this case, Padmasambhava—so that later generations, more fit to understand it, might uncover it in secret locations.[9] The text's power is vouchsafed, in its native context, by sacred transmission, and by yogic practices leading to the divine eye. Phases of the death illumine the mind in ways that overlap with Buddhist Vajrayana practices and, as the Dalai Lama points out, death and the in-between processes provide opportunities, for those with training, to encounter pure radiant awareness.[10]

With or without yogic practices, the text can be read as a bizarre adventure. Its genre is the instruction manual for a great journey, guided by counsel from an elder or shaman familiar with the journey, and who knows its sites and sights. With tantric rituals of prayer, mantra, and visualization, the imagination—as in literature—is brought into play. The many deities and guardians in the text are said to be only apparently existent, or hallucinatory. Turning points for possible liberation are when recognition takes place, that is, when the whole scene is perceived to be dreamlike, illusory, and fictional. The deceased, or what one might call the "*bardo person*," is urged to be mindful, and to pierce through the illusionary façade so dazzlingly described.

The text thereby calls attention to its own illusoriness, so like our passing lives themselves. It may bring to mind novels by Italo Calvino that set a scene, and then call attention to its invented status. Images of the bardo are merely "*projections*," and need to be recognized as the "*play of your mind*" (41, 51). Not only are the text and its characters illusory, but so is the deceased, dissolving from stage to stage of the death process. The bardo person is poignantly called to by name, and his or her narrative is carried on to the bitter end—namely, rebirth.

A Sad Story

The plot with such an ending is a downward progression taking place, if completed, in forty-nine days. The story begins with the dying of the main figure being read to, and ends, unless liberation transpires, with the unfortunate entry of that figure into the womb, from which a new life will spring. The bardo, or in-between time, is an interval, a turning point, a transition, or a gap between the end of one phase and the start of another. The death bardo is one among others, including those of life, meditation, dream, dharmatā, and existence.[11] Each bardo presents a time of ambiguity, a crossroads at which some major choice must be made. Like all humans, we are continually experiencing death and birth, as scenes pass away and new ones emerge to replace them. The journey of death is one that we all are making, have already made, and doubtless will make again.

The occasion of death can be prepared for, however, as in Western skull contemplations. It can also be prepared for in tantra, or the "effect vehicle," that is, a training in the effects that one is trying to achieve—becoming like, and then merging with, one's deity, thereby attaining buddhahood. The deities are empty, dreamlike and self-produced, so another tantric practice is to recognize one's dreams as dreams even while sleeping or, in preparation for death, to imagine an opening at the top of the head (the Brahma aperture) through which the essental spiritual fluids, the *bindu*, will emerge at the time of one's passing. One performs these practices in close consultation with one's guru, who induces, or greatly helps to induce, the visualizations.[12]

The Power of Recitation

Throughout the Buddhist tradition, monks have been enjoined, in the absence of family and household, to take care of one another in times of sickness and dying. The preceptor–disciple relationship in particular, as Gregory Schopen shows, was one of mutual caregiving.[13] In monastic funerals in India, monks were expected to perform a ritualized recitation from sacred texts prior to the corpse's cremation. The recitation was meant to separate the dead monk from "robe and bowl"—that is, from attachments to personal belongings. The merit made by recitation would be transferred to the deceased, and the reciter, in turn, would rightfully inherit whatever property the deceased may have left behind.[14] A version of this compassionate and beneficial tradition could be extended, as in the *Bardo Thödol*, to average yogins or lay practitioners. The oral reader recites well-known rituals, composed with instructions by Padmasambhava and the tradition, and handed down to the most recent oral reader. The recitation is spread over many days, since a comparatively lengthy period was assumed between one life and the next.

The death bardo is divided into three phases. The first phase lasts three or four days, though times are variable, and days are not usually perceived by the deceased.[15] It is called the *chikhai bardo*, in which the clear light appears, though it might not be seen, at the time of death. The second phase, unfolding over fifteen days[16] or fewer, is the *chönyid bardo*, in which various deities appear, along with differently colored seductive lights, leading into the six realms. The third phase, which may last for many days, depending on karmic conditioning, is the *sidpa bardo*, which involves closing or avoiding the womb or, if that fails, finding the best womb for rebirth. The whole sequence, as Carl G. Jung has observed, moves in a downward and disappointing series of developments.[17] The spiral is a litany of missed opportunities or failed efforts, leading to the tragically unhappy, even demeaning, outcome of rebirth.

The *Tibetan Book of the Dead* thus creates a schematic postmortem "biography" for the dead person, and it thereby invents a way to give life—in this case, continued life and the possibility of address or apostrophe—to that person. The "end" of life is really a journey of initiation, a movement toward childhood, or toward a new childhood. Not accidentally, what we are reading is itself a scene of reading: parents read stories to children, teachers read to students who traditionally are told, as the bardo person is, to "repeat after me." The postmortem process is thus pedagogical. At a time when the conventional self has dissolved into elements, the truths of *anattā* and emptiness become more immediate and experiential: the person addressed is no longer an "entity," but at best an an amorphous non-something, a locus of energies and winds. Lacking identity, the bardo person becomes infantile and is treated accordingly. Vulnerable and in need of loving care, he or she is addressed by name, as if still part of the community, even though the usual body is no more, and the name is increasingly irrelevant. This person, after all, is on the way to (re-)becoming, if unliberated, an embryo and a new-born baby.

The process of reading provides a hint of what might be going on: reading, Paul de Man says, is "the endless prosopopeia by which the dead are made to have a face and a voice which tells the allegory of their demise, and allows us to apostrophize them in our turn."[18] The guru reader of the *Bardo Thödol* seems to speak in a direct address (to someone present), yet is reading rather than talking spontaneously, and may thus also seem to be making an apostrophe (speaking indirectly, or invoking someone absent), and at times, as we will notice, a prosopopoeia (giving the deceased a voice).

Communication Problems

If the deceased journeyer is not really listening—which often seems to be the case—then the scene of oral reading is hardly reassuring. There is a question as to what kind of communication, if any, transpires. Perhaps the oral reader, despite contrary intentions, is performing a dramatic monologue, and the only beneficiaries are listeners customarily present at the scene, or we the readers. The bardo person, by contrast, having been gradually deprived of the five skandhas, is left in a confused condition, or is stunned and amazed. This person's learning disabilities seem galling, even so, since (we're told) special, compensatory capacities arise, even if muteness is always a given. The bardo person, who fails to liberate, cannot otherwise indicate whether, or how well, the guru reader and company are getting through, while they, by contrast, seem quite able to determine where he or she is "located" and what is happening—or more usually, not.

There is no single voice in the text, and any communication moves strictly in one direction, with no give and take. This situation is familiar to readers of modern literature. In T. S. Eliot's multivoiced *The Waste Land*, death-like sterility and isolation are indicated when someone asks a desperate question, but any possible response is left unspoken.

> "Do
> *You know nothing? Do you see nothing? Do you remember*
> *Nothing?"*
> *I remember*
> *Those are pearls that were his eyes.*
> *"Are you alive or not? Is there nothing in your head?"*[19]

The questions are in quotes, but the "response" (not a reply) is not. Partly cited from Shakespeare, it is unattributed to a speaker—thus coming from some detached, unlocalized source. Possibly they are thoughts of a hearer who will not or cannot speak, thus exacerbating a situation of persons who may be dead, or who, as the last question indicates, are unsure about whether they are alive or dead.

The bardo person, too, is unsure. But the *Bardo Thödol*, by assuming there is a journeying someone to hear, if not to reply, could be considered a figurative postmortem biography. Unlike *The Waste Land*, it is also an instruction manual, telling its oral guru readers how to deal with persons soon to die, or recently deceased, and periodically laying out "*the method of instruction*" (34–36). Composed in the language of yoga, it provides a description of the death process ("*when respiration is ceased, prāna is absorbed into the wisdom dhūti*"), and combines this language with invocations to tantric deities (33, 35). The term *liberation* in the title refers to any time during the bardo when the process can be cut short, with the deceased becoming a buddha (68). Just as accomplished Zen adepts will pass unhindered through the *Gateless Barrier*, here the best practitioners had been trained in the ejection or transference of consciousness, as described in another gTerma text,[20] and they are liberated soon after dying.

Difficult Cases

Our text deals with the remaining, more difficult, cases, including those who need to travel through the entire process into a new life. The *Bardo Thödol* could thus be described as an emergency troubleshooting handbook, and it is constantly alert to crises, failures, and a need to make renewed efforts.

The typical directions ("*one should say these words*") provide a text to be spoken to the dead person, as follows:

> *"O [child] of awakened family, (name), now the time has come for you to seek a path. As soon as your breath stops, what is called the basic luminosity*

> *of the first bardo . . . will appear to you. . . . Recognise then, and rest in that state . . .".* (35 m)

The "(*name*)" is a blank, as on an application form, to be filled in for whomever the text may refer. As in Shantideva's poem, compassion goes out for all and any. The "*you*" is a generic figure, and "*you*" will apply to all cases running the full gamut between one life and another. Even when imagined as more than a fill-in-the-name blank, he or she is in a state of ongoing dissolution. This person, who apparently does not or cannot follow directions, is an Everyman: flat, typical, and hypothetical. The bardo person exists entirely as an addressee, as someone being guided through a precarious adventure. The stress is on communicating to this person, who is often in terrible anguish, and who moves through a peculiar mental landscape.

The narrative, since there is no one in it, may be thought of as a dress rehearsal with a script to be fixed in mind, a training in ritual, an occasion that has taken place many times, and will take place again in some similar manner. The story capitalizes on the trope of address, and is told vividly enough so that we envisage a "real" advisor and reader addressing a "real" bardo person. We imagine these hypotheticals to be genuine—and that is just what we do in reading fiction, and imagining an unfolding plot.

The Guru Reader

The literary technique is remarkable. With quotes within the passage quoted, the translated text is multiply framed, and several persons seem to be working together. We, as the outermost readers, learn how the instructor in the story, instructed in turn by Padmasambhava and a benevolent deity, advises the oral advisor, or guru reader, about what to say or read.

The figure we are calling the guru reader is said to be psychically in communication with the dead person, knowing just what is happening and what to do when liberation in the bardo fails to occur. Comfortingly, the entire postmortem landscape, and the dead subject's usual developments, are mapped out in advance. The bardo person who is being read to—that is, the innermost, framed subject—is told what mental attitude to assume. The dead person is solemnly addressed:

> *"O child of awakened family, (name), listen. Now the pure luminosity of the dharmatā is shining before you; recognise it. . . . At this moment your state of mind is by nature pure emptiness. . . . To recognise this is all that is necessary. When you recognise this pure nature of our mind as the buddha, looking into your own mind is resting in the buddha mind.* (37 m)

The text and guru reader speak unflinchingly, and with impressive familiarity of what, to most of us, is mysterious and unknown.

The dead person is reminded of any prior tantric practice of cultivating luminosity. If there had been such cultivation, the result will be all that is available at the hour of death. Everything else must be left behind, which is why nonattachment in life was, and is, of paramount importance. Thoughts matter, as in the opening of the *Dhammapada*, and emptiness is to be recognized, as in the *Heart Sutra*.

The Sustaining Voice

The dead enact, once passed into the bardo, a one-way farewell. Grieving loved ones can be observed by the newly dead (a point also made in recent near-death testimonies), but there is no way to communicate with them: "*He can see them, but they cannot see him, and he can hear them calling but they cannot hear him calling them*" (39–40). The subject is able to look back on the world once familiar, now already being put to other uses—his or her bed taken apart, the name called out, though responses are no longer possible. Here again is the scene:

> *One should call him by name and say these words:*
>
> *"O child of awakened family, that which is called death has now arrived, so you should adopt this attitude: 'I have arrived at the time of death, so now, by means of this death, I will adopt only the attitude of the enlightened state of mind, friendliness and compassion, and attain perfect enlightenment for the sake of all sentient beings as limitless as space . . .'"*. (36 m)

Bodhicitta and the Bodhsattva Vow, so vital for Shantideva, have an imperative, salvational role here in the death realm. In a radical absence of voice, the text uses prosopopoeia, that is, the trope in which another's voice is imaginarily provided. The literary technique, again using quotes within quotes, performs a multiple framing, and an ideological reinforcement. The guru reader, following instructions, assumes the role of the bardo person by saying, almost ventriloquistically, what that person might, or should, say.

Death is thus a displaced name, as Paul de Man remarks, for a specifically linguistic predicament: we cannot normally speak to the dead, nor can we expect replies. We can only apostrophize them, and imagine, through prosopopoeia, that they have the living name, face, and voice we recall, and with which we would now re-endow them. We can even, unsatisfactorily, give them liturgical lines to think, much as the guru reader presents the bardo person with familiar prayers to recite mentally. The name "death" is displaced, since the predicament of deprivation occurs any time words need to be used, and not merely in the absence usually called death.[21] Prosopopoeia imaginarily attempts to overcome privation and to repopulate a world of absences.

In the *Bardo Thödol*, prosopopoeia works in conjunction with the trope of address, and any listeners or readers are given the sense that, since the address is being loudly and clearly spoken, "someone" must be there to receive the words. A certain sadness attends this gesture, especially if a corpse lies plainly before the guru reader, and mourners are present. For even if the bardo person is in some sense alive, as the bardo teachings presume, that person cannot respond, but remains mute. The guru reader nonetheless bravely and lovingly continues with the recited instructions.

Role of the Master

Still today the Tibetan lama or guru, the master teacher, is of inestimable importance. Sogyal Rinpoche's best-selling popularization, the *Tibetan Book of Living and Dying*, begins with a brief biographical sketch that omits mention of parents, preferring to specify only his birthplace, his tulku status, and of course his loving and beloved master.[22] This "fairytale-like opening," as Eve Kosofsky Sedgwick comments, "plunges a reader disorientingly into an unfamiliar systems of analogues and incarnations."[23] Bemused readers may or may not be reassured by recurrent deferential references to "my master," to various masters Sogyal knows who provide orientation, who are widely rumored to be experts, and who introduce would-be disciples to the bardo states.[24] More than in the Chan tradition of tough love, the master replaces parents, keeping the disciple in a perpetually dependent, childlike position. The guru reader and the benevolent guardian deities have similar duties, protecting and leading the bardo person in the right direction.

That bardo person is at an opposite remove from the speaker in Rainer Maria Rilke's first *Duino Elegy*, doubtfully wondering, "*Who, if I cried out, would hear me among the angels' orders?*"[25] Here, on the contrary, saintly helpers hope that the bardo person will hear them, and they are continually present. The bardo person is like a wayfarer with earphones of encouragement announcing whom to pray to on every occasion. The constant assumption is that this figure is terrified, and so the penetrating voice says that it's all ritually familiar, and that emergency invocations of divine assistance will surely be of help.

Not surprisingly, the ideal oral reader for a newly dead person is someone who had been his or her master. The average person may not have a guru, but if not, then a disciple of the guru, or a close dharma friend will do (36). Optimally, there should be some close connection between the oral reader and the deceased, all the more so when abilities in imaginative visualization are urgently needed. Such abilities, Stephan Beyer has found, are one reason why, in Tibetan culture, great value is placed on having a yogin present at rituals "to impose his contemplative control upon the appearances of reality."[26] In the passages cited earlier, there surely seems a control imposed, though any efficacy is unstated. The process of dying had been described as a dissolving: "*earth [dissolves into] . . . water, water into fire, fire into air, air into consciousness*" (36). Yet even when the process is being completed, the deceased is addressed by name (former name?), and an "I" is still implied.

While the voice of the guru reader makes its way into the dead person, it is also apprehended by us, the readers at a large distance in time and space who will also die one day, and have felicitously discovered, in our own ways, Padmasambhava's treasure. The text, buttressed by belief in "sudden" enlightenment, is marked by an interplay of closeness and distance, by flexibility and resourcefulness in the face of repeated failures, and by an openness to fresh opportunities.

Assisting Deities

When the first luminosity fades, "*the second luminosity will shine*" (38). A deity, the "*yidam*," somewhat like a guardian angel or tutelary spirit, is closer to the bardo person than others, and can be more intimately consulted: "*concentrate intensely on your yidam. Visualise him as an appearance without substance of its own, like the moon in water . . .*" (38). The realizing of emptiness ("without substance") implies that the yidam, close though it may be, cannot be grasped or always relied upon. As in earlier practices, the deity, like the deceased, is dissolved, and a kind of release ensues:

> *During the second bardo, his consciousness, which did not know whether he was dead or not, suddenly becomes clear; this is called the pure illusory body. If he understands the teaching at this time, the mother and son dharmatās meet, and he is no longer dominated by karma. Just as the light of the sun overcomes darkness, so the power of karma is overcome by the luminosity of the path, and liberation is attained.* (39)

This passage, even in translation, has a brilliant and uplifting clarity. The ignorance of the dead person gives way to an "illusory body," like the moon's reflection. An understanding of emptiness teachings modulates, mysteriously, into an overcoming of karma. There may be magic here, with the sudden and gracious luminosity of the sun, and one is tempted to believe that some Buddhist counterpart to grace emerges, in kinship with the gratuitous generosity of compassion.

In the story's downward spiraling, we are reminded constantly of the "*light ray hook of compassion*" (44) going out from the Buddha families, and we again meet with aspirational prayers, or visualized wish-paths:

When through intense aggression I wander in samsāra
on the luminous light-path of the mirror-like wisdom,
may the blessed Vajrasattva go before me,
his consort Buddha-Locanā behind me;
help me to cross the bardo's dangerous pathway
and bring me to the perfect buddha state. (44)

The tableau, recurring with different sets of deities coming before and after, is of a procession, like a convoy with sherpas leading and following, making its way through some mountainous Himalayan terrain. Such a landscape is likely to have been familiar to peoples of that region, and similarly, the deities invoked are culturally specific. Yet we do not need to know or believe in these gods to understand what is happening. For example, any "*intense aggression*" or "*violent anger*" results in a constantly erring search for new objects, here tempered by the advice given and by the bardo's danger, its "*fearful ambush*" (EW 110) leading in the direction of perfection. We must confront aggressions before going anywhere: "*the road of excess,*" prophesies William Blake, "*leads to the palace of wisdom.*"[27]

Elusive Liberation

In the *Bardo Thödol*, prayers might need to have unusual potencies: perhaps one is "*confused, even after saying the prayer,*" or "*afraid, . . . even after being shown in this way*" (42, 44). The plight of the bardo person is dramatized in urgent choices: "*Do not take pleasure in the soft blue light of human beings. . . . If you are attracted to it you will fall into the human realm and experience birth, old age, death and suffering . . . . Do not be attracted to it, do not yearn for it*"; instead, say the inspiration prayer given with deep devotion, and dissolving "*into rainbow light in the heart of Blessed Ratnasambhava and his consort, and become a sambhogakāya buddha*" (45). Faced with a delicious carrot (becoming a buddha) and a depressing stick (worldly suffering yet again), the preference should be obvious. But "*there are people whose good opportunities have run out,*" and they will miss a fine possibility (45–46).

With the right combination, however, of prayers and well-directed choice—which the author and guru reader are providing—liberation is inevitable: "*it is impossible not to be liberated*" (47). One is not told when liberation will happen, but the deceased subject is as yet unable to do the right thing, and remains enslaved. Each failure of recognition reinforces and recreates the world from which the bardo person has departed,[28] and rebirth becomes increasingly likely. It is not enough to tell the deceased to give up your "*unconscious tendencies [habitual propensities]*" (47; EW 114). Once an addiction develops, long periods of retraining are required, and even then, no assurances are possible. The in-between state is a special situation, to be sure, but days are passing. And the more days that pass, the graver the situation becomes: "*sentient beings . . . wander downward to the fifth day of the bardo state*" (47). Possibly the guru reader feels under pressure to produce results, is increasingly frustrated, and now, in the sixth day, comes close to reprimanding the bardo person:

> *"Even though . . . the light of each of the five families appeared until yesterday, under the influence of bad tendencies you were bewildered by them, and so you have remained here until now. . . . So now watch without distraction."* (49–50)

Crisis Control

What follows, in this emergency plight, is a huge, ritualized convocation of all five buddha families, all four wisdom figures, and an array of wrathful guardians of the gates. The bardo person has missed many chances, and now is confronted with assembly of personages who, like anxious parents, show up in force as part of a special pageant, watching and quietly rooting for the "*child of awakened family*." From the hearts of five buddhas, piercing light rays of compassion stream out, shining on the bardo person's heart (50–52).

The deceased is cautioned once again not to be tempted by the soft lights from the six impure realms—the white light of the gods, the red light of the jealous gods, the blue light of humans, the green light of the animals, the yellow light of the hungry ghosts, and the smoky light of the hell beings (52). These lights, to give a mundane parallel, are like those in a lavish mall where one is warned by a thrifty spouse not to be taken in by the window displays, or by special sales. The spouse also points to much better deals elsewhere, probably entirely outside the mall. The shopping expedition proceeds, and despite good advice, capital is squandered. Similarly, the guru reader keeps warning the deceased to stay away from those soft lights, urging that better, sharper lights be noticed. The guru reader gives advice, but is not obeyed. He says, "*listen without distraction*"; these deities are here just for you, and are "*the primordial spontaneous play of your mind*"; they are just right, "*neither small nor large, but perfectly proportioned*" (51–52). But alas, none of this seems to register!

The advisor and guru reader do hope, however, that something might be getting through. As the story continues, the situation of the bardo person becomes ever more desperate. "*There are many who are not liberated, but wander downwards*," and they are confronted by monstrously huge and nasty-looking wrathful deities (57). The deities are presented in gory detail, tearing bodies apart, eyes straining, teeth snarling, drinking blood from skulls, eating entrails, carrying human corpses. Despite the gore, liberation is all the more available ("*if there is a little recognition, liberation is easy*"). Even if the yogin is "*the lowest of the low*" and merely "*looked at . . . images drawn in pictures*," he will feel as though meeting with old friends, and "*merging inseparably with them [will] become a buddha*" (57).

The deities are named in lists, and they emerge in formalized postures, carrying symbolic objects like swords or vajras, and having many arms and the heads of wolves, foxes, vultures, etc. However gigantic and horrible they may seem, they "*emerge from within your brain*" (66), and this provides a clue to their status. They are portrayed painstakingly in their order and direction of origin, but perhaps some leeway is possible as to which deities appear to whom, depending on the bardo person.

Ways of Seeing

Although they perform actions, the figures are flatly allegorical (Mahadevi is a Great Goddess, Lobha personifies Greed, etc.). Pictorial or presentational, they perform timelessly or in slow motion, in fixed boundaries and without interacting with each other. As in a children's story, they make scary noises: the Glorious Great Buddha-Heruka, with three heads and six arms, "*laughs aloud with shouts of 'a-la-la!' and 'ha-ha' and sends out loud whistling noises of 'shoo-oo!'*" (60). Despite their huge, terrifying dimensions, they are unthreatening, and the bardo person needs to see them for what they are:

> *It is just like seeing a stuffed lion, for instance: he feels very frightened if he does not know that it is only a stuffed lion, but if someone shows him what it is, he is astonished and no longer afraid* . . . (64)

The deities are thus like toy animals, and the text had to some degree depicted them in that way. With recognition, the entire course of events can be reversed and transformed.

Apparently, a kind of awareness (of say, a "stuffed lion") gives way to a release. There are parallels here to ideology critique, or to psychoanalysis, when the patient recovers as obsessions are brought into consciousness. There may be parallels to the Buddha's recognizing—and thereby defeating—Māra. And we are not far from a related term, descriptive of the point of reversal in Greek tragedy: what Aristotle calls *anagnorisis*, also often translated as "recognition." The turning point in tragedy is when Oedipus, for example, makes a discovery about events and his relation to those events: "*recognition . . . is a change from ignorance to knowledge, . . . [and] the best form of recognition is coincident with a change of the situation.*"[29] The reversal changes everything, and in the *Bardo Thödol* it signals a cutting through appearances that is equivalent to liberation.

The text's constant counsel, conveyed through the guru reader, is that there is no need to fear: "*recognize whatever appears as the play of mind*" (65). Contrary to the subject's dread, the apparitions are empty. The play of mind, when seen through, is known, thereby becoming a saving pointer to emptiness everywhere.

> *You are really the natural form of emptiness, so there is no need to fear. The Lords of Death arise too out of your own radiant mind, they have no solid substance.* (69)

At this point, the text praises itself and commends yogic practice—that is, it addresses itself to the living, who still have some time left, however indefinite, to develop their practice.

How are they to do so? It may be difficult for ordinary people, if they lack yogic training or come from another culture, to cultivate proper attitudes toward tantric deities. The postmortem bardo world, filled with regional divinities and rituals, is constructed for a local audience (just as Dante's inferno is filled not with Chinese, but with local, mostly Italian, acquaintances). There are variations in advice on how to adapt to this situation. One commentator stresses the importance, if practical results are to be achieved, of exact visualisations of deities described in tantric texts; another allows that anyone at all may read the text to a familiar corpse, simply substituting images and deities from their own tradition.[30] As readers and as living beings, we need not decide how to proceed, and our options for practice are open. The bardo person whom we are following, by contrast, is unstoppably headed towards re-entry into life. Part Two starts with a new invocation to deities, yidams, and gurus, and the deceased is now, on the tenth day, entering the *Sidpa bardo*, or into what may be the text's most difficult section.

Back to the Womb

Like other Buddhist expositions on the subject, the *Bardo Thödol* needs to give some explanation as to how the karmically-tinged mental stream moves (pours? flies? jumps?) from one life to another, how memories of the old life fade away, and how cravings for a new life become entwined with a lovemaking couple, a fertilized ovum, and an embryo growing into birth.

The process, since it requires forgetting the old life and getting a foothold in some new life, is not well understood and not easily visualized. Even without multiple lives to contend with, Laurence Sterne, following the embryological theories of his time, dramatized the birth process with a "*little man*," a homunculus, that is escorted by fallible "*animal spirits*," whose business it was to take him hand-in-hand to his mother's womb, that is, "*the place destined for his reception.*"[31] Instead of a homunculus starting a first life, the *Bardo Thödol* will speak of the movement, between old and new lives, of a "*mental body.*" There will be no escort, though the guru reader comes close to fulfilling that role.

Before even thinking of a womb, the deceased is advised about the tricky process of avoiding a womb entirely. But if that effort fails, then the next task is to attempt entry into the best possible womb available. The task is made easier in that the mental body has greater capacities than an incarnate body:

> *"O child of awakened family, . . . you are a mental body and your mind is separated from its support, you have no material body, so now you can pass back and forth even through Mount Meru, the king of mountains, or anywhere except your mother's womb and the vajra seat [where Gautama Buddha attained enlightenment]. This is a sign that you are wandering in the bardo of becoming [sidpa bardo], so remember your guru's teaching . . ."* (73)

In everyday life, we hear that returning to the womb is greatest wish of all. Here, though, one's mother is strictly off-limits. And someone wandering around, at this late date, about to be reborn, has no right to the Buddha's seat. The bardo person, having drifted on for a long while, is endowed with supernormal powers, but can they be put to use?

Aware of a mental body, the deceased is at the same time compelled to acknowledge the lack of a physical body, and to notice that samsāric instability is intensified:

> *"O child of awakened family, blown by the moving wind of karma, your mind, without support, helplessly rides the horse of wind like a feather, swaying and swinging."* (74)

This lack of support requires a mental discipline in short supply. Since all is so airy, speeding and swaying, the great temptation (and here the story gets weird) is for the bardo person, in desperation, to try to re-enter his or her old body:

> *"Even if you enter your own corpse up to nine times, winter will have frozen it or summer made it rot, or else your relatives will have burned it or buried it in the grave or given it to the birds and wild animals, . . . so you will find nowhere to enter."* (76)

These gruesome situations are the stuff of gothic romance and horror movies. If the dead person were to get back into a body, the story might start to resemble the cult film *Night of the Living Dead.* But re-entry, however desirable, is not a realistic possibility.

The remedy instead is to recognize one's condition, to supplicate the three jewels, and to meditate upon the Great Symbol (76–77). Unless one does so fervently, one will not be able overcome karmic results. One thus will need to encounter an archetypal judgment day, presided over by the Lord of Death.

> *"Then the Lord of Death will say, 'I will look in the mirror of karma,' and when he looks in the mirror, all your sins and virtues will suddenly appear in it clearly and distinctly, so although you have lied, it is no use."* (77)

The Lord of Death uses a mirror, and counts pebbles standing for the objectivity of karmic law. The bardo person is assumed to have lied, reinforcing a sense of fallibility and a need for warning. With the mirror, a fuller and more accurate vision is encouraged, for the Lord of Death will not be deceived. Yet the entire scene of guilt will itself pass away: punishment, though painful, is empty (77).

Trying Again

The day of judgment seems unpropitious for liberation, and the guru reader and bardo person are both told, "*it is very important to make another effort.*" The deceased is given several tips: avoid entrance into the womb by closing the womb door, or by stopping the person trying to enter. The womb thus becomes a taboo place, and indeed the bardo persons's wish to "get between" lovers already runs into Oedipal complexities. A future male feels "*violent aggression toward the father, and jealousy and desire for the mother*"; and vice versa if the bardo person is a future she. Once entered into the sexually-charged womb, "*you will experience self-existing bliss,*" and a family romance is under way earlier than anyone might have suspected (84). The womb might not even be human, and in that case, the result will be peculiar and degrading: one may be born—horrible surprise—as a dog, or a pig, or even as an ant or worm, and "*there is no returning here, [but] . . . all kinds of suffering from . . . stupidity and ignorance*" (84).

Desperate measures are clearly called for, along with special prayers to close the womb (82–83). The scene is literary, in the sense of being starkly defamiliarized. Common elements of that scene are usually known separately—lovemaking, the womb, a door to be closed, a forbidden act, an emergency situation—but rarely are they brought together. We often think of mothers but not often, even symbolically, of the physiology of wombs, nor of wombs having doors, nor of a "person" wanting entrance there, nor of a warning against entry into that particular place.

We are witnessing a highly charged erotic scene and may wish to become involved. Despite (or because of) being warned away, we may have strong cravings, and here the combination of elements is infatuating! The process of rebirth is dark, sordid, humiliating—yet dangerously tempting. It is to be prevented if at all possible: "*there is nothing more powerful or terrifying*" than to be circling around in the six realms, constantly going through murky, lustful wombs (84). The guru reader must become resigned, even so, to the increasingly evident fact that the bardo person, alas, will be driven by karma toward a new birth. A longer account than usual is given to elaborate on how "*it is impossible not to be liberated*"

(86). This much-repeated declaration is not easily explained, since in the story, despite that fine claim, the bardo person fails to become liberated.

Wombs on Display

This being so, the bardo person's next mission is to choose the best of wombs: "*examine where you are going to be born, and choose the continent*" (87). The bardo person is given a preview of each place, much as a real estate client might look at photographs of properties on sale. One potential place has "*luxurious, beautiful dwellings*" and is recommended. Others boast of such amenities as "*a lake adorned with cattle*" or "*beautiful groves, or what seem to be wheels of fire,*" but they are to be resisted, since "*the dharma does not flourish there*" (88). From these wombs with a view, the six realms are identified. Most of them are unattractive: the hungry ghost realm, for example, has "*tree stumps and black shapes sticking up,*" and the bardo person would go toward them only when pursued "*by the avengers of karma,*" which W. Y. Evans-Wentz compares to the Furies in Aeschylus (88; EW 89). At this point, the yidam prayers are that the avengers be escaped from and a wise choice of wombs be made.

The bardo person's plight is oddly like that of the future Buddha in the *Jātaka-nidāna*, when he looks down from Tushita upon the samsāric world, deciding where and when to take birth. The deities inform him that "*the moment has come for your Buddhahood, Sir,*" much as the bardo person is informed of moments having arrived for his death and rebirth. The future Buddha is advised that, in a time of long life spans, birth in unpropitious, and he sees that "*in three of the continents*" visible in great detail, Buddhas are not born (J 64–65); he thus makes a wise choice of parents and birthplace. Although the bardo person is not similarly able to choose his parents, and his landscape views are of the six realms, the parallel may bring out the Buddha-nature residing in all beings, making the act of rebirth seem less terrible.

The guru's desperate plea, now very much an emergency reading, is to avoid rebirth in any way possible. Since liberation, as usual for the bardo person, is not possible, then please have some discrimination: "*Do not go into whatever womb-entrance appears*" (90). If one must be born, one would best do so for the benefit of others. And so the last wishful prayer is to be born as a "*universal emperor for the good of all sentient beings . . . [or] in a family of pure lineage in dharma . . .*" (91). But even the best rebirth, into a dharma family or as a bodhisattvic emperor, is assumed to be second to liberation.

Indeed, the *Bardo Thödol* increasingly subordinates the deceased's plight to the ideal of liberation, and to its negatively described opposite, rebirth. The text ideologically recommends itself, urging that it be recited continuously and memorized: "*it is a profound instruction which liberates just by being seen and heard and read.*" There is thus a certain automaticity in the liberation process, and mechanical metaphors are offered—a pipe put into a broken water channel, a catapault, a huge tree trunk carried away by water, a horse with a bridle—all demonstrating smooth, purposeful progress (93–94).

The "profound instruction" fails to have been apprehended by the bardo person, despite lengthy reading and listening. That undistinguished person provides a paradigm, however, enabling readers to see a full unfolding of the bardo process, and enabling the advisor and guru reader to exhibit a continuously ongoing compassion. Toward the end, compassion expands outward: hypothetical voices and their hypothetical addressee subtly give way to living addressees, as well as to some author (who set up, or recalled, the typical situation) speaking now with more directness, it seems, to us. It is in this light that we may regard the recurrent assertions that this text, if viewed correctly, "*cannot fail*," and "*will certainly liberate*" (47, 86, 93). Such promises of efficacity, like Shantideva's concluding wishes, are skillful acts of kind encouragement.

Counterpart Visions

Does the *Bardo Thödöl* answer the old, fearfully troubling questions about what's in store with death and about how to prepare for it? Perhaps so, but the text is not for everyone. Stephen Levine cites the case of a dying person for whom it would be culturally alien, and to whom it should not be read; but he finds it useful, rewritten or reconceived, as a "scenario for investigation."[32] Much depends on the quality of our imagining, living, and practice. These elements variably nourish supreme fictions, at best providing guidance through troubled times, and a satisfying worldview. We are never without such fictions, though possibly believing otherwise. If we so decide, the Tibetan text may be just another story, but it also may work its way into our imaginations and eventually merge with other envisionings.

What might such other envisionings be? One counterpart to the *Bardo Thödol* might be found in the concluding myth in Plato's *Republic* where Er was killed in battle, but his corpse, like those of certain Tibetan saints, did not decay. Er was presumed dead, but on the twelfth day, "*already laid on the funeral pyre, he revived and, having done so, told about what he had seen in the world beyond.*"[33] Much as in the *Bardo Thödol*, a number of deities are observed in their proper places. Classical Greek heroes are shown selecting lives and, in a close equivalent to Buddhist karma, "*for the most part, their choice depended upon the character of their former life.*"[34]

Even closer perhaps to the Tibetan text is Dante's *Inferno*, whose famous opening lines describe a gap, a bardo, an intermission:

In midst of the pathway of our life
I found myself in a dark forest,
For the right way had been lost. (1.3)[35]

Dante the pilgrim (as distinguished from Dante the poet, who fictionally recalls and records) is not yet dead or disintegrating. But his experience is a deathlike crisis and his ignorance is a moral loss or an obscuration of the right way.

Lost in murkiness, the pilgrim sees a dawning (1.37–40), but there is no easy exit from this hell he is required to pass through. The way is blocked by three beasts, allegorizing his impurities—a leopard ("*with a spotted hide*"), a lion ("*ravenous with hunger*"), and a she-wolf (with "*craving in her leanness*"). They force him back "*to where the sun is speechless*," as if (like the bardo person) he has somehow not entirely or clearly seen the light, and has missed his chance (1.32–35, 60). Fortunately, he is presented with a guide—his beloved predecessor poet, Virgil, who informs Dante what is happening, urging him not to be afraid and, at times, gently reprimanding him. The repeated motif is to focus the mind, to proceed calmly, and to be undistracted (1.76–81, 2.34–51,121–32).

Pilgrims as Messengers

While the *Bardo Thödol* offers advice (albeit reluctantly) about where to take rebirth, Dante's text directs the pilgrim toward the honor of dwelling, once again, among the living. One of the shades in hell asks if Dante can recognize him, and if so, on returning, to please send greetings to friends in the sweet world of the living: *il dolce mondo* (6.88). The pilgrim thereafter becomes a messenger between the dead and the living, bringing news of the dead to the living, though at times he seems to be neither one nor the other:

> *. . . I did not die and was not alive;*
> *Think for yourself, if you have any wit,*
> *What I became, deprived of both life and death.* (34.25–27)

Like the bardo person, he does not feel part of either realm. But all along the encouraging assumption is that, chastened and purified, he will one day be able to re-enter the sweet, lovely, sunlit world of earthly life.

The bardo person is in a gray landscape, buffeted about by the winds of karma (74–75), while the pilgrim reaches "*a place where every light is muted, which bellows like the sea beneath a tempest,*" and he dies several times over: "*I fainted as if I had met my death. / And then I fell as a dead body falls*" (5.28, 141–42). To emerge from hell may be more difficult, who knows, than to enter into a womb, but clinging to Lucifer-Satan's body and struggling, Dante the pilgrim ultimately emerges into life's "*bright world*" (33.134).

Although rebirth is viewed negatively in the *Bardo Thödol*, the living and dead are both advised to strive, as Dante does, for renewal in a world propitious for spiritual practice. Dante the pilgrim and the bardo person, having journeyed, offer us messages. We may believe them, or suspend belief, or take some middle way in between. But some day, soon enough, the hour of our own death will arrive, and those messages may resonate.

Epilogue

Images in the Reader

. . . She was the maker of the song she sang.

—Wallace Stevens, *The Idea of Order at Key West*

To read Buddhst sacred texts as literature, that is, from a poetic and rhetorical perspective, is to perceive them in promising and fruitful ways. Literary images haunt and persuade; they are the stuff of imagining, of dreams, of wishes, of terrors; they are sparks to creativity and vision, and make up our ongoing panoramas at the time of death. The images cited in earlier chapters supersede and give flavor to Buddhist discourses, remaining long after argumentative subtleties have faded away.

We may assent to suffering's truth stated in formulae, but readers—certainly this reader—can never forget the hyperbolic images, and a voice speaking of "*the flood of tears which, weeping and wailing, you have shed upon this long way—hurrying and hastening through the round of rebirths, . . . [more than] the waters of the four oceans.*" And there are others: the man heedless of karma "*who goes along the south bank of the Ganges killing and slaughtering*"; Gautama in his "*remote jungle-thicket resting places,*" where "*a wild animal would come up . . . , or a peacock would knock off a branch.*" And then comes the night in which "*darkness was banished, and light arose,*" and later the wheel of dharma starts rolling that "*cannot be stopped by any recluse or brahmin or god or Māra or Brahma or anyone in the world.*"

In the *Dhammapada* we read with joy that "*the scent of the virtuous goes against the wind,*" and are elated when geese make an upward flight, "*on the path of the sun.*" We are sobered by "*seeing these white bones, which are scattered like gourds in autumn,*" or by the broken roofbeams of the house we call our own, and indeed, ourselves. We are moved by Avalokita in the *Heart Sutra* looking down to see that there are "*no eyes, no ears, no nose, no tongue, no body, no mind,*" or by the Zen stories of a cliffhanging wild strawberry or of the Buddha handing a flower to his special disciple, only to be called a hawker of dog meat.

And how could anyone forget Maddī, searching frantically for her missing children, while her Great Being of a generous husband sits by and says nothing? We also keep in mind Shantideva, generous as well, alarmed that his life is "*slipping by, slipping by*" yet eager, for the same reason, to be "*an isle for those who yearn for landfall, / And a lamp for those who long for light.*" Last but not at all least, readers will long remember someone (like ourselves one day) who is compassionately called to urgent alertness because "*now the time of death has arrived,*" and "*the pure luminosity of the dharmatā is shining,*" beckoning toward a journey with protecting divinites going before and following behind, and a friend's voice warning earnestly against the horrors of rebirth.

In all such hyperboles and parables, a handful of images is worth more than a truckload of arguments, helpful though each may be to the other. Images are invaluable, then, so it matters what we do with them. In Stevens's *The Idea of Order at Key West*, a woman walks along the shore, singing, and the ocean's heaving noise cannot be ignored, but it is only the background to human doings: the singing. Does she offer an image of purposeful behavior, of fantasy, or of both? We readers have a role in responding to such a question, and it is an active and productive one, if we so choose.

We read literature to escape, to change the scene, to enter other worlds—but often without wanting to escape too far away. Judging from the best-seller lists, people love tales of skulduggery, romantic intrigue, detection and eventual justice, but always with a plenitude of facts, of fascinating facts: who did what underhanded deed, in which exotic capital, with what high-tech means? Nor do most readers want too much serious didacticism: George Orwell's *1984* or James Joyce's *Ulysses* are, for many, too suffocatingly like the inescapable worlds they daily inhabit. The combination of qualities in recent literary works, as in Buddhist texts, answers to our mixed motives in reading them: high adventure, spiritual inspiration, intellectual curiosity, and practical instruction. These motives are all intertwined.

The intertwining allows us to read Buddhist images slightly eccentrically—as literature. Wishing for escape, we still are greedy for facts, for knowing "the way things are," for truths noble or otherwise, for figuring out what to do and how to live. Literary readers—respectful yet undominated by issues of philology, therapy, or even the dharma itself—may notice sidelights not usually stressed: the Buddha's boasting, Zen heteroglossia, Shantideva's disdain for pesky companions, the enframing of voices in the *Book of the Dead*. As literary readers, we refrain from claiming, except ironically, that we see the texts "as they really are." But careful reading allows us witness how images work, in revisionings of Buddhist ways, or partings of ways: the curiously convenient deaths of the Buddha's teachers; lurking floral dangers and renamings in the *Dhammapada*; cancellations and magical escapes in the *Heart Sutra*; reinventions and restructurings in Zen, in Shantideva, in the *Book of the Dead*. The revisions open into new ideological directions—reversals, gaps, sublime bodhicitta, koan masters, mortuary compassion. All of these changes make themselves felt in special imaginative phrasings and re-phrasings.

Circumspectly, we need to take account of the Buddha's disapproval of the arts as temptation and self-deception: poetry is much less valuable than the teachings; a theatrical magical show set up in public deceives us; an intricate painting is like the misleading intricacies of our mind (SN 2.20.27; 22.95.2; 100.8). The Buddha's and his followers' discourses are filled, even so, with a plenitude of images and tales. She of Stevens's poem is the exuberant maker of the song she sings, while Buddhist nuns of the *Therīgāthā* sing songs that, in their modest rightness, show lyricism as another side to familiar formulae. Singers with very few songs, however, or a single way of singing, may become monotonous. Stories of ourselves, in particular, may grow stale, and we need to stay open to new, and other, stories. To what extent is this possible? Literary theorists speak of "ideal readers," but actual readers put literary elements together ways that range from the comfortingly ordinary to the surprisingly apt. How people read is as different as how they walk, dance, or sing.

Fortunately, there is a common space for differing styles of reading. The archetypal heroic career is seminal enough to find fertile soil in the most diverse cultural climates. Literature's central axis, to invoke Northrop Frye once again, has moved between "mythic" and "ironic" (or "naturalistic") levels. Over the ages, and with variations between cultures, the axis has tended to be displaced downward through tragedy, romance, and comedy. Similar images, heroes, or linguistic figures can be read on multiple levels, with varying degrees of "making strange." The earliest and most recent Buddhist texts reach beyond their contexts to be heard by readers in differing, idiosyncratic situations.

Some readers of Buddhist scriptures, like earlier hearers, will be struck by images, and prompted to respond wholeheartedly, in unreserved ways. They are able to answer to the texts' hyperboles, myths, and sublimity, its great events and deeds, its epic battles. Other readers, who have been duly respected here, may have misgivings about more expansive elements in the texts: supernormal powers and feats, divine eyes, nirvana. Factors promoting these doubts are, as remarked, ideology critique, a reductive psychology of motive, "realistic" or scientific queries about what's possible, a sense of outdatedness in worldview. Readers may at times be of either kind, but what remains for both is imaginatively to recreate other visions, other worlds.

Notes

1. Fictions of Reading: Westerners and Buddhist Texts

1. Bernard Faure, *Double Exposure: Cutting Across Buddhist and Western Discourses*, trans. Janet Lloyd (Stanford: Stanford University Press, 2004), 6; Roger-Pol Droit, *The Cult of Nothingness: The Philosophers and the Buddha*, trans. David Streight and Pamela Vohnson (Chapel Hill: University of North Carolina Press, 2003), 66.

2. G. W. F. Hegel, *Vorlesungen über die Philosophie der Religion*, I (Frankfurt am Main: Suhrkamp, 1969), 377.

3. *On the Genealogy of Morals*, trans. Walter Kaufmann and R. J. Hollingdale (New York: Random House, 1969), 32; *Beyond Good and Evil*, trans. Walter Kaufmann (New York: Random House, 1966), 116.

4. *The Connected Discourses of the Buddha: A New Translation of the Samyutta Nikāya* (Boston: Wisdom, 2000), trans. Bhikkhu Bodhi; abbreviated SN, with references by sutta number, section, and (when given) subsection. Habits of carelessness still continue. In the Buddhist magazine *Shambhala Sun*, a popular Western teacher cites a well-known canonical passage in which the Buddha speaks. The teacher adds words of his own to the passage, so that they seem to come from the Buddha. In a subsequent issue, an unhappy reader writes in, urging the editors to require that contributors quote responsibly (*Shambhala Sun* 15.6 [2007]: 41, and 16.1 [2007]: 15).

5. See, for example, Richard Hayes, *Land of No Buddha: Reflections of a Sceptical Buddhist* (Birmingham: Windhorse, 1998); Harvey Aronson, *Buddhist Practice on Western Ground* (Boston: Shambhala, 2004).

6. Hans-Georg Gadamer, *Philosophical Hermeneutics* (Berkeley: University of California Press, 1976), xxv.

7. See Edward Said, *Orientalism* (New York: Vintage, 1979); Charles Hallisey, "Roads Taken and Not Taken in the Study of Theravada Buddhism," in Donald S. Lopez, Jr., ed., *Curators of the Buddha: The Study of Buddhism under Colonialism* (Chicago: University of Chicago Press, 1995), 31–61.

8. Cited by Hallisey in Lopez, *Curators of the Buddha*, 56.

9. M. M. Bakhtin, *Speech Genres and Other Late Essays*, trans. Vern W. McGee, eds. Caryl Emerson and Michael Holquist (Austin: University of Texas Press, 1986), 7 (Bakhtin's emphasis).

10. Northrop Frye, *The Secular Scripture: A Study of the Structure of Romance* (Cambridge: Harvard University Press, 1976), 16–32.

11. Frye, *The Secular Scripture*, 16.

12. Frye, *The Secular Scripture*, 30.

13. Wallace Stevens, *The Necessary Angel*, in *Collected Poetry and Prose* (New York: Library of America, 1996), 663.

14. *The Study of Poetry*, in Lionel Trilling, ed., *The Portable Matthew Arnold* (New York: Viking, 1949), 300.

15. Slavoj Žižek, *The Puppet and the Dwarf: The Perverse Core of Christianity* (Cambridge: MIT Press, 2003), 7.

16. Wolfgang Iser, *The Implied Reader* (Baltimore: Johns Hopkins University Press, 1974), 279.

17. Iser, 290.

18. Norman N. Holland, "Unity Identity Text Self," in Jane P. Tompkins, ed., *Reader-Response Criticism: From Formalism to Post-Structuralism* (Baltimore: Johns Hopkins University Press, 1980), 121, 123–25.

19. *The New Yorker* LXXX (34): 8 Nov. 2004.

20. Samuel T. Coleridge, *Biographia Literaria*, ed. G. Watson (London: Dent, 1975), chap. 14, 168–69.

21. See Stephen Batchelor, *Buddhism Without Beliefs: A Contemporary Guide to Awakening* (London: Bloomsbury, 1997).

22. The story can be found in *Poems of Early Buddhist Nuns (Therīgāthā)*, trans. C. A. F. Rhys Davids and K. R. Norman (1909; Oxford: Pali Text Society, 1997), 88–91, 156 (abbreviated T); also in E. A. Burtt, ed., *The Teachings of the Compassionate Buddha* (New York: New American Library, 1955), 43–46.

23. Bhikkhu Ñanamoli and Bhikkhu Bodhi, trans., *The Middle Length Discourses of the Buddha: A New Translation of the Majjhima Nikāya* (Boston: Wisdom, 1995); abbreviated MN; references are by sutta number and section.

24. See, for example, *The Literary Guide to the Bible*, eds. Robert Alter and Frank Kermode (Cambridge: Harvard University Press, 1987); Northrop Frye, *The Great Code: The Bible and Literature* (New York: Harcourt, 1983); Stephen D. Moore, *Literary Criticism and the Gospels: The Theoretical Challenge* (New Haven: Yale University Press, 1989).

25. Jeff Humphries, *Reading Emptiness: Buddhism and Literature* (Albany: State University of New York Press, 1999), xxi.

26. Humphries, xxi.

27. Joseph Campbell, ed., *The Portable Jung* (New York: Viking, 1971), 67.

28. Northrop Frye, *The Anatomy of Criticism* (Princeton: Princeton University Press, 1957), 107.

29. Joseph Campbell, *The Hero with a Thousand Faces* (Princeton: Princeton University Press, 1949), 30.

30. Joseph Campbell, *The Masks of God: Oriental Mythology* (London: Souvenir, 1962), 252–55.

31. Frye, *Anatomy of Criticism*, 187.

32. Frye, *Anatomy of Criticism*, 187.

33. Heinrich Zimmer, *Myths and Symbols in Indian Art and Civilization* (Princeton: Princeton University Press, 1946), 64.

34. Maurice Walshe, trans., *Thus Have I Heard* (Boston: Wisdom, 1987). This translation of *The Long Discourses of the Buddha*, the *Digha Nikāya*, is abbreviated DN; references are by sutta and verse.

35. Victor Shklovsky, "Art as Technique," in K. M. Newton, ed., *Twentieth-Century Literary Theory: A Reader* (New York: St. Martin's Press, 1988), 24.

36. See *Readings in Classical Rhetoric*, eds. Thomas W. Benson and Michael H. Prosser (Bloomington: Indiana University Press, 1969); Jacqueline de Romilly, *Magic and Rhetoric in Ancient Greece* (Cambridge: Harvard University Press, 1975).

37. For example, Paul de Man, *Allegories of Reading: Figural Language in Rousseau, Nietzsche, Rilke, and Proust* (New Haven: Yale University Press, 1979), and *The Rhetoric of Romanticism* (New York: Columbia University Press, 1984); Gérard Genette, *Figures of Literary Discourse*, trans. Alan Sheridan (New York: Columbia University Press, 1982); Richard Lanham, *The Motives of Eloquence: Literary Rhetoric in the Renaissance* (New Haven: Yale University Press, 1976); Barbara Johnson, *The Critical Difference: Essays in the Contemporary Rhetoric of Reading* (Baltimore: Johns Hopkins University Press, 1980); Ralph Flores, *The Rhetoric of Doubtful Authority: Deconstructive Readings of Self-Questioning Narratives, St. Augustine to Faulkner* (Ithaca: Cornell University Press, 1984); Cynthia Chase, *Decomposing Figures: Rhetorical Readings in the Romantic Tradition* (Baltimore: Johns Hopkins University Press, 1986). For a critical assessment of rhetorical criticism, see John Guillory, *Cultural Capital: The Problem of Literary Canon Formation* (Chicago: University of Chicago Press, 1993), 176–265; on the work of de Man, see Rodolphe Gasché, *The Wild Card of Reading: On Paul de Man* (Cambridge: Harvard University Press, 1998).

38. de Man, *Allegories of Reading*, 10, 15.

39. See Trevor Ling, *The Buddha: Buddhist Civilization in India and Ceylon* (Harmondsworth: Penguin, 1976), 72–75; Richard F. Gombrich, *Theravāda Buddhism* (London: Routledge, 1988), 58–59.

40. Gombrich, *Theravāda Buddhism*, 80.

41. Terry Eagleton, *Criticism and Ideology: A Study in Marxist Literary Theory* (London: Verso, 1978), 72, 76.

42. See A. K. Warder, *Indian Kāvya Literature*, vol. 1 (Dehli: Motilal Banarsidass, 1972), 169.

43. Stephen Webb, *Blessed Excess: Religion and the Hyperbolic Imagination* (Albany: State University of New York Press, 1993), xiii.

44. Henry Clarke Warren, ed., trans., *Buddhism in Translation* (Delhi: Motilal, 1986). See also the translation in Bhikkhu Bodhi, SN.

45. John Schroeder, *Skillful Means: The Heart of Buddhist Compassion* (Honolulu: University of Hawaii Press, 2001), 10, 36.

46. *The Itivuttaka: The Buddha's Sayings*, trans. John D. Ireland (Kandy: Buddhist Publication Society, 1991); abbreviated It; references by section. See also Rune E. A. Johansson, *The Psychology of Nirvana* (Garden City: Anchor, 1970).

47. See Guy Welbon, *The Buddhist Nirvana and Its Western Interpreters* (Chicago: University of Chicago Press, 1967); Steven Collins, *Nirvana and Other Buddhist Felicities* (Cambridge: Cambridge University Press, 1998); Robert E. Buswell Jr. and Robert M. Gimello, eds., *Paths to Liberation: The Mārga and Its Transformations in Buddhist Thought* (Honolulu: University of Hawaii Press, 1992), 11.

48. Frye, *Anatomy of Criticism*, 33–34.

49. *Anatomy of Criticism*, 33.

50. *Anatomy of Criticism*, 39, 170.

51. T. W. Rhys Davids, *Buddhist India* (1903; Dehli: Motilal, 1993), 180–82.

52. Frye, *Anatomy of Criticism*, 318.

53. *Anatomy of Criticism*, 319.

54. *Anatomy of Criticism*, 193.

55. *Anatomy of Criticism*, 193.

2. A Prince Transformed: The *Nikāyas*, the *Nidānakathā*, and Aśvaghoṣa's *Acts of the Buddha*

1. See Malcolm D. Eckel, *To See the Buddha: A Philosopher's Quest for the Meaning of Emptiness* (Princeton: Princeton University Press, 1992), 53.

2. See J. W. de Jong on the work of Emile Sénart and Hermann Oldenberg, in *A Brief History of Buddhist Studies in Europe and America* (Dehli: Sri Satguru, 1987), 23–31.

3. The myth is paraphrased in Hermann Oldenberg, *Buddha: His Life, His Doctrine, His Order* (Dehli: Motilal, 1997), 72. See also Edward J. Thomas, *The Life of the Buddha as Legend and History* (1960; Dehli: Motilal, 1997), 21, 46.

4. Étienne Lamotte, *History of Buddhism from the Origins to the Śaka Era*, trans. Sara Webb-Boin (Louvain: Peeters, 1988), 15–23; 648–62. And see Oldenberg, 108 ("the historical critic is unable to return a verdict"); Rupert Gethin, *The Foundations of Buddhism* (Oxford : Oxford University Press, 1988), 15 ("the historian can make no judgment" on the awakening experience).

5. Paul Ricoeur, *Freud and Philosophy*, trans. D. Savage (New Haven: Yale University Press, 1970), 27, cited in Frederic Jameson, *The Political Unconscious* (Ithaca: Cornell University Press, 1981), 284.

6. A. Foucher, *La Vie du Bouddha* (Paris: J. Maisonneuve, 1993), 72.

7. Phra Khantipalo, ed., *The Splendour of Enlightenment: A Life of the Buddha* (Bangkok: Mahamut Rajavidyalaya, 1990), vol. 1, 1.

8. T. W. Rhys Davids, *The History and Literature of Buddhism* (1896; New Dehli, Munshiram Manoharlal, 1999), 46.

9. Foucher, 67–68.

10. Translations of the *Nidānakathā* used here are in Warren, *Buddhism in Translations*, 1–110, and *The Story of Gotama Buddha (Jātaka-nidāna)*, trans. N. A. Jayawickrama (Oxford: Pali Text Society, 2002); abbreviated W and J respectively.

11. Jonathan Culler, *The Pursuit of Signs: Semiotics, Literature, Deconstruction* (London: Routledge, 1981), 36–41, 51–87.

12. Jacques Derrida, *Of Grammatology*, trans. Gayatri Chakravorty Spivak (Baltimore: Johns Hopkins University Press, 1974): "To name, to give names, . . . was the originary violence of language which consists in inscribing within a difference, in classifying. . . . A second violence is reparatory, protective, . . . prescribing the effacement and obliteration of the so-called proper name" (112).

13. Derrida, *Of Grammatology*, 166.

14. Paul Williams, *Buddhist Thought: A Complete Introduction to the Buddhist Tradition* (London: Routledge, 2000), 17.

15. *Aśvaghoṣa's Buddhacarita, or Acts of the Buddha*, ed., trans. E. H. Johnston (Dehli: Motilal, 1936). References are by canto and verse.

16. Here in the translation in Khantipalo, vol. 1, 102.

17. H. W. Schumann, *The Historical Buddha* (London: Arkana, 1989), 99–100.

18. Oldenberg, 98; Julius Evola, *The Doctrine of Awakening: The Attainment of Self-Mastery According to the Earliest Buddhist Texts*, trans. H. E. Musson (1943; Rochester: Inner Traditions, 1995), 15–16.

19. Here in the translation by John D. Ireland, *Samyutta Nikāya: An Anthology* (Kandy: Buddhist Publication Society, 1967), 7.

20. See Sigmund Freud, *Three Essays on the Theory of Sexuality*, trans. James Strachey (New York: Basic Books, 1962), 47–49, 88–91; Jacques Lacan, *Ecrits*, trans. Bruce Fink, et al. (New York: Norton, 2002), 31–106; Mikkel Borch-Jacobsen, *Lacan: The Absolute Master*, trans. Douglas Brick (Stanford: Stanford University Press, 1991) 200–204. The Prince, in leaving home, may be driven by fetishism. As the Lacanian Slavoj Žižek explains, the fetish, a substitute "for the lacking (maternal) phallus [understood as an imaginary or symbolic object], turns into a harbinger of this very lack"; and the fetish or phobic object "articulates the fear of castration" (*The Plague of Fantasies* [London: Verso, 1997], 104; abbreviated PF). In Buddhist texts, images of renunciation as feared, and thus symbolized, castration (for example, a cut-off palm tree stump) appear obsessively. Also relevant are studies on the Buddha's attitude toward women, and on women in Buddhism: see for example, I. B. Horner, *Women in Early Buddhist Literature* (Kandy: Buddhist Publication Society, 1961); Rita M. Gross, *Buddhism After Patriarchy:*

A Feminist History, Analysis and Reconstruction of Buddhism (Albany: State University of New York Press, 1993).

21. Schumann, 195.

22. Sigmund Freud, "Beyond the Pleasure Principle," *The Standard Edition*, trans. James Strachey, vol. 18 (London: Vintage, 2001), 36–39, 54.

23. See, for example, Ernest Jones, "The Oedipus Complex as an Explanation of Hamlet's Mystery: A Study of Motive," *American Journal of Psychology* 21.1 (1910): 72–110; also Jacques Lacan, *Four Fundamental Concepts of Psychoanalysis*, trans. Alan Sheridan (New York: Norton, 1978), 34–35; Julia R. Lupton and Kenneth Lupton, *After Oedipus: Shakespeare in Psychoanalysis* (Ithaca: Cornell University Press, 1993), 60–118.

24. *Hamlet* 1.2.146. Citations from this and other plays to be mentioned are from *The Complete Works of Shakespeare*, ed. Hardin Craig (Chicago: Scott, 1961).

25. Buddhaghosa, *Path of Purification*, 18.26, trans. Ñanamoli (Kandy, Buddhist Publication Society, 1991), 612.

26. Steven Collins, *Selfless Persons: Imagery and Thought in Theravāda Buddhism* (Cambridge: Cambridge University Press, 1982), 171.

27. Georges Bataille, cited in Jacques Derrida, *Writing and Difference*, trans. Alan Bass (Chicago: University of Chicago Press, 1978), 251–77.

28. References, by original chapter and section, are in Nyanaponika Thera and Bikkhu Bodhi, trans., *Numerical Discourses of the Buddha: An Anthology of Suttas from the Anguttara Nikāya* (Lanham: AltaMira, 1999); abbreviated AN.

29. Trevor Ling, *The Buddha: Buddhist Civilization in India and Ceylon* (Harmondsworth: Penguin, 1976), 113–16, 151–79. For more on selflessness and community, see William Pietz, "Persons," in Donald S. Lopez, Jr., ed., *Critical Terms in the Study of Buddhism* (Chicago: University of Chicago Press, 2005), 188–210.

30. Here in the more succinct translation in Nyanamoli, trans., *A Treasury of the Buddha's Words from the Majjhima Nikāya* (Bangkok: Mahamut Rajavidyalaya, n.d.), vol. 3, 200; abbreviated N.

31. Frye, *The Secular Scripture*, 50.

32. Derrida, "Signature Event Context," trans. Samuel Weber and Jeffrey Mehlman, in *Limited Inc* (Evanston: Northwestern University Press, 1988), 21 (Derrida's emphases).

33. Frye, *Anatomy of Criticism*, 43.

3. The Buddha Awakening: The *Nikāyas*

1. René Girard, *Violence and the Sacred*, trans. Patrick Gregory (Baltimore: Johns Hopkins University Press, 1972), 146.

2. Girard, *Violence and the Sacred*, 13, 96.

3. See Ling, 67; Gombrich, *Theravāda Buddhism*, 68.

4. Aśvaghoṣa, *Buddhacarita* 6.15, translation cited in Khantipalo, vol. 1, 123.

5. John Strong, *The Buddha: A Short Biography* (Oxford: OneWorld, 2001), 51.

6. René Girard, *Things Hidden since the Foundation of the World* (Stanford: Stanford University Press, 1987), 26.

7. Foucher, 129.

8. *Vinaya* 1.8, *Mahāvastu* 3.326, cited in Khantipalo, vol. 1, 142, 195.

9. Jacques Derrida, *Without Alibi*, trans. Peggy Kamuf (Stanford: Stanford University Press, 2002), 93 (Derrida's emphasis).

10. Girard, *Violence and the Sacred*, 310.

11. Andrew J. McKenna, *Violence and Difference: Girard, Derrida, and Deconstruction* (Urbana: University of Illinois Press, 1992), 33.

12. Cited in *The Girard Reader*, ed. James G. Williams (New York: Crossroad, 2002), 183. On murder as the founding event of religions and cultures, see René Girard, *I See Satan Fall Like Lightning*, trans. James G. Williams (Maryknoll: Orbis, 2001), 82–94.

13. Trevor Ling, *Buddhism and the Mythology of Evil* (Oxford: OneWorld, 1997), 59; also A. Foucher, *La vie du Bouddha*, 152–53; Stephen Batchelor, *Living with the Devil: A Meditation on Good and Evil* (New York: Riverhead, 2004), 17–38.

14. Donald S. Lopez, Jr., "Memories of the Buddha," in Janet Gyatso, ed., *In the Mirror of Memory* (Albany: State University of New York Press, 1992), 24.

15. "On the Sublime," in Hazard Adams, ed., *Critical Theory since Plato* (New York: Harcourt Brace Jovanovich, 1971), 77.

16. Edwin Arnold, *The Light of Asia* (1908; Twickenham: Senate, 1998), 108–9.

17. Michel de Certeau, *The Mystic Fable*, trans. Michael B. Smith (Chicago: University of Chicago Press, 1992), vol. 1, 97, 98.

18. K. N. Jayatilleke, *Early Buddhist Theory of Knowledge* (Dehli: Motilal,1963), 466.

19. Frye, *The Secular Scripture*, 61.

20. Edward Conze, *Buddhist Thought in India* (New Dehli: Motilal, 1996), 17–36.

4. Winning Conversions: The *Nikāyas*

1. Richard F. Gombrich, *How Buddhism Began* (Dehli: Manoharlal, 1997), 21.

2. See *Samyutta Nikāya*, trans. John Ireland (Kandy: Buddhist Publication Society, 1967), 34, n. 10.

3. See Gethin, *Foundations of Buddhism*, 60; T. W. Rhys Davids and William Stede, *Pali-English Dictionary* (1921–1925; Dehli: Motilal, 1993), 668, s.v. *sacca*; and *Ten Jātaka Stories: A Pali Reader*, ed. I. B. Horner (Bangkok: Mahāmakut, 1993), xviii.

4. The Pāli can be found in Rune E. A. Johansson, *Pali Buddhist Texts* (London: Curzon, 1977), 23.

5. Th. Stcherbatsky, *The Central Conception of Buddhism* (1922; Dehli: Motilal, 1994), 48–49.

6. Johansson, *Pali Buddhist Texts*, 26.

7. See Bruce Matthews, *Craving and Salvation* (1983; Dehli: Satguru, 1994), 74–89.

8. Mircea Eliade, *Yoga: Immortality and Freedom* (Princeton: Princeton University Press, 1958), 50.

9. See Janet Gyatso, "Sex," in Lopez, Jr., *Critical Terms for the Study of Buddhism*, 271–90.

10. See Peter Harvey, *The Selfless Mind* (Richmond: Curzon, 1995), 155–79.

11. John Keats, *On First Looking into Chapman's Homer*, in *The Portable Romantic Poets: Blake to Poe*, ed. W. H. Auden and Norman H. Pearson (New York: Penguin, 1977).

12. Gombrich, *How Buddhism Began*, 66.

13. Maurice Walshe, ed., trans., *Samyutta Nikāya: An Anthology*, vol. 3 (Kandy: Buddhist Publication Society, 1985).

14. Max Weber, "The Sociology of Charismatic Authority," in *From Max Weber*, ed. H. H. Gerth and C. Wright Mills (New York: Oxford University Press, 1946), 245–50.

15. See Schumann, 162–63.

16. For Trevor Ling, since the Buddha's teaching in its earliest form did not espouse belief in God, it could not in that sense be considered a religion, and instead "is best described as a theory of existence, [or] an ideology" (Ling, 141).

17. Richard H. Robinson, et al., *The Buddhist Religion* (Belmont: Wadsworth, 1997), 48.

18. Thanissaro Bhikkhu, *The Wings to Awakening* (Barre: Dhamma Dana, 1996), 14, 22.

19. "The *Mātikās*: Memorization, Mindfulness, and the List," in Gyatso, ed., *In the Mirror of Memory*, 153.

20. Frank J. Hoffman, *Rationality and Mind in Early Buddhism* (Dehli: Motilal, 1992), 42–43, 98.

21. Collins, *Selfless Persons*, 78; the term "Buddhist ideology" is used by Hallisey, in Lopez, ed., *Curators of the Buddha*, 46, and is a guiding motif in Steven Collins, *Nirvana and other Buddhist Felicities*.

22. Harvey, *The Selfless Mind*, 43.

23. Terry Eagleton, *Ideology* (London: Verso, 1991), 45.

24. Eagleton, 56.

25. Cited in Schroeder, 35.

26. Bhikkhu Ñānananda, *Concept and Reality in Early Buddhist Thought* (Kandy: Buddhist Publication Society, 1971), 13, 19, 38–40.

27. Slavoj Žižek, *The Sublime Object of Ideology* (London: Verso, 1999), 21.

28. Žižek, 99,102.

29. Kenneth Burke, *The Rhetoric of Religion* (Berkeley: University of California Press, 1970), 33, 172.

30. Ferdinand de Saussure, *Course in General Linguistics*, trans. W. Baskin (New York: Fontana, 1974), 114.

31. See Ernesto Laclau, "Why Do Empty Signifiers Matter in Politics?" in *Emancipation(s)* (London: Verso, 1996), 37.

32. Lewis Carroll, *Alice's Adventures in Wonderland* & *Through the Looking Glass* (New York: Signet, 1960), 136.

33. William James, *The Varieties of Religious Experience: A Study in Human Nature* (1902; New York: Penguin, 1985), 84–86, 101, 79.

34. Here in the translation in Bhikkhu Bodhi, ed., *In the Buddha's Words: An Anthology of Discourses from the Pali Canon* (Boston: Wisdom, 2005), 215.

35. Walpola Rahula, *What the Buddha Taught* (1959; Bangkok: Kurusapa, 1990), 28.

36. Rimal Matilal, "Ignorance or Misconception? A Note on Avidyā in Buddhism," in Somoratna Balasooriya, et al., eds., *Buddhist Studies in Honor of Walpola Rahula* (London: Gordon Fraser, 1980), 159–61.

37. Bhikkhu Bodhi, trans., ed., *The Great Discourse on Causation* (Kandy: Buddhist Publication Society, 1984), 2–4.

38. Hajime Namakura, "The Theory of 'Dependent Origination' in its Incipient Stage," in Balasooriya, 165–72.

39. Frauwallner, I.156.

40. Ireland, trans., *Udāna* 8.3; Johansson, *The Psychology of Nirvana*, 39.

41. Collins, *Nirvana*, 27, 33. On *différance* and the strange logic of the supplement (which completes what is already complete), see Derrida, *Of Grammatology*, 141–64, and *Margins of Philosophy*, trans. Alan Bass (Chicago: University of Chicago Press, 1982), 3–27.

42. Collins, *Nirvana*, 112–13.

43. See Bhkkhu Bodhi, ed., *In the Buddha's Words*, 318–19.

44. Collins, *Nirvana*, 212.

45. Collins, *Nirvana*, 189. See also Gérard Genette, "Flaubert's Silences," in *Figures of Literary Discourse*, 194–95.

46. Frederic Jameson, *The Political Unconscious*, 287, 289; on utopia, see also *The Jameson Reader*, eds. M. Hardt and K. Weeks (Oxford: Blackwell, 2000), 359–92.

5. Passing On: *The Nikāyas*

1. Rupert Gethin, *The Buddhist Path to Awakening* (Oxford: OneWorld, 1992), 33–34.

2. Walshe, DN, n. 625.

3. Žižek *The Puppet and the Dwarf*, 31; see also Brian D. Victoria, *Zen War Stories* (London: Routledge Curzon, 2003).

4. Robert H. Scharf, "Buddhist Modernism and the Rhetoric of Meditative Experience," *Numen*, 42 (1995): 228–83. A wider perspective than usual, however, is articulated in Wes Nisker, *Buddha's Nature: A Practical Guide to Discovering Your Place in the Cosmos* (New York: Bantam, 1998). And as Rupert Gethin points out, "much of ordinary, everyday Buddhist devotional practice takes the form of some kind of recollection" of the three jewels, and thus there is "a real sense in which nearly all Buddhists . . . can be considered 'meditators'": *Foundations of Buddhism*, 179.

5. Ven. U Silananda, *The Four Foundations of Mindfulness*, trans. Ruth-Inge Heinze (Boston: Wisdom, 1990), 18; Gethin, *The Buddhist Path to Awakening*, 59–68.

6. Winston L. King, in *Theravāda Meditation* (Dehli: Motilal, 1992), asserts that the Buddha's contribution was insight meditation; Johannes Bronkhorst, in *The Two Traditions of Meditation in Ancient India* (Dehli: Motilal, 1993) asserts that it was the practice of the *jhānas*. The issue has long been debated: see Gethin, *Foundations of Buddhism*, 200.

7. For example in Jātaka 538, *Resolute Determination*, when Queen Canda cannot obtain a boon immediately, she bargains down the time: "five, four, three, two years, [or] one year, [or] seven, six, five, four, three, two months, one month," etc.: in Horner, ed., *Ten Jātaka Stories*, 73.

8. Robert Browning, "In Three Days," and "Meeting at Night," in *The Poetical Works of Robert Browning* (London: Oxford University Press, 1960).

9. See Heinz Bechert and Richard Gombrich, eds., *The World of Buddhism* (London: Thames and Hudson, 1982), 31.

10. K. N. Jayatilleke, *Early Buddhist Theory of Knowledge*, 426, 404, 442.

11. Sangharakshita, *The Eternal Legacy: An Introduction to the Canonical Literature of Buddhism* (London: Tharpa, 1985), 28.

12. See Harvey, *The Selfless Mind*, 68.

13. *The Dhammapada*, 10.9–12, trans. T. Cleary (London: Thorson's, n.d.), 48.

14. References are by book, chapter and section to T. W. Rhys Davids, trans., *The Questions of King Milinda*, 2 vols. (New York: Dover, 1963); abbreviated QM.

15. See Ayya Khema, *Visible Here and Now* (Boston: Shambhala, 2001).

16. Gethin, *The Buddhist Path to Awakening*, 98–101.

17. Frye, *Anatomy of Criticism*, 33, 136. For meditators, jhānas and supernormal powers are real experiences bordering on myth or magic, and thus difficult to articulate. A range of similes may need to be used, as in the *Visuddhimagga* 4.97: "*Momentary happiness* is like flashes of lightning at different moments. *Showering happiness* breaks over the body again and again like waves on the sea shore" (141).

18. Further references to this sutta will be by section and verse only.

19. T. W. Rhys Davids, *Dialogues of the Buddha* (1899; Dehli: Motilal, 2000), vol. 2, 71–77.

20. Jacques Derrida, "Plato's Pharmacy," in *Dissemination*, trans. Barbara Johnson (Chicago: University of Chicago Press, 1981), 61–171.

21. Derrida, *Dissemination*, 130.

22. See Jacqueline I. Stone, "Death," in Lopez, Jr., *Critical Terms in the Study of Buddhism*, 59.

23. *Lycidas*, lines 165–167, in John Milton, *The Major Works*, eds. Stephen Orgel and Jonathan Goldberg (New York: Oxford University Press, 2003).

24. P. B. Shelley, *Adonais*, stanza 39, in Auden and Pearson, *Portable Romantic Poets*.

25. Maria Torok, "The Illness of Mourning," in Nicolas Abraham and Maria Torok, *The Shell and the Kernel*, trans. N. T. Rand (Chicago: University of Chicago Press, 1994), 114.

26. Torok, 116, 114.

27. John S. Strong, *Relics of the Buddha* (Princeton: Princeton University Press, 2004), 4. See also Gregory Schopen, *Stones, Bones and Buddhist Monks: Collected Papers on the Archaeology, Epigraphy and Texts of Monastic Buddhism in India* (Honolulu: University of Hawaii Press, 1997), 126–35.

28. Strong, *Relics of the Buddha*, 7, 8.

29. Eckel, 53–54.

30. Derrida, *Specters of Marx: The State of Debt, the Work of Mourning, and the New International*, trans. Peggy Kamuf (New York: Routledge, 1994), 97.

6. Figures of Right Speech: *The Dhammapada*

1. *The Mahavagga*, I.11, in *Vinaya Texts*, trans. T. W. Rhys Davids, et al. (1885; Dehli: Motilal, 1965), vol. 1, 112.

2. Thanissaro Bhikkhu (Geoffrey DeGraff), *Dhammapada: A Translation* (Barre: Dhamma Dana, 1998), ix.

3. Thanissaro, vi–x.

4. The author's translation is used or, as indicated in the text, those of Thomas Cleary, *The Dhammapada* (London: Thorson's, n.d.); K. R. Norman, *The Word of the Doctrine* (Oxford: Pali Text Society, 1997); John Carter and Mahinda Palihawadana in a bilingual edition, *Dhammapada* (Oxford: Oxford University Press, 1997); abbreviated as C, N, and CP respectively; the translations are sometimes modified, as indicated by the added abbreviation, m. Numbering is as in the Norman edition.

5. Carter and Palihawadana, 109.

6. *Romeo and Juliet* 1.1.51–58.

7. *Merchant of Venice* 2.8.14–16. For a recent analysis of this passage in its Elizabethan context, see Marjorie Garber, *Shakespeare After All* (New York: Pantheon, 2004), 282–312, esp. 298–99.

8. Collins, *Selfless Persons*, 218–21.

7. Joyous Negations: *The Heart Sutra*

1. See John S. Strong, ed., *The Experience of Buddhism: Sources and Interpretations* (Belmont: Wadsworth, 1995), 132–33.

2. Donald S. Lopez, Jr., *Elaborations on Emptiness* (Princeton: Princeton University Press, 1996), 7, 27–28.

3. Composite translation, with author's modifications and numbering of the sections. The Sanskrit can be found in the bilingual, annotated edition, *Buddhist Wisdom: The Diamond Sutra and the Heart Sutra*, trans. Edward Conze (1958; New York: Random House, 2001).

4. Paul Williams, *Mahāyāna Buddhism* (London: Routledge, 1989), 48.

5. Lewis Carroll, *Alice's Adventures in Wonderland*, 38.

6. See Karl Potter, *The Presuppositions of India's Philosophies* (Englewood Cliffs, NJ: Prentice Hall, 1963), 188. See also C. W. Huntington, Jr., *The Emptiness of Emptiness: An Introduction to Early Indian Mādhyamaka* (Honolulu: University of Hawaii Press, 1989): in Indian philosophy, a negation can either affirm the existence of something or else leave nothing in its place, but the Mādhyamaka school (with affinities here to the *prajñāpāramitā*), "negates the reality of the world, [but] affirms neither a something nor a nothing in its place" (58).

7. Gilles Deleuze and Felix Guattari, *Anti-Oedipus: Capitalism and Schizophrenia* (Minneapolis: University of Minnesota Press, 1983), 8.

8. The example is taken from Nina van Gorkom, *Abhidamma in Everyday Life* (London: Triple Gem Press, 1969), 32–33; see also Herbert V. Guenther, *Philosophy and Psychology in the Abhidharma* (Dehli: Motilal, 1974).

9. Deleuze and Guattari, 6.

10. "Rāhulabhadra's Verses in Praise of Perfect Wisdom," in Strong, ed., *The Experience of Buddhism*, 139.

11. Edward Conze, *Buddhist Thought in India*, 203.

12. See David Loy, "The Deconstruction of Buddhism," in Harold Coward and Toby Foshay, eds., *Derrida and Negative Theology* (Albany: State University of New York Press, 1992), 227–53.

13. These terms are from Huntington, xiii.

14. Harold Bloom, *The Anxiety of Influence* (New York: Oxford University Press, 1971), 8.

15. Aristotle, *Rhetoric* 1405a, in George A. Kennedy, trans., *Aristotle on Rhetoric: A Theory of Civil Discourse* (Oxford: Oxford University Press, 1991), 223.

16. Bloom, 14–16. The phenomenon can be found in other arts: Robert Schumann, in his *Phantasie in C Major*, gives a musical quotation from Beethoven but then reworks it, Charles Rosen points out, so as to make it his own: "at the end of Schumann's first movement, the quotation from Beethoven . . . becomes self-reference: [it] seems as much to derive from what has preceded as to be the source" (Charles Rosen, *The Romantic Generation* [Cambridge: Harvard University Press, 1995], 103).

17. A contesting of earlier traditions, in Zen, has been described using Harold Bloom's scheme: see Steven Heine, *Dōgen and the Kōan Tradition: A Tale of Two Shōbōgenzō Texts* (Albany: State University of New York Press, 1994), 133–38; Bernard Faure, *The Rhetoric of Immediacy: A Cultural Critique of Chan/Zen Buddhism* (Princeton: Princeton University Press, 1991), 219; Dale S. Wright, *Philosophical Meditations on Zen Buddhism* (Cambridge: Cambridge University Press, 1998), 156.

18. Lopez, *Elaborations on Emptiness*, vii–viii; Conze, 82.

19. Mu Soeng, trans., *The Diamond Sutra: Transforming the Way We Perceive the World* (Boston: Wisdom, 2000), 135.

20. Bhikkhu Ñānananda, ed., trans., *Samyutta Nikāya*, pt. 2 (Kandy: Buddhist Publication Society, 1972), 61.

21. Here cited from Maurice Walshe, ed., trans., *Samyutta Nikāya*, 63.

22. Conze, 97.

23. Lopez, *Elaborations on Emptiness*, 136.

24. Williams, *Buddhist Thought*, 132–33.

25. See Nāgārjuna, *The Fundamental Wisdom of the Middle Way*, 24.1–15, trans. Jay L. Garfield (New York: Oxford University Press, 1995).

26. Edward Conze, *Selected Sayings from the Perfection of Wisdom* (Boulder: Prajna, 1955), 98.

27. Gethin, 232; Williams, 53.

28. Lopez, *Elaborations on Emptiness*, 72–79; 105–9.

29. Conze, *Selected Sayings from the Perfection of Wisdom*, 81.

30. Sigmund Freud, *Beyond the Pleasure Principle*, trans. J. Strachey, *The Standard Edition*, vol. 18 (1955; New York, 2001), 14–15.

31. Bloom, 15–16.

32. Campbell, *The Hero with a Thousand Faces*, 69.

33. Conze, *Thirty Years of Buddhist Studies*, 140.

34. Lopez, *Elaborations on Emptiness*, 180.

35. Thich Nhat Hanh, *The Heart of Understanding* (New Dehli: Full Circle, 1997), 10, 15.

36. Conze, *Selected Sayings from the Perfection of Wisdom*,16.

37. Page references are to Joseph Conrad, *Heart of Darkness and the Secret Sharer* (New York: Bantam, 1981). On Conrad's techniques, see Richard Ambrosini, *Conrad's Fiction as Critical Discourse* (Cambridge: Cambridge University Press, 1991), 84–115.

38. *Saptaśatikā*, in Conze, *Selected Sayings . . .* , 77-78.

39. Samuel Beckett, *Worstward Ho* (New York: Grove, 1983), 15.

40. Obora, "On *The Heart Sutra*," in *The Tiger's Cave*, trans. T. Leggett (Rutland: Tuttle, 1964), 104.

8. Masters of Emptiness: *The Gateless Barrier* and Zen Folktales

1. Rick Fields, *How the Swans Came to the Lake* (Boston: Shambhala, 1980), 168–272; John McRae, *Seeing through Zen: Encounter, Transformation, and Genealogy in Chinese Chan Buddhism* (Berkeley: University of California Press, 2003), 101–3; Thomas Kasulis, *Zen Action/Zen Person* (Honolulu: University of Hawaii Press, 1985), 32–38, 72–75.

2. Robert H. Scharf, "The Zen of Japanese Nationalism," in Donald S. Lopez, Jr., ed., *Curators of the Buddha* (Chicago: University of Chicago Press, 1995), 124–25; also Bernard Faure, *Chan Insights and Oversights: An Epistemological Critique of the Chan Tradition* (Princeton: Princeton University Press, 1993), 54.

3. *The Platform Sutra of the Sixth Patriarch*, ed. Philip B. Yampolsky (New York: Columbia University Press, 1967), 130–32; abbreviated PS.

4. Robert E. Buswell, Jr., "The 'Short-cut' Approach of *K'an hua* Meditation," in *Sudden and Gradual: Approaches to Enlightenment in Chinese Thought*, ed. P. N. Gregory (Honolulu: University of Hawaii Press, 1987), 325.

5. Buswell, in Gregory, 344.

6. Jacques Derrida, *On the Name*, ed. Thomas Dutoit, trans. David Wood, et al., (Stanford: Stanford University Press, 1995), 75.

7. Katsuki Sekida, trans., *Two Zen Classics: Mumonkan and Hekiganroku* (New York: Weatherhill, 1977), 45.

8. Bernard Faure, *The Rhetoric of Immediacy: A Cultural Critique of Chan/Zen Buddhism* (Princeton: Princeton University Press, 1991), 11.

9. Faure, *Rhetoric of Immediacy*, 67; McRae, 339, 348; Robert Gimello, "Marga and Culture: Learning, Letters, and Liberation in Northern Sung Ch'an," in Buswell and Gimello, ed., *Paths to Liberation*, 374.

10. McRae, 7–8, 18–19; Mu Soeng, *Trust in Mind: The Rebellion of Chinese Zen* (Boston: Wisdom, 2004), 39–46; Dale Wright, *Philosophical Meditations on Zen Buddhism* (Cambridge: Cambridge University Press, 1998), 96–103.

11. See Jacques Derrida, *Dissemination*, trans. Barbara Johnson (Chicago: University of Chicago Press, 1981), 186, n. 14.

12. Faure, *Rhetoric of Immediacy*, 53–61.

13. Steven Heine, *Opening a Mountain: Kōans of the Zen Masters* (Oxford: Oxford University Press, 2002), 19.

14. References are by case number to Robert Aitken, trans., *The Gateless Barrier: the Wu-Men Kuan (Mumonkan)* (New York: Farrar, Straus and Giroux, 1991); abbreviated M. Elsewhere as indicated, Zenkei Shibayama's translation (with the Japanese names) is used: *Zen Comments on the Mumonkan* (New York: Mentor, 1974); abbreviated S.

15. D. T. Suzuki, *An Introduction to Zen Buddhism* (New York: Grove, 1964), 31.

16. *The Zen Teachings of Master Lin-Chi: A Translation of the Lin-chi lu*, trans. B. Watson (New York: Columbia University Press, 1993), 44; abbreviated L.

17. Campbell, *The Hero with a Thousand Faces*, 82, 97.

18. Heine, *Opening a Mountain*, 8–9, 21.

19. Steven Heine, *Shifting Shape, Shaping Text: Philosophy and Folklore in the Fox Koan* (Honolulu: University of Hawaii Press, 1999), 83.

20. T. Griffith Foulk, "The Form and Function of Koan Literature: An Historical Overview," in Steven Heine and Dale S. Wright, eds., *The Koan: Texts and Contexts in Zen Buddhism* (Oxford: Oxford University Press, 2000), 35; also Faure, *Rhetoric of Immediacy*, 22.

21. Robinson, *The Buddhist Religion*, 204–5.

22. Foulk, 39–40.

23. Franz Kafka, *Selected Short Stories*, trans. Willa and Edwin Muir (New Dehli: Srishti, 1998), 67–132, 148–50.

24. Wright, in *The Koan*, 202.

25. Richard J. Lynn, "Sudden and Gradual in Chinese Poetry Criticism," in Gregory, *Sudden and Gradual*, 388, 384.

26. Faure, *Chan Insights and Oversights*, 208; also Burton Watson, "Zen Poetry," in Kenneth Kraft, ed., *Zen: Tradition and Transition* (London: Rider, 1988), 113–14.

27. In Thomas Hoover, *Zen Culture* (London: Routledge and Kegan Paul, 1978), 206.

28. In Maria Tatar, ed., *The Classic Fairy Tales* (New York: Norton, 1999), 15.

29. Suzuki, 42.

30. Wright, *Philosophical Meditations on Zen Buddhism*, 130.

31. Foulk, 42.

32. Isshu Miura and Ruth F. Sasaki, *The Zen Koan: Its History and Use in Rinzai Zen* (New York: Harcourt Brace, 1965), 11–12.

33. Chang Chung-Yuan, ed., *Original Teachings of Ch'an Buddhism Selected from "The Transmission of the Lamp"* (New York: Vintage, 1969), 201–2, abbreviated TL; Heine, *Opening a Mountain*, 49–50.

34. Wright, in *Koan*, 209.

35. Heine, *Opening a Mountain*, 4–8.

36. Faure, *Rhetoric of Immediacy*, 218–21; Heine, *Opening a Mountain*, 101.

37. Jacob Grimm and Wilhelm Grimm, *Grimms' Fairy Tales* (1823; New York: Penguin, 1996), 71.

38. Homer, *The Odyssey* 10.302–472, trans. Robert Fagles (New York: Penguin, 1996).

39. *The New Science of Giambattista Vico*, ed. Thomas G. Bergin and M. H. Fisch (Ithaca: Cornell University Press, 1948), sections 404, 375.

40. In Paul Reps, ed., *Zen Flesh, Zen Bones: A Collection of Zen and Pre-Zen Writings* (New York: Doubleday, 1961), 22–23; also cited in M.5 comm.

41. M. M. Bakhtin, *The Dialogic Imagination: Four Essays*, ed. Michael Holquist, trans. Caryl Emerson, et al. (Austin: University of Texas Press, 1981), 342.

42. Marcel Proust, *The Remembrance of Things Past*, trans. C. K. Scott Moncrieff and Terence Kilmartin, vol. 1 (New York: Vintage, 1982), 54–55.

43. *Hamlet* 3.2.145–47.

44. Bakhtin, *Dialogic Imagination*, 296.

45. Albert Welter, "Mahākāsyapa's Smile: Silent Transmission and the Kung-an (Kōan) Tradition," in *The Kōan*, 75–109.

46. Welter, 98, 101n12.

47. See Gary S. Morson and Caryl Emerson, *Mikhail Bakhtin: Creation of a Prosaics* (Stanford: Stanford University Press, 1990), 220–23; Bakhtin, *Dialogic Imagination*, 344–46.

48. Heine, *Opening a Mountain*, 51–52. The full text can be found in *The Blue Cliff Record*, trans. Thomas Cleary and J. C. Cleary (Boston: Shambhala, 1992), 22–30.

9. Extreme Giving: *The Vessantara Jātaka* and Shantideva's *A Guide to the Bodhisattva Way of Life*

1. Gethin, *The Buddhist Path to Awakening*, 179–80.

2. Harvey Aronson, *Love and Sympathy in Theravada Buddhism* (Dehli: Motilal, 1980), 71.

3. See Ven. Henepola Gunaratana, *Mindfulness in Plain English* (Boston: Wisdom, 1991), 140.

4. References are by section number to Jātaka no. 547, in *The Jātaka, or Stories of the Buddha's Former Lives*, ed. Edward B. Cowell, trans. H. T. Francis (Cambridge: Cambridge University Press, 1895–1913). A more recent translation, with illustrations, is *The Perfect Generosity of Prince Vessantara: A Buddhist Epic*, trans. Margaret Cone and Richard F. Gombrich (Oxford: Clarendon Press, 1977); abbreviated CG.

5. Robinson, *The Buddhist Religion*, 61, 101.

6. Citations in the text will be by chapter and verse to the translation from the Sanskrit by Kate Crosby and Andrew Skilton, *The Bodhicaryāvatāra* (New York: Oxford University Press, 1996) or to the translation from the Tibetan (sometimes numbered slightly differently) by the Padmakara translation group, *Shantideva: The Way of the Bodhisattva* (Boston: Wisdom, 1988); abbreviated P.

7. Jan Nattier, *A Few Good Men: The Bodhisattva Path Acording to the Inquiry of Ugra (Ugrapariprcchā)* (Honolulu: University of Hawaii Press, 2003), 134–35.

8. Here in the translation of Gil Fronsdal, *The Dhammapada* (Boston: Shambhala, 2005). The word for "welfare" may also be translated as "purpose," "needs," or "interests."

9. Har Dayal, *The Bodhisattva Doctrine in Buddhist Sanskrit Literature* (1932; Dehli: Motilal, 1999), 31–35.

10. Nattier, 80–105, 145–47.

11. Ernst R. Curtius, *European Literature and the Latin Middle Ages*, trans. Willard R. Trask (New York: Harper and Rowe, 1953), 83, 407–13.

12. Robinson, 18–19.

13. *The Confessions of St. Augustine*, trans. John K. Ryan (New York: Doubleday, 1960), esp. books 1–2; and see Flores, 44–65.

14. Sigmund Freud, *Civilization and Its Discontents*, pt. 5, trans. James Strachey (New York: Norton, 1961), 66–67. Similarly, Jacques Lacan remarks that "We place no trust in altruistic feeling, we who lay bare the aggressivity that underlies the activity of the philanthropist, the idealist, the pedagogue, and even the reformer" (*Écrits*, trans. Alan Sheridan [New York: Norton, 1977], 6–7). Shantideva's compassion, as his text will show, is intertwined with aggressivity against himself, against others, and finally against the cosmic moral order.

15. Sir Philip Sidney, *An Apology for Poetry*, in Adams, 168.

16. I. B. Horner, cited in Gregory Schopen, *Buddhist Monks and Business Matters* (Honolulu: University of Hawaii Press, 2004), 172.

17. See John C. Fenton, trans., *The Gospel of Saint Matthew* (London: Penguin, 1963), 90–91.

18. Friedrich Nietzsche, *Beyond Good and Evil*, trans. Walter Kaufman (New York: Vintage, 1966), 225; *Jenseits von Gut und Böse*, in Karl Schlechta, ed., Friedrich Nietzsche, *Werke* (München: Carl Hanser Verlag, 1981), vol. 3, 689.

19. Nietzsche, *Daybreak: Thoughts on the Prejudices of Morality*, section 133, trans. R. J. Hollingdale (Cambridge: Cambridge University Press, 1982), 84; *Morgenröte*, in Schlechta, vol. 2, 105.

20. Nietzsche, *Daybreak*, 84; Nietzsche's emphasis.

21. Charles Darwin, *The Origin of Species*, chap. 3, in Philip Appleman, ed., *Darwin*, 3rd ed. (New York: Norton, 2001), 107–11; in the same volume, see also Michael Ruse and Edward O. Wilson, "The Evolution of Ethics," and Matt Ridley, "The Origins of Virtue," 506, 519–24.

22. For example, Jātaka no. 316, *Dāna*, in Horner, 4–5.

23. Charles Baudelaire, *Oeuvres complètes*, ed. C. Pichois (Paris: Gallimard, 1961), 29.

24. See Kelsang Gyatso, *The Joyful Path to Good Fortune* (London: Tharpa, 1990).

25. Tenzin Gyatso, *A Flash of Lightning in the Dark of Night* (Boston: Shambhala, 1994), 1.

26. Aristotle, *Rhetoric* 1356b, in Kennedy, 40–41.

27. Richard Weaver, *The Ethics of Rhetoric* (Chicago: Regnery, 1965), 23.

28. Percy Bysshe Shelley, *A Defense of Poetry*, in Adams, 512–13.

29. Translators' introduction, P, 7.

30. Sidney, in Adams, 157; and see *Engaged Buddhism: Buddhist Liberation Movements in Asia,* eds. Christopher S. Queen and Sallie B. King (Albany: State University of New York Press, 1996).

31. *The Holy Teaching of Vimalakirti: A Mahāyāna Scripture*, trans. Robert A. F. Thurman (Dehli: Motilal, 1991), 21.

32. Webb, xiii.

10. Final Emergency Reading: *The Tibetan Book of the Dead*

1. Donald S. Lopez, Jr., *Prisoners of Shangri-La* (Chicago: University of Chicago Press, 1998), 46–86.

2. T. Y. Evans-Wentz, ed., *The Tibetan Book of the Dead.* 3rd ed. (New York: Oxford University Press, 1957), ix.

3. Robert Thurman, trans., *The Tibetan Book of the Dead* (New York: Harper Collins, 1994), 10.

4. See, for example, Ian Stevenson, *Twenty Cases Suggestive of Reincarnation* (Charlottesville: University of Virginia Press, 1980); Raymond Moody, *Life after Life* (San Francisco: Harper, 2001); Kenneth Ring, *Life at Death* (New York: Quill, 1980); Michael Sabom, M.D., *Recollections of Death: A Medical Investigation* (New York: Harper & Row, 1982).

5. Sherwin B. Nuland, *How We Die: Reflections on Life's Final Chapter* (New York: Random House, 1995), 123.

6. Friedrich Nietzsche, *The Gay Science*, trans. Walter Kaufmann (New York: Vintage, 1974), 168.

7. "Birth and Death," in Kazuaki Tanahashi, ed., *Moon in a Dewdrop: Writings of Zen Master Dōgen* (New York: North Point Press, 1985), 74.

8. Citations are by page number to Francesca Fremantle and Chogyam Trungpa, trans., *The Tibetan Book of the Dead: The Great Liberation through Hearing in the Bardo* (Boston: Shambhala: 1987); if modified, followed by m (parts of the translation were redone by Francesca Fremantle in *Luminous Emptiness: Understanding the Tibetan Book of the Dead* [Boston: Shambhala, 2003]). Sometimes the translation cited alternates with that in the Evans-Wentz edition; abbreviated EW. A recent annotated translation by Gyurme Dorje of the complete text is *The Tibetan Book of the Dead,* eds. Graham Coleman and Thupten Jinpa (New York: Penguin, 2005); abbreviated GD.

9. Janet Gyatso, "Drawn from the Tibetan Treasury: the *GTer ma* Literature," in *Tibetan Literature*, ed. J. I. Cabezon, et al. (Ithaca: Snow Lion, 1996), 151.

10. In GD, xviii–xxiii.

11. Fremantle, 53–69.

12. Padmasambhava, *Natural Liberation*, comm. Gyatrul Rinpoche, trans. Alan Wallace (Boston: Wisdom, 1998), 52, 200, 208; also GD, esp. 38–91.

13. Schopen, *Buddhist Monks and Business Matters*, 21.

14. Schopen, *Buddhist Monks and Business Matters*, 96–97.

15. Fremantle, 346.

16. Detlev Lauf, *Secret Doctrines of the Tibetan Books of the Dead* (Boston: Shambhala, 1989), 96.

17. In T. Y. Evans-Wentz, li.

18. Paul de Man, *The Rhetoric of Romanticism* (New York: Columbia University Press, 1984), 122.

19. *The Waste Land*, lines 121–126, in T. S. Eliot, *The Complete Poems and Plays: 1909–1950* (New York: Harcourt, Brace and World, 1952).

20. Padmasambhava, 195–223.

21. de Man, *The Rhetoric of Romanticism*, 80–81.

22. Sogyal Rinpoche, *Tibetan Book of Living and Dying*, eds. Patrick Gaffney and Andrew Harvey (New York: HarperSanFranciso, 1993), xi.

23. See Eve Kosofsky Sedgwick, "Pedagogy," in Lopez, Jr., ed., *Critical Terms for the Study of Buddhism*, 166–68.

24. For example, Sogyal Rinpoche, 110, 262.

25. *Duino Elegies*, in *The Selected Poetry of Rainer Maria Rilke*, bilingual edition, trans. Stephen Mitchell (New York: Random House, 1987), 151 (translation modified).

26. Stephan Beyer, *The Cult of Tara* (Berkeley: University of California Press: 1974), 75.

27. From "Proverbs of Hell," in Mary Lynn Johnson, et al., eds., *Blake's Poetry and Designs* (New York: Norton, 1979), 89.

28. Stephen Hodge, et al., trans., ed., *An Illustrated Tibetan Book of the Dead* (New York: Sterling, 1999), 53.

29. Aristotle, *Poetics* XI.2, in Adams, 54.

30. Lama Thubten Yeshe, *The Tantric Path of Purification* (Boston: Wisdom, 1995) 46; Thurman, 72–73, 135. See also the Dalai Lama, *Advice on Dying, and Living a Better Life* (London: Ryder, 2002).

31. Laurence Sterne, *The Life and Opinions of Tristram Shandy, Gentleman*, ed. James Work (1759–1767; New York: Odyssey, 1940), 5.

32. Stephen Levine, *Who Dies? An Investigation of Conscious Living and Conscious Dying* (Garden City: Anchor, 1982), 272–89.

33. Plato, *Republic* 614b, in *The Republic*, trans. G. M. A. Grube (Indianapolis: Hackett, 1992), 285. The myth of Er is discussed in Evans-Wentz, 49–53.

34. Plato, *Republic*, 617c–d, 620a.

35. Dante Alighieri, *The Divine Comedy: Inferno*, bilingual edition, trans. Allen Mandelbaum (New York: Bantam: 1982), cited by canto and line (translation modified).

Bibliography

Abraham, Nicolas, and Maria Torok. *The Shell and the Kernel.* Translated by Nicholas T. Rand. Chicago: University of Chicago Press, 1994.

Adams, Hazard, ed. *Critical Theory since Plato.* New York: Harcourt Brace Jovanovich, 1971.

Aitken, Robert, trans. *The Gateless Barrier: the Wu-Men Kuan (Mumonkan).* New York: Farrar, Straus and Giroux, 1991.

Alter, Robert, and Frank Kermode, ed. *The Literary Guide to the Bible.* Cambridge: Harvard University Press, 1987.

Anguttara Nikāya. Numerical Discourses of the Buddha. Translated by Nyanaponika Thera and Bhikkhu Bodhi. London: Altamira, 1999.

Aristotle. *On Rhetoric.* Translated by George A. Kennedy. New York: Oxford University Press, 1991.

Arnold, Edwin. *The Light of Asia.* 1908; Twickenham: Senate, 1998.

Aronson, Harvey. *Love and Sympathy in Theravada Buddhism.* Dehli: Motilal, 1980.

Auden, W. H., and Norman H. Pearson, eds. *The Portable Romantic Poets: Blake to Poe.* New York: Penguin, 1977.

Auerbach, Erich. *Mimesis: The Reprssentation of Reality in Western Literature.* Translated by W. Trask. Princeton: Princeton University Press, 1953

Augustine. *The Confessions of St. Augustine.* Translated by J. K. Ryan. New York: Doubleday, 1960.

Ayya Khema. *Visible Here and Now.* Boston: Shambhala, 2001.

Bakhtin, M. M. *The Dialogic Imagination: Four Essays.* Edited by Michael Holquist, translated by Caryl Emerson, et al. Austin: University of Texas Press, 1981.

———. *Speech Genres and Other Late Essays.* Translated by Vern W. McGee, edited by Caryl Emerson, et al. Austin: University of Texas Press, 1986.

Balasooriya, Somaratna, et al., eds. *Buddhist Studies in honor of Walpola Rahula.* London: Gordon Fraser, 1980.

Batchelor, Stephen, trans. Shantideva, *A Guide to the Bodhisattva's Way of Life.* Dharamsala: Library of Tibetan Works and Archives, 1981.

———. *Buddhism without Beliefs: A Contemporary Guide to Awakening.* London: Bloomsbury, 1997.

———. *Living with the Devil: A Meditation on Good and Evil.* New York: Riverhead, 2004.

Baudelaire, Charles. *Oeuvres complètes*, ed. C. Pichois. Paris: Gallimard, 1961.

Beyer, Stephan. *The Cult of Tara*. Berkeley: University of California Press, 1974.

Bechert, Heinz, and Richard Gombrich, eds. *The World of Buddhism.* London: Thames and Hudson, 1982

Beckett, Samuel. *Worstward Ho*. New York: Grove Press, 1983.

Blake, William. *Blake's Poetry and Designs*. Edited by Mary Lynn Johnson, et al. New York: Norton, 1979.

Bloom, Harold. *The Anxiety of Influence*. New York: Oxford University Press, 1971.

Blyth, R. H. *Zen in English Literature and Oriental Classics*. Tokyo: Hokuseido Press, 1942.

———, trans. *Zen and Zen Classics*, vol. 4: *Mumonkan*. Tokyo: Hokuseido, 1966.

Bodhi, Bhikkhu, trans. *The Connected Discourses of the Buddha: A New Translation of the Samyutta Nikaya*. 2 vols. Boston: Wisdom, 2000.

———, trans, ed. *The Great Discourse on Causation*. Kandy: Buddhist Publication Society, 1984.

———, ed., *In the Buddha's Words: an Anthology of Discourses from the Pali Canon*. Boston: Wisdom, 2005.

Bronkhorst, Johannes. *The Two Traditions of Meditation in Ancient India*. Dehli: Molitlal, 1986.

Browning, Robert. *The Poetical Works of Robert Browning*. London: Oxford University Press, 1960.

Broughton, Jeffrey L., ed. *The Bodhidharma Anthology. The Earliest Records of Zen*. Berkeley: University of California Press, 1999.

Buddhaghosa. *The Path of Purification*. Translated by Ñanamoli. Kandy: Buddhist Publication Society, 1991.

Burke, Kenneth. *The Rhetoric of Religion*. Berkeley: University of California Press, 1970.

Buswell, Robert E., and Robert Gimello, eds. *Paths to Liberation: The Mārga and Its Transformations in Buddhist Thought*. Honolulu: University of Hawaii Press, 1992.

Campbell, Joseph. *The Hero with a Thousand Faces*. Princeton: Princeton University Press, 1949.

———. *The Masks of God: Oriental Mythology*. London: Souvenir, 1962.

Carrithers, Michael. *The Buddha*. Oxford: Oxford University Press, 1983.

Chase, Cynthia. *Decomposing Figures: Rhetorical Readings in the Romantic Tradition*. Baltimore: Johns Hopkins University Press, 1986.

Clarke, J. J. *Oriental Enlightenment*. London: Routledge, 1997.

Cleary, Thomas, and J. C. Cleary, trans. *The Blue Cliff Record.* Boston: Shambhala, 1992.

Cleary, Thomas, trans. *Unlocking the Zen Koan.* Berkeley: North Atlantic, 1993.

Coleman, James. *The New Buddhism.* Oxford: Oxford University Press, 2001.

Coleridge, Samuel T. *Biographia Literaria.* Edited by G. Watson. 1817; London: Dent, 1975.

Collins, Steven. *Nirvana and Other Buddhist Felicities: Utopias of the Pali Imaginaire.* Cambridge: Cambridge University Press, 1998.

———. *Selfless Persons: Imagery and Thought in Thervada Buddhism.* Cambridge: Cambridge University Press, 1982.

Cone, Margaret, and Richard F. Gombrich, trans. *The Perfect Generosity of Prince Vessantara: a Buddhist Epic.* Oxford: Clarendon Press, 1977.

Conrad, Joseph. *Heart of Darkness and the Secret Sharer.* New York: Bantam, 1981.

Conze, Edward. *Buddhist Thought in India.* New Dehli: Molital, 1996.

———. trans., *Buddhist Wisdom: The Diamond Sutra and The Heart Sutra.* 1958; New York: Random House, 2001.

———. ed., *Selected Sayings from the Perfection of Wisdom.* Boulder: Prajna, 1955.

———. *Thirty Years of Buddhist Studies.* New Dehli: Manoharlal, 2000.

Coward, Harold, and Toby Foshay, eds. *Derrida and Negative Theology.* Albany: State University of New York Press, 1992.

Crosby, Kate, and Andrew Skilton, trans. and comm., *Śantideva, The Bodhicaryavatara.* New York: Oxford University Press, 1996.

Culler, Jonathan. *The Pursuit of Signs: Semiotics, Literature, Deconstruction.* London: Routledge, 1981.

Dante Alighieri. *The Divine Comedy: Inferno.* Translated by Allen Mandelbaum. New York: Bantam, 1982.

Dayal, Har. *The Bodhisattva Doctrine in Buddhist Sanskrit Literature.* 1932; Dehli: Motilal, 1999.

De Certeau, Michel. *The Mystic Fable,* vol 1. Translated by Michael B. Smith. Chicago: University of Chicago Press, 1992.

Deleuze, Gilles and Felix Guattari. *Anti-Oedipus: Capitalism and Schizophrenia.* Translated by Robert Hurley, et al. Minneapolis: University of Minnesota Press, 1983.

De Man, Paul. *Allegories of Reading: Figural Language in Rousseau, Nietzsche, Rilke, and Proust.* New Haven: Yale University Press, 1979.

———. *The Rhetoric of Romanticism.* New York: Columbia University Press, 1984.

Derrida, Jacques. *Dissemination.* Translated by Barbara Johnson. Chicago: University of Chicago Press, 1981.

———. *Of Grammatology.* Translated by Gayatri Chakravorty Spivak. Baltimore: Johns Hopkins University Press, 1974.

———. *On the Name.* Edited by Thomas Dutoit. Translated by David Wood, et al. Stanford: Stanford University Press, 1995.

———. *Specters of Marx: The State of the Debt, the Work of Mourning, and the New International.* Translated by Peggy Kamuf. New York: Routledge, 1994.

———. *Without Alibi.* Translated by Peggy Kamuf. Stanford: Stanford University Press, 2002.

de Romilly, Jacqueline. *Magic and Rhetoric in Ancient Greece.* Cambridge: Harvard University Press, 1975.

Dhammapada. Translated by John Ross Carter and Mahinda Palihawandana. Oxford: Oxford University Press, 1997.

———. Translated by Thomas Cleary. London: Thorsons, n.d.

———. *The Word of the Doctrine.* Translated by K. R. Norman. Oxford: Pali Text Society, 1997.

———. Translated by Thanissaro Bhikkhu. Barre: Dhamma Dana, 1998.

———. Translated by Gil Fronsdal. Boston: Shambhala, 2005.

Dōgen, Eihei. "Life and Death," in *Moon in a Dewdrop.* Translated and edited by Kazuaki Tanahashi. New York: North Point Press, 1985.

Dorje, Gyurme, trans. *The Tibetan Book of the Dead.* Edited by Graham Coleman, et al. New York: Penguin, 2005.

Droit, Roger-Pol. *The Cult of Nothingness: The Philosophers and the Buddha.* Translated by David Streight and Pamela Vohnson. Chapel Hill: University of North Carolina Press, 2003.

Eagleton, Terry. *Ideology: An Introduction.* London: Verso, 1991.

Eckel, Malcolm D. *To See the Buddha: A Philosopher's Quest for the Meaning of Emptiness.* Princeton: Princeton University Press, 1992.

Eliade, Mircea. *Yoga: Immortality and Freedom.* Princeton, NJ: Princeton University Press, 1958.

Eliot, T. S. *The Complete Poems and Plays: 1909–1950.* New York: Harcourt, Brace and World, 1952.

Evans-Wentz, W. Y., ed. *The Tibetan Book of the Dead.* Third ed. New York: Oxford University Press, 1957.

Evola, Julius. *The Doctrine of Awakening.* Translated by H. E. Musson. 1943; Rochester: Inner Traditions, 1995.

Faure, Bernard. *Chan Insights and Oversights.* Princeton: Princeton University Press, 1993.

———. *Double Exposure: Cutting Across Buddhist and Western Discourses.* Translated by Janet Lloyd. Stanford: Stanford University Press, 2004.

———. *The Rhetoric of Immediacy: A Cultural Critique of Chan/Zen Buddhism*. Princeton: Princeton University Press, 1991.

Ferguson, Andy, ed. and trans. *Zen's Chinese Heritage*. Boston: Wisdom, 2000.

Fields, Rick. *How the Swans Came to the Lake*. Boston: Shambala, 1981.

Flores, Ralph. *The Rhetoric of Doubtful Authority: Deconstructive Readings of Self-Questioning Narratives, St. Augustine to Faulkner*. Ithaca: Cornell University Press, 1984.

———. "Ungrounding Allegory: The Dead-Living Letter in Hawthorne's *The Scarlet Letter*." *Criticism* 29.3 (1987): 313–40.

Foucher, A. *La Vie du Bouddha*. Paris: J. Maisonneuve, 1993.

Frauwallner, Erich. *History of Indian Philosophy*. 2 vols. Dehli: Motilal, 1973.

Fremantle, Francesca. *Luminous Emptiness: Understanding the Tibetan Book of the Dead.* Boston: Shambhala, 2003.

——— and Chogyam Trungpa, trans. *The Tibetan Book of the Dead: The Great Liberation through Hearing in the Bardo*. Boston: Shambhala, 1975.

Freud, Sigmund. *Beyond the Pleasure Principle*. Translated by James Strachey. *The Standard Edition*, vol. 18. London: Vintage, 2001.

———. *Civilization and Its Discontents*. Translated by James Strachey. New York: Norton, 1961.

———. *General Psychological Theory*. Edited by Philip Rieff. New York: Crowell-Collier, 1963.

———. *Three Essays on the Theory of Sexuality*. Translated by James Strachey. New York: Basic Books, 1962.

Frye, Northrop. *The Anatomy of Criticism*. Princeton: Princeton University Press, 1957.

———. *The Great Code: The Bible and Literature*. New York: Harcourt, 1983.

———. *The Secular Scripture: A Study of the Structure of Romance*. Cambridge: Harvard University Press, 1976.

Gadamer, Hans-Georg. *Philosophical Hermeneutics*. Berkeley: University of California Press, 1976.

———. *Truth and Method*. New York: Continuum, 1989.

Gasché, Rodolphe. *The Wild Card of Reading: On Paul de Man*. Cambridge: Harvard University Press, 1998.

Genette, Gérard. *Figures of Literary Discourse*. Translated by Alan Sheridan. New York: Columbia University Press, 1982.

Gerth, H. H., et al., eds. *From Max Weber*. Oxford: Oxford University Press, 1946.

Gethin, Rupert. *The Buddhist Path to Awakening*. Oxford: OneWorld, 1992.

———. *The Foundations of Buddhism*. Oxford: Oxford University Press, 1988.

Girard, René. *I See Satan Fall Like Lightning*. Translated by James G. Williams. Maryknoll: Orbis, 2001.

———. *Violence and the Sacred.* Translated by Patrick Gregory. Baltimore: Johns Hopkins University Press, 1972.

Gombrich, Richard F. *How Buddhism Began*. Dehli: Manoharlal, 1997.

———. *Theravāda Buddhism*. London: Routledge, 1988.

Griffiths, Paul J. *Religious Reading: The Place of Reading in the Practice of Religion*. New York: Oxford University Press, 1999.

Grimm, Jacob, and Wilhelm Grimm. *Grimms' Fairy Tales.* New York. Penguin, 1996.

Gross, Rita M. *Buddhism After Patriarchy: A Feminist History, Analysis and Reconstruction of Buddhism.* Albany: State University of New York Press, 1993.

Guillory, John. *Cultural Capital: The Problem of Literary Canon Formation.* Chicago: University of Chicago Press, 1993.

Gyatso, Janet, ed. *In the Mirror of Memory.* Albany: State University of New York Press, 1992.

Gyatso, Kelsang Geshe. *The Joyful Path to Good Fortune*. London: Tharpa, 1990.

Gyatso, Tenzin. *A Flash of Lightning in the Dark of Night*. Boston: Shambhala, 1994.

Hanh, Thich Nhat. *The Heart of Understanding*. New Dehli: Full Circle, 1997.

Harvey, Peter. *An Introduction to Buddhism*. Cambridge: Cambridge University Press, 1990.

———. *The Selfless Mind.* Richmond: Curzon, 1995.

Hayes, Richard. *The Land of No Buddha: Reflections of a Sceptical Buddhist*. Birmingham: Windhorse, 1998.

Hegel, G. W. F. *The Phenomenology of Spirit*. Translated by A.V. Miller. New York: Oxford University Press, 1977.

———. *Vorlesungen über die Philosophie der Religion*, I. Frankfurt am Main: Suhrkamp, 1969.

Heine, Steven, and Dale S. Wright, eds. *The Kōan: Texts and Contexts in Zen Buddhism.* Oxford: Oxford University Press, 2000.

Heine, Steven. *Opening a Mountain: Kōans of the Zen Masters*. Oxford: Oxford University Press, 2000.

———. *Shifting Shape, Shaping Text: Philosophy and Folklore in the Fox Koan*. Honolulu: University of Hawaii Press, 1999.

Hoffman, Frank J. *Rationality and Mind in Early Buddhism*. Dehli: Motilal, 1992.

Homer. *The Odyssey*. Translated by Robert Fagles. New York: Penguin, 1996.

Horner, I. B., ed. *Ten Jātaka Stories: A Pali Reader.* Bangkok: Mahāmakut, 1993.

———. *Women in Early Buddhist Literature.* Kandy: Buddhist Publication Society, 1961.

Humphries, Jeff. *Reading Emptiness: Buddhism and Literature.* Albany: State University of New York Press, 1999.

Huntington, Jr., C. W. *The Emptiness of Emptiness: An Introduction to Early Indian Mādhyamaka.* Honolulu: University of Hawaii Press, 1989.

Ireland, John D., trans. *The Itivittaka.* Kandy: Buddhist Publication Society, 1991.

———, trans. *Samyutta Nikāya: An Anthology.* Kandy: Buddhist Publication Society, 1967.

———, trans. *The Udāna.* Kandy: Buddhist Publication Society, 1990.

Iser, Wolfgang. *The Implied Reader.* Baltimore: Johns Hopkins University Press, 1974.

Jackson, Roger R., et al., eds. *Buddhist Theology: Critical Reflections by Contemporary Buddhist Scholars.* Richmond: Curzon, 2000.

James, William. *The Varieties of Religious Experience: A Study in Human Nature.* 1902; New York: Penguin, 1985.

Jameson, Frederic. *The Jameson Reader.* Edited by M. Hardt and K. Weeks. Oxford: Blackwell, 2000.

———. *The Political Unconscious: Narrative as a Socially Symbolic Act.* Ithaca: Cornell University Press, 1981.

The Jātaka, or Stories of the Buddha's Former Lives. Edited by Edward B. Cowell, and translated by H. T. Francis. Cambridge: Cambridge University Press, 1895–1913.

Jayawickrama, N. A. *The Story of Gotama Buddha (Jātaka-nidāna).* Oxford: Pali Text Society, 2002.

Jayatilleke, K. N. *Early Buddhist Theory of Knowledge.* Dehli: Motilal, 1980.

Johansson, Rune E. A., ed. *Pali Buddhist Texts.* London: Curzon, 1977.

———. *The Psychology of Nirvana.* Garden City: Anchor, 1970.

Johnson, Barbara. *The Critical Difference: Essays in the Contemporary Rhetoric of Reading.* Baltimore: Johns Hopkins University Press, 1980.

Johnston, E. H. *Aśvaghoṣa's Buddhacarita, or Acts of the Buddha.* Dehli: Motilal, 1936.

Jung, Carl G. *The Portable Jung.* Edited by Joseph Campbell. New York: Viking, 1971.

Kafka, Franz. *Selected Short Stories.* Translated by Willa and Edwin Muir. New Dehli: Srishti, 1998.

Kalupahana, David J. *Buddhist Philosophy: A Historical Analysis.* Honolulu: University Press of Hawaii, 1976.

Kasulis, Thomas. *Intimacy or Integrity.* Honolulu: University of Hawaii Press, 2002.

———. *Zen Action/Zen Person.* Honolulu: University of Hawaii Press, 1985.

Keith, A. Barriedale. *A History of Sanskrit Literature.* Dehli: Motilal, 1993.

Phra Khantipalo, ed. *The Splendour of Enlightenment: A Life of the Buddha.* Bangkok: Mahamut Rajavidyalaya, 1990.

King, Winston L. *Theravada Meditation.* Dehli: Motilal, 1992.

Lacan, Jacques, *Écrits.* Translated by Alan Sheridan. New York: Norton, 1977.

———. *Four Fundamental Concepts of Psychoanalysis: The Seminar of Jacques Lacan, XI.* Translated by Alan Sheridan. Edited by Jacques-Alain Miller. New York: Norton, 1977.

Laclau, Ernesto. *Emancipation(s).* London: Verso, 1996.

LaFleur, William R. *The Karma of Words: Buddhism and the Literary Arts in Medieval Japan.* Berkeley: University of California Press, 1983.

Lamotte, Étienne. *History of Buddhism from the Origins to the Śaka Era.* Translated by Sara Webb-Boin. Louvain: Peeters, 1988.

Lanham, Richard. *The Motives of Eloquence: Literary Rhetoric in the Renaissance.* New Haven: Yale University Press, 1976.

Laozi. *Dao De Jing: The Book of the Way.* Translated by Moss Roberts. Berkeley: University of California Press, 2001.

Lauf, Detlev. *Secret Doctrines of the Tibetan Books of the Dead.* Boston: Shambhala, 1989.

Levine, Stephen. *Who Dies? An Investigation of Conscious Living and Conscious Dying.* Garden City: Anchor, 1982.

Ling, Trevor. *The Buddha: Buddhist Civilization in India and Ceylon.* Harmondsworth: Penguin, 1976.

———. *Buddhism and the Mythology of Evil.* Oxford: OneWorld, 1997.

Lopez, Jr., Donald, ed. *Critical Terms for the Study of Buddhism.* Chicago: University of Chicago Press, 2005.

———. *Curators of the Buddha: The Study of Buddhism under Colonialism.* Chicago: University of Chicago Press, 1995.

———. *Elaborations on Emptiness.* Princeton: Princeton University Press, 1996.

———. *Prisoners of Shangri-La.* Chicago: University of Chicago Press, 1998.

Magliola, Robert. *Derrida on the Mend.* West Lafayette: Purdue University Press, 1984.

Matthews, Bruce. *Craving and Salvation.* 1983; Dehli: Satguru, 1994.

McKenna, Andrew. *Violence and Difference: Girard, Derrida, and Deconstruction.* Urbana: University of Illinois Press, 1992.

McRae, John R. *Seeing through Zen: Encounter, Transformation, and Genealogy in Chinese Chan Buddhism.* Berkeley: University of California Press, 2003.

Middle Length Discourses. Translated by Bhikkhu Bodhi and Bhikkhu Ñanamoli. Boston: Wisdom, 1995.

Miura, Isshu, and Ruth F. Sasaki. *The Zen Koan: Its History and Use in Rinzai Zen.* New York: Harcourt Brace, 1965.

Moody, Raymond. *Life after Life.* 2nd ed. San Francisco: Harper, 2001.

Moore, Stephen D. *Literary Criticism and the Gospels: The Theoretical Challenge*. New Haven: Yale University Press, 1989.

Nāgārjuna. *The Fundamental Wisdom of the Middle Way*. Translated by Jay L. Garfield. New York. Oxford University Press, 1995.

Ñanananda Bhikkhu, ed., *Samyutta Nikāya*, pt. 2. Kandy: Buddhist Publication Society, 1972.

Ñānananda Bhikkhu. *Concept and Reality in Early Buddhist Thought*. Kandy: Buddhist Publication Society, 1971

Nattier, Jan. *A Few Good Men: The Bodhisattva Path According to the Inquiry of Ugra (Ugraparipṛcchā)*. Honolulu: University of Hawaii Press, 2003.

Newton, K. M. *Twentieth-Century Literary Theory: A Reader*. New York: St. Martin's Press, 1988.

Nietzsche, Friedrich. *Beyond Good and Evil*. Translated by Walter Kaufmann. New York: Random House, 1966.

———. *Daybreak: Thoughts on the Prejudices of Morality*. Translated by R. J. Hollingdale. Cambridge: Cambridge University Press, 1982.

———. *On the Genealogy of Morals*. Translated by Walter Kaufmann and R. J. Hollingdale. New York: Random House, 1969.

Nisker, Wes. *Buddha's Nature: A Practical Guide to Discovering Your Place in the Cosmos*. New York: Bantam, 1998.

Nuland, Sherwin B. *How We Die: Reflections on Life's Final Chapter*. New York: Random House, 1995.

Nyanamoli, trans. *A Treasury of the Buddha's Words from the Majjhima Nikaya*. 3 vols. Bangkok: Mahamut Rajavidyalaya, n.d.

Nyanaponika Thera. *The Heart of Buddhist Meditation*. London: Rider, 1983.

Nyanaponika Thera, and Bikkhu Bodhi, trans., ed. *Numerical Discourses of the Buddha: An Anthology of Suttas from the Anguttara Nikāya*. Lanham: AltaMira, 1999.

O'Flaherty, Wendy D., trans., ed., *The Rig Veda: An Anthology*. Baltimore: Penguin, 1981.

Oldenberg, Hermann. *Buddha: His Life, his Doctrine, his Order*. Translated by William Hoey. New Dehli: Motilal, 1997.

Padmakara Translation Group, trans. *Shantideva, The Way of the Bodhisattva*. Boston: Shambhala, 1997.

Padmasambhava. *Natural Liberation*. Commentary by Gyatrul Rinpoche. Translated by Alan Wallace. Boston: Wisdom, 1998.

Plato. *The Republic*. Translated by G. M. A. Grube. Indianapolis: Hackett, 1992.

Potter, Karl. *The Presuppositions of India's Philosophies*. Englewood Cliffs, NJ: Prentice Hall, 1963.

Powers, John. *Introduction to Tibetan Buddhism.* Ithaca: Snow Lion, 1995.

Prebish, Charles S. *Luminous Passage: The Practice and Study of Buddhism in America.* Berkeley: University of California Press, 1999.

Proust, Marcel. *The Remembrance of Things Past.* Translated by C. K. Scott Moncrieff and Terence Kilmartin. New York: Vintage, 1982.

Queen, Christopher S., and Sallie B. King, eds. *Engaged Buddhism: Buddhist Liberation Movements in Asia.* Albany: State University of New York Press, 1996.

Rahula, Walpola. *What the Buddha Taught.* Bangkok: Kurusapa, 1990.

Ray, Reginald. *Buddhist Saints in India.* New York: Oxford University Press, 1994.

Reps, Paul, ed. *Zen Flesh, Zen Bones.* Rutland: Tuttle, 1957.

Rhys Davids, T. W. *Buddhist India.* Dehli: Motilal, 1993.

———. trans., ed. *Dialogues of the Buddha.* Dehli: Motilal, 2000.

———. *The History and Literature of Buddhism.* New Dehli, Munshiram Manoharlal, 1999.

———. trans. *The Questions of King Milinda.* New York: Dover, 1963.

Robinson, Richard H., Willard L. Johnson, et al. *The Buddhist Religion: A Historical Introduction.* Belmont: Wadsworth, 1997.

Said, Edward. *Orientalism.* New York: Vintage, 1979.

Sangharakshita. *The Eternal Legacy: an Introduction to the Canonical Literature of Buddhism.* London: Tharpa. 1985.

Sekida, Katsuki. *Two Zen Classics: Mumonkan and Hekiganroku.* New York: Weatherhill, 1977.

Schopen, Gregory. *Buddhist Monks and Business Matters: Still More Papers on Monastic Buddhism in India.* Honolulu: University of Hawaii Press, 2004.

———. *Stones, Bones and Buddhist Monks: Collected Papers on the Archaeology, Epigraphy and Texts of Monastic Buddhism in India.* Honolulu: University of Hawaii Press, 1997.

Schroeder, John. *Skillful Means: The Heart of Buddhist Compassion.* Honolulu: University of Hawaii Press, 2001.

Schumann, H. W. *The Historical Buddha.* London: Arkana, 1989.

Shakespeare, William. *Complete Works.* Edited by Hardin Craig. Chicago: Scott, 1961.

Shibayama, trans., comm. *Zen Comments on the Mumonkan.* New York: Mentor, 1975.

Soeng, Mu, ed. *Trust in Mind: the Rebellion of Chinese Zen.* Boston: Wisdom, 2004.

———, trans. *The Diamond Sutra: Transforming the Way We Perceive the World.* Boston: Wisdom, 2000.

Sogyal Rinpoche. *Tibetan Book of Living and Dying.* Edited by Patrick Gaffney and Andrew Harvey. New York: HarperSanFranciso, 1993.

Sophocles. *The Three Theban Plays: Antigone, Oedipus the King, Oedipus at Colonus.* Translated by Robert Fagles. New York: Penguin, 1982.

Spenser, Edmund. *Edmund Spenser's Poetry: Authoritative Texts, Criticism.* Edited by Hugh Maclean and Anne L. Prescott. New York: Norton, 1993.

Stcherbatsky, Theodor. *The Central Conception of Buddhism.* Dehli: Motilal, 1994.

Sterne, Laurence. *The Life and Opinions of Tristram Shandy, Gentleman.* Edited by James Work. New York: Odyssey, 1940.

Stevens, Wallace. *Collected Poetry and Prose.* Edited by Frank Kermode. New York: Library of America, 1997.

Stevenson, Ian. *Twenty Cases Suggestive of Reincarnation.* Charlottesville: University of Viginia Press, 1980.

Strong, John. *The Buddha: A Short Biography.* Oxford: Oneworld, 2001.

———, ed. *The Experience of Buddhism: Sources and Interpretations.* Belmont: Wadsworth, 1995.

———. *Relics of the Buddha.* Princeton: Princeton University Press, 2004.

Suzuki, D. T. *An Introduction to Zen Buddhism.* New York: Grove, 1964.

Tatar, Maria, ed. *The Classic Fairy Tales.* New York: Norton, 1999.

Thanissaro Bhikkhu (Geoffrey DeGraff), trans. *Dhammapada: A Translation.* Barre: Dhamma Dana, 1998.

———. *The Wings to Awakening.* Barre: Dhamma Dana, 1996

Thomas, Edward J. *The Life of the Buddha as Legend and History.* 1960; Delhi: Motilal, 1997.

Thurman, Robert A. F., trans. *The Holy Teaching of Vimalakirti: A Mahāyāna Scripture.* Dehli: Motilal, 1991.

Tompkins, Jane P. *Reader-Response Criticism: From Formalism to Post-Structuralism.* Baltimore: Johns Hopkins University Press, 1980.

Van Gorkom, Nina. *Abhidamma in Everyday Life.* London: Triple Gem, 1969.

Vico, Giambattista. *The New Science of Giambattista Vico.* Translated by Thomas G. Bergin and Max H. Fisch. Ithaca: Cornell University Press, 1948.

Victoria, Brian D. *Zen War Stories.* London: Routledge Curzon, 2003.

Wallace, Alan, and Vesna Wallace, trans. *Śantideva, A Guide to the Bodhisattva Way of Life.* Ithaca: Snow Lion, 1997.

Walshe, Maurice, trans. *Samyutta Nikāya: an Anthology.* vol 3. Kandy: Buddhist Publication Society, 1985.

———, trans. *Thus Have I Heard: The Long Discourses of the Buddha.* Boston: Wisdom, 1987.

Warder, A. K. *Indian Kāvya Literature.* 2 vols. Dehli: Motilal, 1974.

Warren, Henry Clarke, ed. *Buddhism in Translations.* New Dehli: Motilal, 1986.

Watson, Burton, trans., ed. *The Essential Lotus: Selections from the Lotus Sutra.* New York: Columbia University Press, 2002.

Weaver, Richard. *The Ethics of Rhetoric.* Chicago: Regnery, 1965.

Webb, Stephen. *Blessed Excess: Religion and the Hyperbolic Imagination.* Albany: State University Press of New York, 1993.

Welbon, Guy. *The Buddhist Nirvana and Its Western Interpreters.* Chicago: University of Chicago Press: 1967.

Wellek, René, and Austin Warren. *Theory of Literature.* 3rd ed. New York: Harvest, 1984.

White, Hayden. "Ethnological 'Lie' and Mythological 'Truth.'" *Diacritics* 8 (1978): 2–9.

Williams, Paul. *Buddhist Thought: A Complete Introduction to the Buddhist Tradition.* London: Routledge, 2000.

———. *Mahāyāna Buddhism.* London: Routledge, 1989.

Wright, Dale S. *Philosophical Meditations on Zen Buddhism.* Cambridge: Cambridge University Press, 1998.

Yeats, William Butler. *The Collected Poems of W. B. Yeats.* New York: Macmillan, 1959.

Youxuan Wang. *Buddhism and Deconstruction: Towards a Comparative Semiotics.* Richmond: Curzon, 2001.

Zimmer, Heinrich. *Myths and Symbols in Indian Art and Civilization.* Princeton, NJ: Princeton University Press, 1946.

Žižek, Slavoj. *The Plague of Fantasies.* London: Verso, 1997.

———. *The Puppet and the Dwarf: The Perverse Core of Christianity.* Cambridge, MA: MIT Press, 2003.

———. *The Sublime Object of Ideology.* London: Verso, 1999.

Index